Signs of Life

Signs of Life

A Memoir

Natalie Taylor

W F HOWES LTD

This large print edition published in 2011 by
W F Howes Ltd
Unit 4, Rearsby Business Park, Gaddesby Lane,
Rearsby, Leicester LE7 4YH

1 3 5 7 9 10 8 6 4 2

First published in the United States of America in 2011
by Broadway Books

While this is a true story, some names and details have been
changed to protect the identity of those who appear in the pages.

'Stopping by Woods on a Snowy Evening' from the book THE
POETRY OF ROBERT FROST, edited by Edward Connery
Lathem. Copyright © 1923, 1969 by Henry Holt and
Company. Copyright © 1951 by Robert Frost. Reprinted by
arrangement with Henry Holt and Company, LLC.

A CIP catalogue record for this book is available
from the British Library

ISBN 978 1 40749 351 0

Typeset by Palimpsest Book Production Limited,
Falkirk, Stirlingshire
Printed and bound in Great Britain
by MPG Books Ltd, Bodmin, Cornwall

MIX
Paper from
responsible sources
FSC
www.fsc.org   FSC® C018575

For the two loves of my life, Josh and Kai

AUTHOR'S NOTE

While this is a true story, the names of all of my students and the individuals who participated in the single mothers' group and the grief group have been changed to protect their identities.

This memoir is a compilation of journal entries that I wrote following my husband's death. It is not a reflection that was written after time passed, it is what was in my brain at that moment. While this book has been edited in the appropriate respects, the experiences and personal thoughts have remained the same since the days they were originally typed into my computer, which is not to say I am proud of all the things I say and do, but it is to say that it is real to the person I was at that time, and, for better or worse, I am still very much the same neurotic, over-analytical nut-job you are about to meet.

PROLOGUE

Mathews walks in the door. It is somewhere in the middle of the night. I wake up. 'Your phone is off.' He says something about trying to call me, that people have been trying to call me. He says something about Josh. Josh has been in an accident. *No big deal*, I think to myself. *Let's just go home*. I picture a broken arm. I have a flash of seeing him in a hospital bed annoyed at an injury. Chris Mathews is one of my good friends – he's Josh's best friend. Mathews and I are in Florida visiting my sister Moo and her husband, David. Josh, my husband, couldn't come because of work, so he's back in Michigan. I just hung up with him right before I lay down. He was out Carveboarding with our friend Nate. We just got to Miami this morning, but I don't care about leaving early – I had reservations about leaving Josh anyway.

But there is something in Mathews's voice that isn't right. In moments, it registers. I know it's more than a broken arm. Josh hit his head, he tells me. The back of his head. I talk to Nate. I ask if he was bleeding. He says yes. I picture a cut on his forehead. 'Where?' I ask. 'His mouth.'

I lie in Moo's bed. All of the lights are off. Mathews is in the front of the house somewhere. Every now and then my left leg starts to shake uncontrollably. I go to the bathroom. I throw up a little. I go back and start shaking again. I go to the bathroom and have diarrhea. I go back and my leg starts shaking again. I put clothes back into my suitcase. I go to the bathroom again. No puke, no diarrhea. Nothing.

Moo comes in; there are a few frantic phone calls back and forth. No one gets on the phone with me. Mom and Dad talk to Moo. Moo relays words. I know. I know. No one says it, but I know.

JUNE AND JULY

Show me how to do like you. Show me how to do it.

—'DO LIKE YOU' BY STEVIE WONDER,
EPIGRAPH FROM ALICE WALKER,
THE COLOR PURPLE

We leave for the airport. I have no idea what time it is. I am on the phone with a doctor. He asks me if Josh's heart stops, do I want to resuscitate him. I ask questions. I do not cry. He says something about severe brain damage, *severe*. I say no, do not resuscitate him. We hang up.

I call my mom.

'The dogs,' I say. 'Can someone go get the dogs?'

'Yes,' she says.

We are on the plane. It is light out. We are sitting on the runway because the plane doesn't have any electricity or something. Moo is crying. I am not. There is a man standing at the front of the plane talking on a phone with his hand on his hip. He has no idea.

We are in the air. I get up to go to the bathroom again. I walk back to my seat. A man says to me, 'You and your sister seem upset.'

'My husband was in an accident. He's suffered a severe injury to his head.' Just like that. I say it just like that. I am not crying.

'Your husband? The father of your baby?' His eyes drop briefly to my stomach. My hand is over my stomach. I am five months pregnant.

'Yeah.'

'Well, these days, I mean, what doctors can do. You shouldn't lose hope.'

'Thanks.' I sit back down.

I walk through the terminal. My family is there. They hug me. Adam, my older brother, hugs me and I feel like he is acting. I feel like he is acting like a sad person. He is doing a really good imitation of a sad person. Haley, my little sister, stares at me with her big blue eyes, but she doesn't say anything. No one really says anything.

We have a long drive. I sit in the middle with a pillow over my stomach. I am so tired. My dad drives. My mom sits in the back next to me and strokes my hair.

'Try to sleep,' she says.

We arrive at the hospital. We take an elevator to the third floor. The elevator opens and dozens of eyes fall on us. I walk to his room. His aunt is in the hallway outside his room. She looks at me, shaking, frantic, her chest heaving. I walk in. Everyone leaves except Uncle Alex. I look at Josh.

He has a scrape on the upper left-hand side of his forehead and there is stubble all around his face. He hadn't shaved since I left yesterday morning. I will remember that hair, those little buds of facial hair on his strong jaw, for the rest of my life.

'Uncle Alex,' I say. 'Can you tell me,' I stop. 'I don't know anything.' I start to cry. Uncle Alex is a doctor. He actually delivered me and he delivered Josh. We thought this was such a testament to the star-aligned quality of our relationship. Now Uncle Alex is standing over Josh's pale, still body explaining to his pregnant wife how he died. But I am happy it's only Uncle Alex in the room. Happy? What does that word even mean now?

Uncle Alex cries. 'He fell backward and hit his head. It crushed his skull into the back of his brain. He died in less than three minutes.'

Last night, right before I went to bed, Josh went out Carveboarding. A Carveboard is a modified skateboard. It rocks side to side and imitates the motion of a surfboard. Carveboards are used on pavement embankments. Josh was not wearing a helmet at the time of the accident. He never wore a helmet.

Uncle Alex leaves. I cry. I cry relentlessly. My whole body shakes. I don't touch him. I don't hold his hand. I do not want to feel him cold.

'I'm not mad at you,' I say. 'I'm not mad at you and I will take care of our son.' Those are the two things I say to him. 'I'm not mad at you. I will

5

never be mad at you. And I will take care of our son.'

I am in the waiting area. Adam and Moo are trying to get me to eat. I haven't eaten for hours. I can't eat. I can't eat anything. I drink some water. Ads buys a granola bar and breaks it off into little pieces. He hands me one small piece of the granola bar.

'Just this little bite, Nat,' he says. I eat it. He lets a few minutes go by and hands me another one.

'Here, Nat. A little more.'

There are a lot of people at the hospital. People hug and cry and stare out the window with red, swollen faces. A little after three o'clock in the afternoon the doctor comes out. Everyone sits together. I sit next to Deedee, Josh's mom, and hold her hand. Ashley, Josh's little sister, sits on the floor in front of her mom. The doctor says something about the injury, the trauma to the head, how they had to wait so many hours and examine it again, just to be sure. And then he says that Josh Taylor was pronounced dead at 3:00 p.m. on Sunday, June 17, 2007. He was twenty-seven years old. It is Father's Day.

The next morning I wake up early. I walk around my parents' house. I sit on the couch in the family room. I get up. I try to pee. I feel like I have to pee, but I don't. I lie back down. I get back up. I try to pee again. I look at the clock. Is it too early to go up to my parents' room? Yes. I walk around the house some more. I sit. I stand. I open the fridge. I shut it. I lie back down. I get up. I turn on the TV. I turn it off. Finally. I go up into my parents' room and get into their bed. I start to cry. They cry too. My mom rubs my back. A few minutes later, I get up again.

'Where are you going?' my mom asks.

'I don't know.' I say.

Ads wakes up.

'Nat. Breakfast?'

'Sure.'

'Eggs?'

'Sure.'

'Omelet?'

'Sure.'

He cooks. I lie on the couch.

'Nat, what do you need? Coffee? You want to read the paper? You want to put in a movie?'

'I don't know, Ads. I don't know.'

Chris, Josh's little brother by less than one year, got on a plane this morning. He lives in Denver, but he was fishing in Estes Park, about twenty miles outside of Denver. The park ranger had to go and find him and tell him. He had to drive back, get a ticket. It was almost a full day before he knew anything. I try to call him but it goes straight to voice mail. I don't leave a message. What the hell would I say?

Deedee stays at the hospital all night. All of Josh's organs are in perfect working order. We decide to

7

donate as many as possible. This process will take a few days, she explains to me over the phone. Then she says, 'You understand why I need to be here, don't you?'

'Yes. I do. And you understand why I can't be there, right?'

'Yeah. I do.'

We hang up.

People come over. Tons of people. All my friends are here. Katie Battersby and Jen, whom I've known since the sixth grade, lie on the floor with me. Terrah, my friend from college, calls all of our friends from out of town. Everyone keeps asking, 'Nat, do you need anything? Water? Food? A back rub? A bath?' I shake my head.

I fall asleep on the carpeting in my parents' family room. I wake up, and almost everyone is gone. I go to bed on the futon in my old room. My friend Maggie sleeps with me. Maggie was Josh's close friend growing up, but she and I became close once Josh and I got married. We used to joke that Josh had two wives. She was always telling him what to do, pointing her finger at him. 'Josh, I don't mean to preclude you from eating these cupcakes,' I heard her tell him last weekend, 'but we do need to wait until—' and then he stuck his finger right in the icing. She got all flustered. He gave her the typical, 'Oh, Margaret, calm down.' She uses words like *preclude*. She is the only person I know who can conjugate *swim, swam, swum* correctly in a conversation. Now she hardly says anything. What do we have to talk about?

The next day my mom takes a small white package from the fridge.

'I bought these burgers on Saturday. I was going to cook them for dinner on Sunday night.' She stares at the white label on the package.

She says, 'It seems like a lifetime ago.'

Later that night I hear the front door of my parents' house open. Chris walks in the door. There is a small group of people around him. He has his blue visor pulled over his eyes a little. Finally, he gets to me. I hug him. We both start to cry. We hug for a long time. I cry into his shoulder. We don't say anything to each other.

Days pass. Josh donates seven organs. We meet with the people at the funeral home. They call us several times a day. We have to answer all sorts of questions about flowers and caskets and times and we have to pick out pictures. Pictures we just took. Someone tells me I have to go to my house to pick out clothes for Josh. I don't want to go. I don't want to go.

But Moo and I get in the car. We stop at the light at Fourteen Mile and Woodward, one block away from my house. I start to cry hysterically.

'I'm never going to be happy again.' I say this over and over. My voice is high. There are tears and snot all over my hands and shirt.

'I'm never going to be as happy as I was.'

'Don't say that,' Moo says. She looks at me. She cries too.

'Don't say that. Josh would hate to hear you say that.'

I keep crying.

I open the door to my house. I walk through the hallway. I try not to look at any of the pictures. I walk into our bedroom. His T-shirts. His shoes. Our bed. His boxer shorts. His dirty laundry. His balled-up socks. His hanging shirts. His pillows. His alarm clock. His carry-out from Friday night in the fridge. His razor in the shower. Everything. Every single thing in the house indicates that two people live here. That one should be back any minute now. I am hysterical. Moo, Deedee, and Ashley start pulling out T-shirts. We pick out clothes for him.

We get to the funeral home in the middle of the afternoon for the first viewing. The funeral home is packed with people. I am wearing a black dress from Banana Republic. That morning I went to Banana Republic with Maggie, Battersby, Terrah, Jen, and Lauren Gentry and Angela Anagnost – my college friends. Just over a year ago, they were all my bridesmaids. Today they helped me pick out an outfit for my husband's funeral. They all walked around me, my secret service, making sure I didn't have to carry anything or drive or walk too far without a snack or something to drink. I bought two dresses. I spent over three hundred dollars on two dresses.

At the viewing, people stand in small circles. They hug me and stare at me.

'Thank you for coming,' I say. People say things like 'You're going to be okay.' 'You're strong.'

I try not to cry at all in front of anyone at the funeral home. I say nice, comforting things to other people.

'We'll be okay.' I nod. I don't know why I say this or what it means; it just comes out of my mouth.

Josh's aunt Barb looks at the pictures. She cries. I hug her and try to say something nice. 'It's okay, Aunt Barb.'

She looks at me, her red eyes serious.

'It's not okay, honey.' She looks right at me. 'It's not okay.' She starts to cry. 'It's *not* okay. You were robbed. You were *robbed.*' I am not mad at her for saying this. I am not upset because I cry in front of people. She's right. I know she is right.

There are over a thousand people at the funeral. First Deedee and Chris speak. Then Pug, one of Josh's best friends growing up, goes next. Then I speak. Somehow I speak.

Then it is over and Vito, my dad, drives us all home. There are six of us crammed in his Volvo. The car is full of orchids, cards, flowers, and the posters with all of our pictures. I feel like we are in the car forever. I feel like I am going to throw up or pee my pants. I feel like I am suffocating in the backseat of my dad's car. We get home. I run to the bathroom. I don't throw up. I try to pee but can't.

I put all of the boards with pictures into my old room at my parents' house. I shut the door. One by one I take all of the pictures down. One by one I look at each picture. I cry and cry and cry.

His credit cards, our gym memberships, his cell phone, his car, his insurance, his bills, his work. Days go by of these phone calls.

'Yes, my husband, Josh, died suddenly in an accident. I would like to cancel his debit card.'

'Oh, I'm sorry to hear that, ma'am. We'll get that taken care of right away.'

'Thank you.'

I get seven copies of his death certificate. I sit in my old room and read his death certificate over and over: 'Date of birth: December 21, 1979. Date of death: June 17, 2007. 1:21 a.m. Trauma to the head.'

I call Social Security. I get a check from them for $273 and zero cents. There is a formal letter attached.

'This lump sum has been issued to you as a result of the death of your husband, Joshua Raymond Taylor.' Another segment reads, 'The marriage of Natalie Taylor and Joshua Taylor was terminated on June 17, 2007, due to the death of Joshua Taylor.'

More days pass. My mom, Hales, and Moo come with me to my obstetrician's office. I called and told them what happened. There are six doctors in the practice. Today I am seeing Dr Ford. I've never met Dr Ford before.

We crowd into the small examination room. I lie on the table. My mom sits next to me. Moo and Hales stand in the corner. A tall, slender man with thick black glasses slinks in the door. He has a large forehead and looks awkwardly at the four of us. He doesn't say anything. I take a deep breath. We all sit in silence for a moment and wait for Dr Ford to say something. Or are we supposed to say something? *Great*, I think to myself. Of course the one time I need a doctor who has a sense of emotional connection, I get the scientist. This jackass has no idea what he has just walked into. My throat starts to tighten at the thought of my mother and sister trying to explain what has happened to me. Finally the silence breaks.

'I know,' he says in a clear, soft voice. 'I know what happened.' He pauses. 'I'm very sorry to hear about your loss.'

'Thank you,' I mutter.

A few moments of silence go by. Then he starts to talk.

'How's your brain?' he asks. He stands still as he says this.

'It's okay,' I shrug.

'That's a lie.' He then slides down the wall behind him and sits on the floor, still holding his clipboard. In any other context, it would be completely bizarre and inappropriate for any doctor to sit on the floor with his knees pulled to his chest. But right now, it feels completely right. He has put all of us at ease. He just wants us to

13

know that this is not a normal doctor's visit and he realizes that.

He goes on to tell me that my body is fine. Everything is moving along wonderfully. He says I can get an ultrasound today or any other day I want. I tell him I'm nervous. I'm nervous because my whole body is in so much pain, it's hard to imagine something growing inside of it. I have this strange anxiety that my grief will somehow physically manifest itself and attack the baby. He does not acknowledge this as a crazy emotion, which I deeply appreciate. I tell him I haven't been eating as much as I used to, my appetite has decreased substantially. He says, 'Natalie, there are women on this earth who eat dirt and ice for nine months and deliver perfectly healthy babies. You will be fine. Your body knows exactly what it needs to do.' He pauses. 'But you need to work on your brain. Your brain isn't fine, and it shouldn't be.'

I feel the tears well up in my eyes.

He asks me a few questions. Then he takes a card out of his breast pocket: DR ELLEN GURIZA, PHD. PSYCHOLOGIST.

'I'm not suggesting that you go see her,' he says. 'I am instructing you, as your obstetrician, that you *have* to go see her. The sooner the better. Call her today. If she doesn't answer the phone, leave a message and say that I referred you and that you would like to come in as soon as possible.' I nod. He looks at my mom.

14

'Make sure she does this. It is *imperative* that she does this.' She nods too.

I don't go back to my house. I stay at my parents'. I sleep on the futon in my old room every night. Maggie sleeps with me every night. Mathews doesn't go back to work. He spends the night in my parents' basement for over a week. He and I never talk about Josh, but in a strange way he is the most comforting person I have. He is the only person who can make me smile. A few days after the funeral we went out to dinner with our friends from out of town. Mathews and I sat next to each other. I told him if he was still single at thirty and hadn't found a man yet (he's gay), we should get married for the tax break. We could be Will and Grace, but I'd be a much more pathetic, less attractive version of Grace. Maggie overheard us and said she wanted to marry Mathews too; we'd have to flip for it. After she turned away, Mathews leaned toward me and said, 'I'll marry you, but I am *not* marrying Maggie.'

During the days before the funeral, people kept dropping off food. Platters and platters of fresh fruit, cheese, lunch meats. It was so generous. We never had to think about food. After a few days Dubs (Moo's husband, David – we call him Dubs) asked if we could do something different for dinner – he was 'kind of sick of cold cuts.' Mathews and I heard him say this and exchanged a look, a 'what a jerk' look. Later that night, Mathews found me in my room, lay down with me, and

15

said, 'Nat, are you so sick of cold cuts or what?'
Mathews provides me with glimpses of relief. A
few seconds where I smile. These moments are
nearly impossible otherwise.

I lie on the futon in my old room. I cry hysterically. I heave and sob. I can hardly see. My mom
is there next to me. She cries too. Her hand is on
my head.

She says, 'If I could take this away from you I
would.' I know she would.

'If I could do this instead of you, I would do it
in a second.' She sounds desperate, as if she is
truly negotiating with someone.

'I never want to be alone again,' I say, through
my heaves of air. She shakes her head. 'You don't
have to be. You don't have to be.'

I look at the ceiling. I try to wipe my face off.
'I never want to go back to my house and I never
want to be alone again.'

The last book I read with my eleventh-grade
class before school got out a few weeks ago was
The Color Purple. In the beginning of the book
there is an epigraph based on Stevie Wonder's
lyrics that reads: 'Show me how to do like you,
show me how to do it.' After reading the book, it
is obvious that the epigraph speaks to the larger
themes of self-discovery. The main character,
Celie, is a poor black woman living in rural
Georgia at the turn of the twentieth century. She
is physically, sexually, emotionally, and psycho-
logically abused. But she 'finds herself' and she

has a sexual, emotional, and religious reawakening owing to the help of some tremendous friends. People show her how to do things. I think of Celie all the time. I think of that epigraph every day. *Will someone please just show me how to do this*? I want to go around asking people who have gone through this, 'Okay, what is the second month like? What is the third month like? How about six months? What happens after a year? What did you do to make yourself feel better? What did you eat? What did you drink? How often did you pee? How do I make myself feel like I'm not going to throw up all the time? What movies did you watch? What books did you read? Who did you talk to? Can I have their numbers? Just tell me how you did it, and then I can do it.'

Susie Daniels, one of my fellow teachers, lost her brother in a car accident when she was sixteen. She called and asked if she could take me to breakfast. *Thank God*! Maybe she can give me some answers. Or I want to call Dennis, another co-worker. He lost his sister in a plane crash. *He'll* tell me how this works. But nobody does. They just shake their heads quietly and try not to cry.

I sit at a table at Caribou Coffee with Battersby and Jen. Battersby lost her mom in a car accident three years ago. She's been giving me practical advice in all of these very strange situations. Right before the first viewing, she told me that she was giving me an invisible stack of STFU cards, which stands for 'shut the fuck up.' So when people come

17

up to me and say, 'How *are* you doing?' or 'This was God's plan' or 'Why wasn't he wearing a helmet?' I could politely smile and hand them an STFU card.

We sit and drink Caribou Coolers. We used to come here all the time in high school. During college when we would come home for breaks, we'd meet here and gossip and catch up on one another's lives. Now they ask me questions about how I'm doing, but in a way that doesn't merit an STFU card. Finally I ask Battersby, 'What is this like? How long does this take?' She shrugs.

'Nat. It's going to be different for you. You know I can't tell you any of that.'

'How long was it before you started to feel okay again?' I ask her. I can tell she is hesitant to give me an answer.

'It took three years until the first thing I *didn't* think about when I opened my eyes in the morning was, "My mom died."'

Fuck, I think to myself. Three years. Three years.

I sit on a very nice leather couch in Dr Guriza's office. She is a slender woman with short black hair. She sits in a big chair across from me.

'Okay, Natalie. Why don't you start by just telling me what happened.'

I start to talk. I get through the first three words, and then my voice cracks and I start to cry.

'My husband, Josh.' I put my head in my hands and cry for a while, maybe a few minutes. I try

18

to talk again, but my voice is very high. I tell her the story. Again, tears and snot everywhere.

It has been three weeks since Josh's accident. I go see Dr G. again.

'Tell me about Josh. What kind of person was he?'

'He was amazing. He was a real man. You know how there are not a lot of real men these days? He was a real man.' I go babbling on through my tears, telling her about how he would do everything – garden, cook, clean, play sports with me, read, joke, bike. He didn't want anything more out of life than to be a dad. He was the best at everything.

'I know you think I'm exaggerating, but I'm not. Ask anyone who knew him. He was the *best* at *every*thing.' I go on to tell her about his bike trip across the country to raise money for a charity, about how he had such good balance, about how he was a great driver, surfer, soccer player – anything. I cry. I cry and cry. She tells me that it is really important for me to go through these memories. I nod. *But sometimes*, I think to myself, *nothing is harder than remembering*. 'You're going to cherish these memories. You may not now, but you will.' I nod again, but I don't really believe her.

I get home. Hales asks, 'How was she?'

I shrug. 'Fine, I guess.'

'Do you think she can help you?'

I shrug again. 'What do you mean, *help*? No, I don't think she is going to help me. I think I'm just going to go and bawl my eyes out and every now and then she'll say something nice and insightful and that'll be it.'

Hales nods.

In the state of Michigan there is a long-standing tradition of traveling to the northern part of the state when the weather gets warm. People camp, stay in cottages, rent condos or hotel rooms. Most northern lakeside cities are lined with lodging for out-of-towners. Most read NO VACANCY from Memorial Day weekend until after Labor Day. We call it 'going up north.' For my entire life, I have been going to Ludington, Michigan, for summer vacations. Ludington is small town on the coast of Lake Michigan. My grandmother's grandfather built our cottage in 1899. My grandparents don't come up anymore, but this is the place we would see them every summer growing up. It is the most beautiful place on the planet in the summertime. It beats the Mediterranean, the beaches of Oahu, the coast of Saint-Tropez. Not that I've ever been to any of those places, but I don't need to when I have Lake Michigan. And it's not just the scenery that makes it great. We never turn on the television. We go for walks and talk to neighbors. The same people come up every summer; families have known one another for generations. We slow down and eat dinner after the sun goes down so it doesn't interfere with lying on the beach. When I

20

think about life up north I have an image of my mother shucking corn on the steps of the cottage in her bathing suit.

Josh's family follows this tradition also. Josh's grandparents, Margaret and Ray, bought a small cottage on Elk Lake shortly after Josh was born. Elk Lake is a small inland lake, about eight miles long and two miles across. It is obviously not as large as Lake Michigan, but Elk Lake and its neighbor, Torch Lake, have this brilliant color to them. On sunny days in the middle of summer, you'd swear you were looking at the Caribbean. Once Josh and I were married, we split our Fourth of July time between Ludington and Elk Lake. We'd stay in Ludington to see the fireworks and then leave the next morning for Elk Lake. Deedee, Chris, and Ashley are at Elk Lake for the Fourth of July, but there's no way I can go there. I don't know if I can ever go there again. Everything in that cottage is Josh.

As we have done every single year since I can remember, my family and I head to Ludington for the Fourth of July this year. Everyone goes. My mom and dad, Adam, Moo and Dubs, Hales, and me. Adam and I drive up together. Adam's fiancée, Ellie, is in Los Angeles working out wedding plans. Adam and Ellie are getting married in two weeks in Aspen, Colorado.

The dogs, Louise and Bug, are with a dog trainer in another part of northern Michigan. The month before Josh's accident, he and I had arranged for them to be sent to a trainer for four weeks. Josh had taken both dogs up north multiple times that spring. He took them fishing and out on walks on the local trails, which they obviously loved. As they had gotten older, keeping them close by was getting more difficult. I was getting increasingly frustrated with them on walks. We found a guy who trains dogs to walk off-leash and it just so happened that they were scheduled to be picked up shortly after Josh's accident. It was so strange to see them before they left. I felt like they kept looking around me. Their eyes darted around my parents' house as if to ask, 'Where is he?' I am relieved I don't have to worry about taking them with us or boarding them. I hardly feel equipped to take care of myself, let alone two animals.

The weather up north is beautiful, but even the beach and the water can only do so much. I wake up. I eat. Sometimes we go out for breakfast. I sit around the cottage. I walk. I try to read stupid magazines. I talk to my family about celebrity gossip. I laugh, I smile. But all of the time, *all* of the time, I am sad. Sad has taken up permanent residency in my body. I keep thinking about Richard Wright's autobiography, *Black Boy*. There is one part where he describes growing up in Memphis and his mother doesn't have enough money for food. He says, 'I would wake to find hunger at my elbow, standing at my bedside, staring at me gauntly.' That's me, only it's not hunger.

We do manage to find things that prove to be therapeutic. We constantly work on a puzzle. Halfway through the week we complete the Coca-Cola puzzle, which to Hales's dismay was missing three pieces. After the Coca-Cola puzzle, we buy two new puzzles. The day before we leave we finish Lighthouses of the Great Lakes. Moo misses the inserting of the final piece of the lighthouse puzzle and is sorely disappointed.

We work on crossword puzzles on a daily basis. Every morning someone goes into town to get a *Detroit Free Press* or a *Ludington Daily News*. We work on the crossword, put it aside, and eventually, among the seven of us, it is complete by the end of the day.

Every day, every single day without fail, I go through a stack of pictures of Josh. There are probably twenty-five pictures in the stack. Most of them had been taken in the last two years, and there are several from a few summers ago. I go through the stack slowly. I look at each picture and I cry. I cry and sometimes I get a knot in my stomach because I have memorized the order of the pictures and I don't want to see certain ones, but I look anyway. Like the one of us dancing at our wedding. We're looking at each other. Just at each other and people are in the background smiling at us. I hate that picture. I hate it and I love it.

Once we get home from Ludington, we start preparing for Adam's wedding in Colorado.

Maggie, who had not originally planned on going, books a flight. I am happy she is coming with us, but I fear the entire trip.

Josh had been looking forward to this trip for months. He was an avid outdoorsman, and Colorado is the doorway to everything he loved to do, and the most appealing part was that he could be with Chris. The two of them had talked endlessly about fishing outings, where they could go rafting, if Ads would want to rent inflatable kayaks, and then they both laughed about Ads in an inflatable kayak. They were going to go biking and climbing and hiking. All of us were excited to be together for the week. Now, without Josh, this trip seems torturous.

On the other hand, I want to go because I will be with my family at all points of the day. I don't have to worry about not sleeping with someone. All meals will be with big crowds of people. I am excited to go. I tell Dr G. all of this. She listens and then initiates another topic.

'Natalie, let's talk about your house.'

I sit there silently.

'You need to start going back there.'

I still sit silently. I don't know what to say. I want to throw up.

'Maybe start with once a week. Then try to go more frequently.' *All right*, I think. *That's enough, sister. Let's not push it.*

I hate going to my house. Everything is horrible. The sound the door makes when it opens. The pictures. The food in the fridge. His car in the driveway. The smell. The smell is enough to kill me. But the worst is the nursery. The day before Josh died, the day before Father's Day, Josh went with my mom and dad and his mom to Pottery Barn Kids. He bought a rug, a crib sheet set, a mobile, and baby towels. He had cleaned out our old office for the new nursery. He was going to redo it while I was in Miami and surprise me when I got home. Now in the old office, the walls are bare. There are wallpaper removal items in the middle of the room and all of the furniture is gone. Everything from Pottery Barn Kids is still in his car. He didn't even get a chance to take it out of his car. Sometimes I forget that I didn't just lose Josh, but I also lost my baby's father. I walk into that empty nursery and something slams into me so hard it almost knocks me to the ground.

It has been over a month since his accident. Over the past couple of weeks, I have been frustrated by my lack of control over my emotions. I feel like I have Tourette's syndrome, only instead of swear words it's hysterical tears. I go to Colorado. I look at the mountains and the trees and I think of Josh.

We are at the rehearsal. I am wearing a hat. I am standing there, silently, literally holding my breath on and off, trying not to burst into tears in the middle of the minister giving us directions. Ads's friend Michael is doing one of the readings. Michael is from Texas and has a deep, slow voice

25

with a rich southern accent. The minister says, 'All right, Michael, go ahead and read your lines.' He starts in on 1 Corinthians. I feel like I am being tortured. It's not the 'love is patient, love is kind' part that gets me. Personally, I think that's a little cliché. I know that it's probably not right to call parts of the Bible cliché, but I just lost my husband and I'm six months pregnant so I'm okay with offending sacred texts. I'd tell it to God himself if he'd hear me. I've got quite a few offensive things to say to God actually, now that I think about it. But anyway, Michael starts in on the most beautiful and hurtful verses you could possibly pick. 'If I speak in the tongues of men and of angels, but have not love, I am only a resounding gong or a clanging cymbal. If I have the gift of prophecy and can fathom all mysteries and all knowledge, and if I have a faith that can move mountains, but have not love, I am nothing. If I give all I possess to the poor and surrender my body to the flames, but have not love, I gain nothing.'

First, my left leg starts to shake, and then, sure enough, it's like a drain opens up. Everyone feels awkward. Everyone stares at me. I pull myself together for the last ten minutes, and then once we're dismissed, I leave immediately. I go for a walk. I find an isolated spot in the woods and cry.

The next day is the wedding at the top of Mount Aspen. It's beautiful. I make it through the ceremony. Almost. Dubs gets up to speak. At the end of his speech, he says that Josh should be standing up there with him. In my brain, I thank Dubs for saying this, then instantly curse Dubs for saying this. I wait for an appropriate time to find my mom and I tell her I am leaving. I speed-walk to the gondola, and then, for the *first* time since the accident, I completely *lose* it, lose it.

You know in the movies when people are screaming over a person who has just died, 'No, God, why? *Why!* Why Jimmy? Why *now*?' and it's very dramatic and intense? I always thought that outrageous reactions like that really did happen right after a person dies. But for me, it didn't. Then, on July 28, 2007, less than an hour after my brother got married, I was alone in a gondola on Ajax Mountain screaming.

'You should be here! *You* should be here! Where the hell are you? You should be *here*!'

I secretly hope I see a sign. Maybe a bird could land on the plastic window. Maybe a bolt of lightning could streak across the sky. I wait for a noise, a voice, anything. But nothing happens. There is just the slow rocking of my gondola car headed down the mountain and my shrieking voice.

When I come home from Aspen, all I want is to be alone. I am finally able to go to my house. I sit in my house and cry. When I am done in one room, I walk to another room and cry. It doesn't make me feel better, but it doesn't make me feel worse. And I prefer it to having people watch me cry uncomfortably. I suddenly feel like no one can

talk to me anymore. No one knows what I am
going through.

And then I read *Harry Potter and the Deathly
Hallows*, which has just been published. There are
two epigraphs. The first one reads:

> *Oh, the torment bred in the race,*
> *the grinding scream of death*
> *and the stroke that hits the vein,*
> *the hemorrhage none can staunch, the grief,*
> *the curse no man can bear.*
> *But there is a cure in the house,*
> *and not outside it, no,*
> *not from others but from them,*
> *their bloody strife. We sing to you,*
> *dark gods beneath the earth.*
> *Now hear, you blissful powers underground –*
> *answer the call, send help.*
> *Bless the children, give them triumph now.*
> —Aeschylus, *The Libation Bearers*

The second one reads:

> *Death is but crossing the world, as friends do*
> *the seas; they live in one another still. For they*
> *must need be present, that love and live in*
> *that which is omnipresent. In this divine glass,*
> *they see face to face; and their converse is free,*
> *as well as pure. This is the comfort of friends,*
> *that though they may be said to die, yet their*

28

friendship and society are, in the best sense, ever present, because immortal.
—William Penn, *More Fruits of Solitude*

Does J. K. Rowling know me? I think to myself. She must. She must have had the book all ready to go, then heard about me and Josh and his accident and how I was pregnant, and so she called her publisher and said, 'Wait! I need to add two epigraphs for Natalie Taylor!'

'Who's Natalie Taylor?' some guy asks in a British accent. She rolls her eyes and scoffs at him. *Of course you wouldn't know who she is*, J. K. thinks to herself. But as another single mother in the world, J. K. knows my story already. She has written this for me.

I have suffered nearly two months of stupid fucking comments from people. 'Oh, it was meant to happen,' 'It's all a part of God's plan,' 'You are so strong, you'll be fine.' So many moronic attempts at sympathy. And then, over the Fourth of July weekend up north, no one said anything to us. People ignored us. Some people avoided eye contact. Like we were lepers! A pregnant widow? Watch out! She might be contagious! You never know! And here comes J. K. and I feel like we are best friends who have never met. I just want to pick up the phone and call her.

'J. K. It's Nat.'

'Finally!' she says, flopping down on her couch

and putting her feet up. We talk at length about how I'm *really* doing. We both cry. She gives me some words that are actually comforting.

At the conclusion of *Harry Potter and the Deathly Hallows*, in a chapter called 'King's Cross,' Harry is nearly killed. But instead of dying he is suddenly transported to a deserted tube station – King's Cross. At King's Cross Harry is reunited with Dumbledore, his hero who was killed fighting the book's villain. Dumbledore sits with Harry and tells him all about the things that Harry doesn't understand about life and death and finding his way. Right before the scene closes, Dumbledore gives Harry one last piece of advice: 'Do not pity the dead, Harry. Pity the living, and, above all, those who live without love.'

I read 'King's Cross' at least fifteen times. It is the only thing that makes any sense to me.

AUGUST

Don Corleone rose from behind the desk. His face was still impassive but his voice rang like cold death. 'We have known each other many years, you and I,' he said to the undertaker, 'but until this day you never came to me for counsel or help. I can't remember the last time you invited me to your house for coffee though my wife is a godmother to your only child. Let us be frank. You spurned my friendship. You feared to be in my debt.'

—MARIO PUZO, *THE GODFATHER*

A few weeks ago my dad bought me a copy of *The Godfather* by Mario Puzo. I had never read it or seen any of the movies, but after a few hours of reading I found myself completely immersed in it. I have become obsessed with the world of the Corleone family. I know they are cold-blooded killers, but there is so much more to them than that. They love each other, they want to protect each other, and they would die for each other. They're not that different from my family once you look past all of the money and guns. In fact, more and more I find myself analyzing scenarios from the perspective of Don Corleone.

Ever since I lost Josh, the world has turned into two classes of people. There are those people who would do anything for me, those to whom I feel more connected than I've ever felt before. Mathews, Battersby, Maggie, Josh's close friends Toby and Brian Elliott, of course my parents, in-laws, and siblings. All of these people have rallied to my side without a moment's hesitation. These people I will now address as The Family. Then there are those with whom I had more of a peripheral relationship before Josh died, but now after making only a few small gestures (or no gestures at all), these people have proven themselves to be unworthy of the Family. There are even a few people who were on the periphery prior to the loss of Josh but, because of their surprising yet welcome acts of kindness and generosity, have been accepted. And like the Corleones, my Family is not necessarily connected by blood or geographic location. They simply have to show their undying loyalty to me, to the rest of us, and they are in for life. And if someone betrays or disgraces one of my Family members, he or she is out for good.

Dr G. explains this as my new perspective of relationships. She doesn't use the Corleone

family as a metaphor and I don't bring it up –
I don't want to alarm her or anything. But she
does reiterate that now that I have experienced
death firsthand, I know the value of having strong
relationships. All of the people in my Family are
closer than they have been before. I talk to them
more often, we are more open with each other
about life in general, and we often express our
feelings more outwardly than we did before. But
on the other side, as Dr G. explains, I have no
tolerance for even the slightest hint of in-
authenticity (that's my word for it). People who
try to be nice but who are not truly there for me
are simply off the list. People who are not there
for me now clearly do not love me as much as
I thought.

For example, the other afternoon I was pulling
into my neighborhood and I saw this creepy guy
who lives in the duplexes at the entrance to my
subdivision watching me. I have always thought
this man was odd; I have seen him walking down
the street in the middle of the day wearing a white
V-neck T-shirt with stains on it and boxer shorts.
He has long greasy hair and a slimey smile. So, I
was thinking, what if this man came over one day
and attempted to forcibly enter my house? What
would I do? Obviously, I would first call the police,
but I can't expect them to be there promptly (the
Don would scoff at this, 'the police!?'), nor can I
expect them to do anything more than 'shoo' the
man away back to his house, which is four houses

down from mine. So whom would I call? I came to the following conclusion: First, I would call Toby. Toby is a close friend of Josh's from college. The summer after they graduated from college, Josh and Toby rode their bicycles across the country together. Josh always said that when they were older, someday they would do the same route on their motorcycles. Toby is first on the list for several reasons. First, he lives closest to my house. Second, Toby is from Indiana, and not that I am generalizing about people from Indiana, I do know that Toby has several firearms in his house (and probably his car), so he could come over armed. Now, obviously I wouldn't ask Toby to use a firearm against someone, but I would use his pistol to threaten the man and if necessary, I would shoot him, probably in the knee or femur. I've watched the *Beverly Hills Cop* trilogy enough times to know where to shoot a guy and not kill him. Axel Foley gets hit in the shoulder a lot (at least he did in the first one), but the shoulder is too close to the heart. Let's get real, I don't want to have this baby in jail. Or if he were really pissing me off, I would just fire away, point-blank, into his genital region. Let's be honest: any man who attacks a pregnant widow deserves to have the symbol of his masculinity blown to bits. It's that simple.

If Toby was not available, I would call Brian Elliott. Elliott and Josh played soccer together in college. Right before Josh died, they had taken up the sport (?) of paintball. It was one of the few activities where they could act like they were twelve and get away with it – a grown man's (?) version of Cowboys and Indians. Elliott is interesting because he does not own a pistol yet he has an entire arsenal of bizarre and lethal weapons (if used correctly). Elliott has a set of nunchucks, a Samurai sword set, and a night-stick that unfolds into something similar to what Donatello carried in *Teenage Mutant Ninja Turtles*. The downside to calling Elliott would be that he would have to go into hand-to-hand combat with my intruder, leaving me powerless in the situation. Elliott, however, unlike Toby, does not act rationally when someone in his family in endangered. He simply runs on ferocious emotion, which makes his wrath all that more terrifying. Toby is more cool and collected, the Rocco Lampone, while Elliott is more of a Luca Brasi. In short, now that I am a single woman living alone it is necessary that I have assigned button men. And I do. If I called them at any point of the day or night and said, 'There is someone in my house, will you come over and help me?' I know that they would be here without fail. They have an unquestionable loyalty, and if necessary they would kill another human being in my defense. That's the stuff that puts people in the Family.

Then there are those who are unworthy. For example, the other night my friends and I were at a restaurant in downtown Royal Oak for Elliott's birthday. We run into this guy, Ted Helms. Ted Helms is a friend from college. Josh adored him and he used to be close to the rest of us. The year after Mathews and I graduated from college (Josh was a year ahead of us) Mathews told Josh he was gay. Josh was the first person Mathews came out to. I was the second. Then slowly Mathews started telling more and more of our friends. Everyone was incredibly supportive. Ted Helms, however, is the only person who told Mathews that it is not okay for him to be gay. Ted sent some ridiculously ignorant e-mail saying something about how this is Mathews's 'choice' and Ted does not agree with it. He said he will never agree with it and he thinks it is morally wrong. Ted also said he does not want to hear anything about Mathews's 'gayness' in the future. What a fucking prick. So while we are out, Battersby, Maggie, and I see Ted Helms. Battersby and Maggie are both incredibly intelligent and graceful. However, in addition to these lovely qualities, they are both also highly confrontational. In every group of friends, there is at least one person who looks for a fight, who likes to mouth off after a few drinks and see who's in the mood. In *Romeo and Juliet* it's the character Mercutio. Everyone has a Mercutio. Battersby is Mercutio with curly brown hair and a manicure. Maggie also has a few of these tendencies. We have always said that Maggie has the identical personality of her miniature dachshund, Lennie: little dog, big attitude. In short, they both find it impossible to be fake to people. We see Ted Helms. We are shocked he showed up to hang out with Mathews and his friends. We see him chat with Mathews, like everything is cool again. Before he's within earshot, Batterbsy stirs her drink and calls him a 'fucking asshole.' Maggie mutters something under her breath about how it is 'certainly egregious of him.' Once he gets up to us, they greet him in that cold, snooty way that most females are capable of, and then Battersby explains to him that 'we'll be moving to another table.' Later on, I have the following conversation with Mathews.

'Mathews, Ted is out of the Family.'

'What?'

'Ted Helms is out of the Family. He has disgraced you.' Mathews gives me this weird look like he wants to say, 'Why are you talking like that?' but he doesn't. I continue. 'Maggie, Battersby [who are both ironically Irish, therefore fitting the character of Tom Hagan, the non-Italian consigliere], and I have discussed it. He is not one of us anymore.' Mathews puts his drink down and tells me something to the effect of 'it doesn't have to be like that.' I nod my head and let him think that, but I don't agree. Mathews is a kinder person than me at this point in our lives, but the strange thing is I don't feel guilty about being so mean to people. I wish he agreed with me. I want to yell at him and say, 'The Don would be disappointed in you!'

So now I embrace a sense of absoluteness when

it comes to friendships. I know that the absoluteness, in part, has also stemmed from my own frustration when people who know me seem to be stupefied in the presence of my grief. One of the most shocking side effects of being recently widowed is how frequently people avoid me. Take, for example, Melissa Murphy. Melissa and I went to high school and college together. She is friends with Mathews and his fraternity guys (again, Mathews is too nice to turn her away). A few days ago I saw Melissa at the gym. She saw me, made eye contact, and before I could say hello or make conversation, her eyes shifted and she darted the other way. Lame. I am tired of being treated like a leper. It pisses me off. So many times I have seen people who know me, who know what happened to me, and they walk away. They are scared or afraid or just too dumb, so they let me see them walk away. A few days later I run into Melissa again at a restaurant. She looks at me, surprised to see me, and says, 'Hey, Natalie, was that you I saw at the gym the other day?' *Oh come on*, I think to myself. *Give me a fucking break. You looked right at me.* I reply, maintaining strong eye contact and no friendly break of a smile, 'Yeah, that was me.' She tosses her blond hair back and uncomfortably adjusts her necklace and says, 'Oh, right, yeah, I saw you, but I didn't know if it was you, but I thought it was you, but like I didn't want to say hi if it wasn't you.' I let her finish completely. I don't interrupt because I want her to know just how stupid she sounds. Finally, she stops talking and looks at me for approval. 'Yeah, it was me,' I say again. But the subtext is, you're a rude bitch. I walk away, again, looking for my table, the table where only Family members can sit.

Just as the Corleone family knows, however, sometimes there are clashes in the Family. Carlo Rizzi is the new brother-in-law at the beginning of *The Godfather*. It is evident that the men in the Corleone family are skeptical of his character, but they must embrace him as their brother. Ashley, Josh's little sister, is my Carlo Rizzi. When Josh was here, he and Ashley had a rocky relationship. We only really saw her on holidays or during the summer at their cottage. But now that Josh isn't here, I see her almost every day of the week.

Ashley is my age and about my height, but she always feels taller than me. She has long blond hair and is ferociously good-looking. She is the type of woman who, when she walks in high heels, announces her presence with the sound of her heels striking the ground. This is an odd way to judge a person, I know, but just watch how some people walk, how loud their shoes are, and see if it doesn't match their personality. Another way I judge women is by when they choose to expose their cleavage. For example, most of my close friends (Maggie, Battersby, and Terrah) would only show their cleavage at a very special occasion – a wedding, for example. So they qualify as Wedding Date

Cleavage. And they would only show their cleavage at a friend's wedding, not a family member's wedding. Moo is more Date-Night Cleavage, but she lives in Miami where everybody is Morning Coffee Cleavage (or at least that's my impression of Miami as a midwestern suburbanite). Hales would blush if you said the word *cleavage*, and my mom hasn't shown off her cleavage since 1974, which classifies her as Back-in-the-Day Cleavage. But Ashley is Workday Cleavage, hands down. Four out of five days, she's showing off the girls. She is a wine rep and works at restaurants and bars, so it is an acceptable venue for cleavage, but still. In my mind, the only bosom display that ranks lower than Workday Cleavage is Religious Ceremony Cleavage. She's not quite there yet. She is extremely confident (most Workday Cleavage women are) and has a loud, definitive voice. I have always been intimidated by her, though I have never admitted this to anyone, most certainly not her. She is an intense human being who will always tell you exactly how she feels, even if her opinion is offensive, outlandish, or uninvited. She is boisterous, and though she would never outwardly admit it, she prides herself on getting what she wants. Aren't most Workday Cleavage women this way? Isn't that after all the objective of Workday Cleavage?

Perhaps the anecdote that best shows Ashley being Ashley stems from an incident that occurred a few weeks after Josh's funeral. When Ads and I were driving home from up north after the Fourth of July, Ashley called my cell phone. She had gone to the Tigers game the night before with Chris and some friends. I think they were excited to do something normal after a month of funeral stuff. I asked how the game was.

'The *game* was fine. Kinda long, but nothing exciting. But, um, it was after the game that a few crazy things happened.' This is a typical Ashley story setup. She acts like she doesn't really want to tell me what happened and now I will have to pry a little to get the details, but in reality she is dying to tell me something juicy. She had called me, after all. And I know I am not the only person who will get this suspenseful story today. She has this well rehearsed. She is looking to *stun* me with some drunken tale from last night.

'Oh *really*. Well, what happened?'

'Well, we were at the bar after the game – we went to the Inn Place in Royal Oak – and who do I see but none other than Brady Ryan.' She says his name slowly, as if to make sure I heard. She wants to solidify a reaction from her audience. Brady Ryan is the guy who directed Josh's funeral. Even before Josh's death, Ashley and her family have always known Brady; he grew up in the same area as they did, and she and Brady were acquaintances throughout high school and college. Obviously, in the days following Josh's death, we were with the guy all the time. He's now in his early twenties and is single and, if I may say so myself, he is a downright beautiful human

41

being. Having said all of that, he still directed her brother's funeral, but just in the tone of her voice, I know where this is going.

'Really. Well, how did that go?'

'Well, we chatted, had a few drinks, and then the next thing I knew he was dropping me off at my place.' She pauses and waits for me to ask what happened next.

'And then?'

'And then somehow it went from a beer at my apartment to a drunken make-out.'

I am officially stunned at this point. Stunned, but not stunned. I can't say it any better than that.

'You had a drunken make-out with Brady Ryan,' I say out loud, so Ads can hear me. He just about swerves off the road.

'Yeah, it was pretty funny, actually.' I can sense she is smiling through the phone. 'But after a little while, we both decided it didn't need to go any further.'

'Good for you, Ash,' I say dryly, still trying to process what she has just told me. I glance over at Ads. He is shaking his head in disbelief.

'Ash, that is funny. Wow. You and Brady Ryan. Maybe this is the beginning of a beautiful relationship. You never know.'

'Yeah, we'll see.' I can tell by the way she says this that she would not be opposed to repeating the experience. Finally I hang up.

As my phone clicks shut I look over at Ads. His jaw is dropped.

'*What?*' he says, slamming one hand down on the steering wheel. I relay the details.

'Nat, I'm not sure what to say right now.' I agree with him. We are both speechless, but we can't stop laughing. Obviously, as everyone in my family knows, Brady Ryan, for being so young, did a tremendous job with Josh's funeral and with helping us through the process. All of us were in awe of his sense of understanding for our grieving family and the way he conducted himself so confidently through the process. But this, this was the real red-blooded American boy coming through.

For the next thirty miles or so, we go back and forth discussing the hilarity of him making out with Ashley. We brainstorm ideas of what we will say next time we see Brady Ryan. 'Brady, hey, just so we're on the same page, I'm not going to get a bill for additional services rendered, am I?' or 'Brady, do you smash face with all of your grieving clients or just the blond ones?' To his credit, Ads and I both concede that with the combination of Ashley's natural saleswoman personality, her Workday turned Date-Night Cleavage, the overwhelming feeling that life is short, and alcohol, the guy didn't stand a chance.

Brady and Ashley never did follow through on the initial spark they had that night. And while I do find the whole thing a little concerning, I have to say that it gave me something to laugh about with Ads instead of thinking about how Josh wasn't the one driving next to me. Ads and I both concluded that Brady certainly did follow through on helping a girl in a time of loss, to say the least. How many funeral directors can put that much sense of life into dealing with death? Maybe I should even send Brady a thank-you card for his comic relief. I even have some leftover stationery from the funeral, courtesy of Brady himself.

I may not fully agree with Ashley's behavior all the time, but she is part of the capital *F* no matter what. But that is the nature of the Family. Sure, she is an in-law, but just like Carlo Rizzi that doesn't mean she's not in.

At my first baby shower Ashley of course shows up looking gorgeous with a full face of makeup and her blond hair looks perfect. She is wearing three-inch heels and clomps around as she excitedly arranges presents around me at the front of the room. Her enthusiasm is overwhelming. I sit with my shoulders rolled forward in a large armchair. I am not wearing makeup. My hair, which has not been highlighted since January, is pulled back in a low ponytail. I have always thought that showers, however generous they may be, are incredibly awkward for the person doing the opening. I feel greedy for asking for all of these things and I feel sad that I'm not even sure about being a single mom. But I have to act excited and happy. It's like being at your own wedding shower when you secretly hate the groom. The panini maker is only a big coverup for the truth: no object wrapped in pretty tissue paper can make the future easier. But we still sit here and do this. Ashley feels entirely different about the process.

Ashley makes me open her gift first in front of the twenty-six women at the shower. She hands me a laundry basket. I pick up the first outfit and am prepared to ooh and ahh and say my thank-you, but I quickly discover that the outfit is clipped to a piece of string, along with another outfit, then another, and another. The laundry line of baby clothes wraps around the entire room so that every single woman at the shower is holding an outfit attached to the clothesline. Everyone claps and gasps at Ashley's generosity. She beams. 'I went a little crazy!' She then announces to the crowd that she opened up a charge card at Baby Gap. Deedee turns to Aunt Kathy: 'Did you hear that? She opened a *charge card* at Baby Gap. That's *so* Ashley.' I am confused. I'm not quite sure whom the shower is for.

The entire time Ashley sits next to me, cleaning up wrapping paper and organizing gifts. She tells me about every present I open, as if I would other-wise be clueless of its function if it weren't for her. Ashley loves babies and children and desperately wants to have children, though at this point she isn't dating anyone. Before she got a job as a wine rep, she spent several summers and postcollege months nannying for a family with a two-year-old boy and triplet baby girls. As a result, she feels qualified to speak to all things baby and children. It seems like everything I hand to her, she gives

45

me her advice and finds it necessary to add in her own experiences with her children, which, again, weren't really her children at all.

'Hey, Nat, just so you know, all the girls had the Graco Snug-Ride car seat, and it was awesome because you can buy a separate base for your mom's car if you want. Lynn! Lynn!' – she is now yelling across the room to my mother – 'I just told Nat you can buy a separate base for this if you want!' Then 'Hey Nat, I know they say to use Dreft detergent with baby stuff, but just so you know, they say that Tide detergent is the worst.' (Is it?) I smile and say thanks and try to keep my cool. No one wants to see a pregnant woman freak out at her own shower. But man, I sure am close.

After the shower I sit and go through all the outfits by myself. The other week I went to breakfast with one of my co-workers, and she kept saying, 'But really, you must be so *relieved* to be pregnant. What a blessing. I mean, you must be *thrilled* to be pregnant, despite everything else.' I just kept nodding and staring at my pancakes, but I couldn't actually verbally agree with her. This is the most frightening thing in the world – to have a baby without my husband. I have absolutely no clue what I am doing. I have no idea what to expect or how to prepare. Am I thrilled? No. I'm downright scared. I'm scared and sad.

I have no urge to go out and buy baby clothes. Ashley always seems more excited than me to have this baby, but maybe that's more my fault than hers. My *fault*? Is that the right word? *Excited*? That can't be the right word either. It's just hard to be excited about anything right now. I am always thinking about Josh, and when I smile or laugh it never feels real. I can tell I'm faking it.

Although I go to my house for small increments of time, I am still living with my parents. No one is pressuring me to move back, but I know they all envision me moving back in at some point. I envision slapping a FOR SALE sign on the front lawn. Deedee suggests painting. She sees it as her mission to finish the nursery that Josh had started. I agree at first but only because I know it would make Deedee feel better, not because I am actually planning on moving in again.

'Well, the first thing we'll do is paint the ceiling white. Don't you think, Nat?' She says this as I stand in the doorway of the nursery. She is standing so close to me when she says this I can feel her body touching mine. And it's hot and humid in my house, not to mention my body has a built-in furnace. Deedee is a close talker and a long hugger, and she kisses right on the lips. I am particular about my personal space, I don't really like hugging people all that much, and I am most certainly not a lip kisser. The little barrier, the unspoken space that existed between us when Josh was here, is gone now. There is no screen, no buffer, that a woman normally has between herself and her husband's mother. No son to say to his

47

mother, 'No, Mom, let's not paint the ceiling.' There is just the mother-in-law and me. 'Till death do us part' may be true of husband and wife, but it's not true of the mother-in-law. She stays no matter where the husband goes. I think of this as she puts her arms around me. I try not to flinch in discomfort. She tells me she is going to finish this room for me. She is going to do it for Josh, and for me, and for my son. This is an incredibly kind gesture, but all I can think is that if she doesn't let go of me, I'm going to start choking for air. I feel like I'm inhaling Saran Wrap. She won't let me leave this house. If I tried, it'd be Tiananmen Square in my driveway.

'Well, you *are* using Benjamin Moore paint, aren't you?' Deedee says later at my parents' dining room table. This is her way of disguising a direction in the form of a question. 'I mean, you can't beat Benjamin Moore paint.' Deedee says this all the time. I've known her for four years now and I have heard her say this exact same sentence at least twenty times. You must be wondering how many times in four years can a group of people talk about paint – not even paint color, but paint *manufacturers*. Amazing, I know. She also says it about her three staple recipes that she has made for twenty-five years. I'm not sure if you've heard, but you can't beat swiss cheese chicken, hamburger soup, or marshmallow sweet potatoes either.

Sure, Benjamin Moore sounds great, I tell her.

I just want to get it over with, though. Just put the paint up so I don't have to think about who wasn't there to do it. Let's hammer this thing out. But once she decides to repaint the nursery, she also decides to repaint Josh's old office and the master bedroom. I don't know if allowing her to do this is okay or if this is what I'm supposed to do. But I don't know what I am supposed to do, so I just kind of go along with it. I won't live in my house as it looks right now, but I feel like I'm not supposed to change things around me so quickly. It seems like you're not allowed to redecorate so shortly after someone dies. I am breaking some sort of undefined law, defying a code of grief. I have this fear that one day two grief auditors will show up and point to the drop cloth and the blue tape and I'll be punished with two more months of losing it in line at Target. I decide to do it anyway, but I want it over and done.

All my life, I've been the type of person who takes the accelerated route. I liked being in advanced classes. Normally it takes people five to six years to complete an education degree, perform the requisite student teaching, and earn teaching certification. I did it in four. When I decide to do something, I want it done quickly. I do not dilly-dally. When Dr G. told me that grief takes time, I wanted to say, 'But what about for the smart kids?' I took Advanced Placement Calculus in high school. Let's talk Advanced Placement Grief. But one of the first things I realize about this stupid emotion is that AP Grief does not exist. Time goes by, weeks pass, a month passes, my belly grows, my hair grows, but when I wake up in the morning it feels exactly the same. Grief goes at its own speed. Because there is such a lack of progress in my emotional healing, I just want to see progress somewhere else. Every time Deedee leans against the wall with another paint swatch, I think that this may be the only way to compensate. My brain is royally screwed up and I feel completely unprepared to have this baby, but maybe paint is the answer. It would be nice if something in my life – even if it's just paint – reflects readiness for this child to come into the world. So the house becomes the project and my mother-in-law decides to spearhead the project with me waddling in tow.

We go to Benjamin Moore. Deedee picks out the colors. Skylark Song for the nursery, French Lilac for the bedroom, and Oklahoma Wheat for the office.

'Anything worth doing is worth doing right,' she says to me as she individually cleans the blinds in the baby's room. She wants to clean the blinds before she starts painting. Every single blind. 'Wednesday,' she says. 'We'll start Wednesday.' But it's too humid on Wednesday, so we move it to Friday. The primer goes on. Then we wait. 'Well, it needs another coat of primer, don't you think? And you are going to paint the ceiling, right?' Again, a direction dressed in a question's clothing.

50

'Anything worth doing . . .' she says to me. I sneak out before she can start in on Benjamin Moore. A million different things come up. A million reasons why we have to postpone the paint. 'You really can't do molding all at once' or 'You know, even the guys [how she refers to the people who work at Benjamin Moore] say that you should allow a full two days for drying.' She is insistent on the details of the process. I just want the results. I hate the process. Pregnancy, grief, paint. Every element of my life feels like I'm wading in molasses. But with the paint, that molasses has a name: Deedee. The AP Grief student in me is deeply, deeply frustrated.

Finally the ceiling gets done. Deedee yells for me to come in and see it. She likes to yell across the house. I walk in. She is standing in the nursery with her hands on her hips, admiring her work. If this were my own father or Josh or my mom, I would walk in and say, 'Looks great. Let's get going with the walls now.' But with Deedee, I can't. There are these little unwritten rules with her that I have to feel out. I remember my first encounter with her seven-layer Jell-O cake on Thanksgiving was almost disastrous. ('No, Deedee, it's not that I don't like it, it's just I'm not a big Jell-O fan. No, it's not that I won't eat *your* Jell-O cake, I just don't like Jell-O in general.') After a half-hour Jell-O conversation, I gave up and I've been eating it ever since. So now, here we are. She really needs me to stand here and take the time to appreciate this ten-by-ten-foot white ceiling, which I didn't even think needed to be repainted and has just set us back by about ten days. She stares at it.

'It just makes the room feel warm,' she says.

'*So* warm,' I say, nodding.

'I think it really does it for the whole room.'

'*Totally* does it.'

'I just love it, don't you?'

'Really really really love it.'

A lifetime of this, I think to myself. *A lifetime of seven-layer Jell-O cake and drawn-out conversations with my mother-in-law and no husband.*

After the ceiling, things slow down again. I suggest hiring a professional. Out of the question, she says. Not only does Deedee work at her own pace, but she has to be in charge of every single detail. The dogs come back next week. I tell Deedee that I want to move in before they get back. I want to be settled before the dogs come home. I think she is so excited by the prospect of me being in my house again that she finally gets her act together.

Oklahoma Wheat starts to transform the office. French Lilac slowly fills my bedroom. I stand in the vacant nursery staring at Skylark Song, amazed at the progress of this little room. Miraculously, all three rooms of my house are completed before the dogs get back from their summer training camp. I walk through my house. The paint sings from the walls. Deedee did an amazing job. As much as she drives me crazy, I am desperately dependent on her help. The only thing more frustrating than the presence of my in-laws is the fact that I really really need their help. I hate admitting this more than anything.

It's my first night alone in my house. The dogs come back tomorrow morning. I know I have to do something. I can't just sit around and stare at old pictures. I need to fall asleep with some sense of accomplishment. I decide to frame the pictures and hang them on the wall.

Last Christmas Deedee bought me a box of ten black frames. Three five-by-sevens, four four-by-sixes, one eight-by-ten, and two two-by-threes. Anyone who knows me can tell you that there is a reason why I let Josh make all of the redecorating decisions. I have a horrible concept of spatial relations. It is very difficult for me to envision and estimate how much space something will take up. A couch, a table, a frame, whatever it is, I have a difficult time figuring out how one thing will look, or if it will fit in a different place. Josh would often tease me about this. He would roll his eyes when I wanted to rearrange furniture, but still he would help me move chairs and tables around, only to laugh when everything had been reassigned to its new location and the couch stuck out two feet into the doorway. And then, laughing at my deficiency, he would help me move it back.

I consider all of this as I look at my stack of ten frames. I consider how if Josh were here he would hammer in all of the nails. He wouldn't even need to think about how he would arrange them first. He would just stand there quietly, hang one frame, look at it, and then hang the next. By the end, it would look perfect. I consider how I am sad that he is not here, not just to hang the frames but that he can't stand in this hallway anymore. He can't look at these pictures with me and laugh about how mad I was that day we went fly-fishing. He can't tell me that he doesn't want to use the one from last Christmas because he was chubby or that he wants to hang the one of Ashley from last summer in her bathing suit because she was chubby and he knows she'll hate it. He can't do any of this. He will never do any of this again. How am I supposed to sleep here tonight? How am I supposed to do anything again, knowing he can never share it with me?

But I get out the toolbox and I take the plastic off the frames. I don't know why this is so important. I don't know why I make myself do this. It's like everything else I do lately. Taking out the garbage, emptying the dishwasher, putting wet laundry in the dryer – every motion that I go through in the house reminds me that Josh used to be here, but I still make myself do it because I want to remember what it used to feel like and I need to know what it feels like now.

I arrange the frames on the floor of my bedroom. I come up with a few arrangements. *Wait and see what Mathews thinks*, I tell myself. But then my body takes over again and I hang the first frame. I measure everything on the wall. I make pencil marks all over the wall. I want to make sure it looks perfect. I want to make sure I know how to make it look perfect. I measure the distance from one frame to the next. I measure the center of the frame. I measure how far down the hook is from the top of the frame. And then finally, I hammer the nail.

As an amateur in the business of hammering nails, I am annoyed at how difficult it is to hammer a nail in straight. The first three nails do not go well at all. The whole wall shakes and it takes me about fifteen strikes with the hammer to get it into position. A couple of times I hit my fingers, bend the nail, or shift it off center. Again, I get sad and frustrated that Josh isn't here to do this. I can picture myself in a parallel world somewhere yelling his name. And he walks up from the basement and silently takes the hammer from me and finishes the rest of the nails. And then when he's done he does something funny like pull up his shirt sleeve and flex his bicep or flip the hammer in the air and catch it after one full turn. I can see all of this. And then I become angry that I can't see any of this. I will never see any of this again. They're just nails and a hammer, just frames on a wall. But he's always there no matter what I'm doing. He's always there reminding me that he can never be there again.

An hour and a half later all ten frames hang on

the office wall. They look perfect. I stand back and look at my work. I am impressed with myself, a little surprised also. I toss the hammer back in the toolbox, a lofty, cocky toss, as if I am its new master.

Later on that night I am lying in my bed. I stare up at the ceiling. I can't sleep. I can't think. I get out of bed and try to find a book to read. I can't read *The Godfather* at night. It scares me. The other day when I read the scene in which Michael has dinner with Sollozzo and McCluskey the cop, I had to stand up and walk around in the middle of it because I was so nervous for Michael. Tonight I just want to read something light and funny. I walk into my living room and look at the bookshelves. I see a small spine in the corner of the shelf. It says *Jelly Belly* in green writing. *Jelly Belly* is a book written for middle-school-aged kids. It's about a boy who goes to fat camp and how he hides food in his swim trunks and stuff like that. *Jelly Belly* is one of my dad's all-time favorite books. We have it in our bookshelf because he gave it to Josh to read. That's the mark of a real gentleman. No matter what stupid thing my dad asked Josh to do – try on his new Keens, go shopping for orchids, or read a sixth-grade book about some chubby kid at fat camp – Josh did it. I open the book and right there in the front cover is a picture of Josh and me dancing at our wedding. We are looking at each other, smiling. A pain pangs in my stomach. I can feel my throat dry up. I know exactly why this picture is here. Josh always used photographs as his bookmarks. So first, it tells me he picked this picture as a bookmark. I think of him looking at it, holding it and thinking, *Yeah, I like this one*, smiling to himself and sliding it into the book. That's part of the crying. The second part is he picked out a bookmark for *Jelly Belly*, which means he had every intention of reading it. He didn't just take it from my dad and say, 'Oh yeah, sure,' and then throw it aside. He was actually going to read it because my dad wanted him to.

Earlier this month Dr G. asked me what I thought of 'spiritual connections.' I said I didn't really know, but on the inside I was rolling my eyes. 'Smoke and mirrors,' is what I wanted to say. She could sense my rigidity to the subject so all she said was, 'Just don't close yourself off.' I can't remember the rest of what she said about it, but I remember that part exactly. I'm not saying I had a spiritual connection with Josh via *Jelly Belly*, I'm just saying I found the book and thought of Dr G.'s words.

I don't read *Jelly Belly*. Eventually I just get back in bed. I lie in bed, in the middle of the bed with one pillow. This is my life. The toolbox belongs to me. The bed only has one pillow and one body. I can only see Josh in pictures. I know I will make it, I know I will survive, but I hate my life. Somewhere, hours later, as I finally drift off to sleep I can feel Josh telling me, Don't hate your life.

It is his desperate message: Don't hate your life.

The next morning Louise and Bug arrive, with wagging tails and boisterous barks. I know they are so happy to see me and I them, but they are also completely unsympathetic to me and my grief. They need attention and care and energy that I just can't seem to summon. Jason, the dog trainer, comes over once every two weeks to help train me in handling them. He tells me how to hold the leash, what to say to command them and how to say it. He emphasizes the point that the person giving the command (me) has to do so in a way that is calm and controlled. He says the dogs will respond to a calm, controlled command. Jason is a very nice man, but when he says this, part of me wants to look at him and report, 'Easier than it sounds, ace.' I am a lot of things right now and calm and controlled are certainly not on the list. But I lie. 'Got it,' I tell Jason. I nod my head and say, 'Sure, I can do that.'

When Jason walks with us the dogs are awesome. For the first couple of hours after he leaves they are great. Even the first walk or two with me at the helm is okay. I feel like I really am in control. But after he's been gone for a few days, they start to come undone. Or maybe it's me coming undone.

When Josh was here, he was the pack leader. Louise and Bug listened to him because they could sense his confidence. Anyone who knew Josh, dog or human, could sense his confidence. I tell myself I am going to be the pack leader, but I know I'm not made of pack leader stock. The dogs know this too. But we walk every day. We practice our new family every day.

Even with two animals in the house, it still feels very lonely. It is strange walking in the door and not having anyone to yell hello to, to fold laundry with no conversation, to go to bed by myself. Sometimes all I want to do is fill this house with people, but I know once everyone got here all I would do is scream for them to get out. Sometimes I resent how involved my in-laws are in my life right now. They are family – no, they are the Family – but it still feels like my in-laws are making an impossible situation more difficult. Ashley comes over and gives me coupons she's collected from Carter's and Target and tells me about how she went shopping for the baby on her lunch hour. I have to tell myself, *She is only helping,* but really she makes me crazy. I feel like she's constantly reminding me that I am not excited enough for this baby. Her loud voice – it's like she talks that way just to try to get my attention. When she sits on my couch, I just think about how I want her to leave. Then when I sit alone I think about how it's almost easier to put up with their uninvited visits than a silent house.

I tell Moo about how my days and nights are so quiet except for Louise and Bug. Moo suggests I start listening to podcasts at night. She listens to a show called *This American Life* hosted by this guy named Ira Glass.

I go for a walk by myself and listen to an episode. The first show I download is called 'Unconditional Love.' The episode is about a woman, Heidi, and a seven-year-old boy she adopted from Romania. Halfway through my walk I am crying all over myself. But the weird part is I don't know exactly why I'm so upset. I'm upset because this kid spent seven years standing in a crib in an orphanage with no parents or grandparents or friends and that makes me really sad. Also, this Heidi woman wanted a child so badly that she adopted a son who was on the cusp of the most difficult age for a boy. And here I am pregnant with a perfectly healthy baby and wishing for a different life. All I want to do is call Heidi and invite her over. I just want to talk to her. I am obsessed with finding people who have seen the universe bear its ferocious teeth and I am entirely sick of people who seem to live free and easy.

No wonder I identify more with Italian mobsters than with the average pregnant woman. The Corleones and I are both entrenched in an ugly world of death. We both see the gruesome part of life that most people spend their lives trying to avoid.

This year Labor Day weekend begins at the end of August. I'm afraid to be alone for the weekend so I decide to go up north with my parents. My single friends will be going to bars and staying out late. My married friends will be going to barbeques with their in-laws. So I just leave to avoid the out-of-placeness and potential rejection.

On the way up north I sit in the back of my dad's car. My dad drives and my mom sits in the passenger's seat. Ads calls my dad's cell phone, but I pick it up. I am in the middle of a conversation with Ads when we hit a dead zone. I hand my dad his phone back and announce that the call broke up. I know my dad is doing everything he can not to ask me, 'Well, is everything okay?,' paranoid that perhaps Ads had to hang up because he got into a car accident or he was suddenly being held at gunpoint. He doesn't ask this because he knows it will really piss me off. I've been a little touchy lately – not surprisingly – and I know my dad is consciously trying to give me space. A few minutes later, my mom's cell phone rings. At first, she picks up my dad's cell phone, whose ring is nothing like hers.

'That's your phone,' he says.

'What?' She looks at him, as if he's the idiot. Clearly the phone she is holding is *his* phone.

'No, the phone that's ringing. That's *your* phone.'

'Oh.' My mom sets my dad's phone down and picks up her iPod, and for just a split second she almost brings it to her ear. Finally, she sets the iPod aside and finds her phone. I grab the phone to relay to Ads the entire ridiculous scenario of Mom almost answering her iPod.

'Stop it!' she yells from the front seat. 'Stop watching me!' Ads and I rap for a few more minutes and then he remembers that he has something to tell Mom. So I hold the phone out to Mom and say, 'Here, Mom, Ads has a funny story.' My mom, who I instantly realize is engrossed in Dr Joy Browne on her iPod, takes the phone and shuts it, leaving Ads waiting on the other line a bit confused.

'Mom!' I yell. She pulls her headphones out.

'What?' she says, again irritated that I am getting on her case for no good reason.

'Ads wanted to tell you a funny story.'

'Oh!' She laughs to herself and calls him back. 'Ads, sorry hun.' I can't hear him, but I know he is reminding her of the time she fell asleep when he was talking to her.

We stop at a Wesco gas station in Evert. I am relieved not only because I have to pee, but because I need a break from being eight months pregnant and sitting in the backseat. Moments later my mom and I are standing outside the car waiting for my dad. He walks to the car slowly, carrying his gas station purchases.

'Are you guys sure you don't want anything?' he asks.

'Yeah,' I say shortly. 'Let's go.'

'What did you get?' my mom asks.

'I got two Chunkies and a piña colada SoBe.' My dad pronounces it 'Sue-be.' I roll my eyes at this, because it is obviously pronounced 'So-be.' It is completely phonetic.

'Oh.' My mom sounds interested.

For the next several minutes of the drive, my dad offers my mom one of his Chunkies, which she initially rejects but then, after his pestering her, accepts. The same thing happens with the SoBe. He takes a sip and then hands it to her. Eventually, she drinks most of it, not realizing it, until the last sip remains.

'You can finish it,' my dad says.

'No, it's too sweet for me,' she says, honestly not realizing she has consumed most of his beverage. So to make her feel like she didn't just take half of his gas station snack, he drinks the rest.

This is how it always works with my parents. At restaurants, gas stations, and wedding buffets. My mom always says she doesn't want any and then steals his to make herself feel like she didn't really eat it. As I sit in the car, I am initially frustrated by this. Why can't my mom just buy her own Chunkies, her own piña colada SoBe? And then, with both grief and happiness coursing through me, I realize that this is how they are. Their actions, however minute, always involve each other. He knows she will take his food, which is why he buys two Chunkies. She knows he will have enough for her. This is what they have developed after thirty-two years of marriage. I am happy for them that they have little things like this, little ways to remind each other that they are there. I am sad that I may never have this again.

Or perhaps that I did. I knew such a feeling. And now I don't.

It's not just the sight of my parents' marriage that evokes this sense of emptiness. I feel like everyone in my life is normal and I'm different. I see women and men pushing strollers and all I feel is anger toward them. I just want to find another Heidi or another me. Maybe I don't want to go shopping because all of the pregnant women at Baby Gap are wearing wedding rings, looking really happy. Maybe I don't want to chat it up with everyone about my pregnancy because all I can think about is how Josh isn't here. Maybe I channel all of my frustration toward my in-laws because the one person who is supposed to be dealing with them is gone, and that's all I can think about when they call. I just want to be around people who aren't normal anymore.

I look at my parents in the front seat. In so many ways they drive me crazy and they are a constant reminder that I never get to have what they have. At the same time I know I am incredibly grateful for them. They have helped me in a way that I will never be able to repay. But that is the credo that holds the Family together. That is the strand that ties us to the Corleones. We both know that without the Family, we don't stand a chance.

SEPTEMBER

So we beat on, boats against the current,
born back ceaselessly into the past.
—F. SCOTT FITZGERALD, *THE GREAT GATSBY*

Summer is over and it's time to go back to
school. In some ways this is wonderful. I
have to get dressed in the morning. I have
to brush my hair and pick out shoes. I am so
relieved that I had an entire summer to not think
about my appearance, but starting each day with
a direction and a destination is a good thing.

In other ways it's really, really scary. I have prac-
ticed not crying in front of people for two months
and somehow I have convinced myself that I will
absolutely not present any of my inner feelings of
weakness while at school. But teenagers are a lot
like dogs in that they can sense things that others
can't. They know, they *know*, when a teacher is
not on sturdy ground. And the thing is, I teach
at a lovely school. We have wonderful students,
but they're still teenagers. This year I decided to
work part-time (Monday, Tuesday, Thursday) so

I can stay home a few days a week when my son is born. I am teaching two sections of ninth-grade English and one section of eleventh-grade English. Ninth-graders are usually incredibly eager to please and try very hard to earn the approval of their teacher. I'm not particularly concerned about them. Eleventh-grade students, however, are typically very cynical and at this point in their high school careers are ready to question everything, especially the teacher and the text. They're not dogs, they're velociraptors.

We start the year with *The Great Gatsby* by F. Scott Fitzgerald. *Gatsby* was published in 1925, but it didn't achieve its fame until after Fitzgerald passed away. The story takes place in New York during the 1920s – the Jazz Age (test question). Jay Gatsby is this hotshot bachelor who lives on the new-money side of the bay, and five years prior to when the story starts he was in love with a woman named Daisy. She loved him too, but he wasn't from her socioeconomic playing field. So he goes off to war. She is sad but then meets this other guy named Tom Buchanan and he's filthy rich (but a real jackass, as we later find out). Tom and Daisy get married and have a daughter. Well, you guessed it, five years later, Gatsby shows up and he's made himself filthy rich in order to win back his golden girl. I won't give away the ending, but you really should read it not only because it's a good story, but also because Fitzgerald is basically a poet who writes novels. He's the Kobe

Bryant of 1920s literature. Finesse, it's all finesse. (Hemingway is Shaquille O'Neal, but Fitzgerald is totally Kobe).

In chapters 5–7 of *The Great Gatsby*, Fitzgerald introduces (or begins to heavily emphasize) the theme of time. Jay Gatsby has been in love with Daisy for 'five unwavering years' and even though she is married and has a child, Gatsby still believes that they can make it work. Fitzgerald gives the reader all sorts of clues that Gatsby is living in the past. There are 'period rooms' throughout his house. The only picture that Fitzgerald chooses to mention is of an old friend, Dan Cody, taken nearly twenty years ago. At one point the narrator, Nick Carraway, describes Gatsby as 'an over-wound clock.' The most obvious reference to time is when Gatsby sees Daisy for the first time in the book. He is so nervous during their awkward meeting that he bumps into the clock on Nick's mantel. It drops and Gatsby, the man who is determined not to let the events of five years ruin his dream, catches the clock and prevents it from breaking.

One of the most blatant references to Gatsby's desire to go back in time is when he describes to Nick his ultimate plan to break up Tom and Daisy and marry Daisy the way it should have been. Nick remarks, 'You can't reinvent the past.' Gatsby replies by saying, 'Can't reinvent the past? Why, of course you can!'

In previous years I always got to this part and

thought, wow, Gatsby needs serious therapy. How can an intelligent human being believe that you can actually go back in time? As one of my students today pointed out, it's like in *Napoleon Dynamite* when Napoleon tries the time machine and the uncle wants to be a high school football star again. And it is. I always believed that Gatsby would, just as foolishly, try the time machine too. That's how bad he wants to go back. Yet it's one of the most basic laws of physics – the clock only goes forward; it is completely impossible to go back in time. And the people who want it to go back, or the people who think it can, must be entirely delusional. Gatsby, Napoleon's uncle – don't they know any better? Don't they know that the past, present, and future can never collide?

But this year I feel like Gatsby and I have a whole lot more in common. We both had a dream. We both pictured our lives working out in certain ways. We worked and planned and spent years trying to build a certain style of life. We both had visions of future Christmas cards, he with Daisy, and me with Josh and the kids. Gatsby pictured himself and Daisy, sitting on a blanket enjoying the scenery of West Egg, talking about nothing, just relieved at the company. I had pictured Josh and me, sitting on the dock at Elk Lake, Josh swinging our baby boy into the water and talking about tying flies for fly-fishing and hunting for frogs. But like Gatsby, there comes a moment when it settles in that all the things we've pictured will never happen. And we both think, *This is as happy as we can ever be*. If this person is not in our lives then there is nothing else to look forward to. There is no image of the future on which we can rest comfortably. That person (me, Josh; him, Daisy) is the 'incarnation' of our dream. For both of us, the dream dies almost as quickly as it came.

You can't reinvent the past. It seems so simple. But for me life has now been abruptly sliced into two categories. Before Josh died and after Josh died. And there are moments when I think that I can somehow go back. Until Josh died, I thought I understood what time was and how it worked. I thought I knew that you couldn't go back. But death gives time a whole new meaning. I have days on which suddenly it will hit me, as if for the first time, and I will say to myself, *Oh my God. I'm never going to see him again*. Every time that thought comes to my mind, no matter when or where I am, it seems to be as painful as the first time. I can't go back. I will never be able to go back. I know that even now, three months later, my brain hasn't fully absorbed that concept. That's what Gatsby and I also have in common. We can't seem to swallow our own realities. Of course, it's not like I'm cooking dinner for two and looking out the driveway waiting for his car to pull up, but I still don't know if I get it.

A few weeks after Josh died I ordered return address labels that only had my name on them. Instead of JOSH AND NATALIE TAYLOR they just said

NATALIE TAYLOR. Around the same time, I took Josh's name off of our checking accounts, and I immediately ordered new checks with only my name on them. Most notably, not even a month after losing Josh, I stopped wearing my wedding ring. I did this because I wanted everyone to know that I got it. I didn't want *anyone* to think that I was in denial about his death (as if Consumers Energy or Comcast Cable care about whether or not I'm in denial). Months later, as I read *The Great Gatsby* again, I think about my return address labels, checks, and wedding ring. I don't get it. I don't understand what has happened. I just try to change things around me to help my brain along. But it doesn't help.

A week into school I talk to all three of my classes about how yes, obviously I am pregnant and will not be here the entire semester. I explain to them that I will be having a baby in the next few weeks, and once I leave, a long-term substitute will be with them until the end of the semester. This is really where you see the difference in age. The ninth-grade students sit frozen in their seats and the boys especially look scared to death that their female teacher, whom they really don't know all that well, is talking about having a baby, you know like, delivering a baby. They seem to sit as still as possible and try to wait until the conversation is over. Once, Hales told me about when she was in the third grade and her teacher, Mrs Sylvan, who was very pregnant,

70

calmly announced to her room of eight-year-olds that her 'water broke.' Haley said that immediately all the kids in class picked their feet up off of the floor, as if the water would soon seep under their desks. I have a strange feeling that the same thing could happen in my ninth-grade class if I were to be so horrifically unlucky.

The eleventh-graders, of course, approach the subject with a brash, arrogant tone. 'Mrs Taylor!' Steven McCain yells from the front of the class. I had Steven in class as a ninth-grade student. I have learned to seat him in the front where he is less likely to verbally assault other students. He is the type of high-school student who claims to be really good at 'debating,' but seems to think debating consists of interrupting people who disagree with him and constantly saying over-dramatized lines from Hollywood portrayals of attorneys like 'Overruled!' or 'Erroneous on all counts!' So here he is, weighing in on my current state of gestation.

'Mrs Taylor! I just want you to know I can drive you to the hospital if you have the baby in class.' This is the other thing: Everyone in the world except women who have actually had a baby assumes that childbirth happens with this tremendous sense of immediacy. It must always happen with someone speeding through traffic lights as the woman holds her stomach with two hands and practices breathing exercises from a decade ago.

I tell Steven that I would rather walk to

Beaumont Hospital but thank him for the offer. Then an argument quickly erupts between Steven and Anthony Myers, who sits on the opposite side of the room (for a good reason), about who would be the better driver.

'I'm in the parking lot on Sunnyknoll, Anthony, and you're all the way over in the Trash Lot [student name for the parking lot on Catalpa]. It would be ridiculous for you to drive.'

'Steven, you just got your license a month ago – you think you should drive a pregnant lady to a hospital after driving for a *month*?'

I pick up the handouts for today and get things going. Like most conversations that Steven McCain initiates, this is a stall tactic.

'I saw you roll right through that stop sign at Catalpa and Henley yesterday, Anthony,' Steven pipes back.

'You didn't see me! I didn't roll through that stop sign, and if I did, there's no way you saw me.'

'You can't prove if I didn't!' Steven looks up at me and changes the tone of his voice, 'Is that the type of guy you want driving you to the hospital, Mrs Taylor? A guy who *rolls* through stop signs?' Anthony tries to counter, but I cut him off before he can form a rebuttal. I tell the front row to take a handout and pass it back. Steven shoots a look to Anthony that says, 'I rest my case!' I tell Steven he can take his argument in the hall if he'd like. He looks at me and says in a way that assures me someday he actually will be a very smarmy lawyer, 'Mrs Taylor, I just want to make sure you are taken care of.' I say thank you and move on with the assignment.

No matter how rowdy my students are, no matter what kind of ridiculous arguments I have to referee, it is nice to think about something other than the pain of grief. I feel okay at school. It's like getting some fresh air. But aside from those eight hours of structure and distraction, it's tough.

Sometimes I debate with myself as to what is now the worst time of day. I used to think it was first thing in the morning. Right after the accident, I would dream about Josh almost every night. He would be there, vivid, and everyone else in the dream would know what happened except him. In one dream I was at work and insisted on leaving early to get home to see Josh. I made a big scene – 'No, I really have to go!' – and I stormed out. One time I dreamed he walked out of the hospital room, good as new. 'You're alive!' I said. He smiled like nothing happened. In my dream, I started to call all of my friends. 'Josh is alive! Yeah, he's right here!' In the dream I thought about how I had to cancel my appointment with Dr G. Lately I've been dreaming that Mathews and I are trying to figure out where he is. 'Has he responded to your e-mails?' I ask Mathews in the dream. I've also had the one where I try Josh's number and he doesn't pick up, or I haven't seen him in a few days and

I start to worry. I know why I have these dreams. Deep down my brain is saying, 'This is too horrible to be real life. This didn't *really* happen to me.' Then I wake up and realize that it did, which is why I used to think waking up was the worst part of the day. It isn't.

You might think the evening is the worst. Especially when the sun goes down and it starts to get dark outside. This is the time when families cook dinner, when people come back from practice or long meetings. I also quickly realized that this is when Josh always would have been home. I call my friends, but they're in for the night. They're with their fiancés eating dinner or watching TV. My mom and dad are washing dishes and *Entertainment Tonight* is on in the background. But I am alone. The dogs are quiet. The house is quiet. This used to scare me, when I would feel the sun setting. But ever since August, I've been listening to my radio shows in the evening. Dr Joy Browne and Ira Glass fill the empty space of my house. I turn on the Tigers if there is a baseball game. Last night I watched the U.S. Open. So the evening is not as bad as it was. It's still bad, I should say, it's just not quite the monster it used to be.

But today I realized that after school is the worst time of day. This is my first week of school and while I am relieved to be busy again, I have also found that all of my actions throughout the day somehow used to involve Josh. He used to leave

74

me funny voice mails on my work phone. I used to call him on my prep hour. I always called him at lunch or on my way home from work. Oftentimes if he didn't work late, he would be home around four. Some days we would be so tired from work we would both take off our work clothes and just lie in our bed at five o'clock in the afternoon talking about our days. I can see him so clearly, hanging up his suit in the closet, wearing his boxer shorts, telling me a funny story from work.

After he changed into comfy clothes, Josh would usually have a lot of errands to run, or so he claimed. He would want to go to Margaret's (his grandma), or his mom's, or want to 'see what my parents were doing for dinner,' or he'd want to go to English Gardens or to Best Buy, and I would complain that I hated English Gardens and I hated Best Buy. But we would always get in the car with only a few things on our list and it would take us hours to get home. But we were together and he made everything fun.

Today I come home from school at three thirty. I lie down for a minute because my feet hurt. I think to myself how I have nowhere to go. I have no errands to run. It's too early to work on stuff for school, and besides, what's the point? Everything is just an excuse to not sit in the quiet and think about how he's not here. I just sit there and stare at the closet and I listen to the sound of my own deep breaths as the tears come out unexpectedly. *He's not home, Nat,* I tell myself. *He's not home.*

Jason ended his biweekly dog-training sessions at the end of August. I have been trying really hard to keep it cool on the walks when the dogs get a little jittery, but I'm not good at it. Every walk gets worse. I get worse so they get worse. Today's walk is a huge disaster.

Relaying the details only makes it more painful. They are horrible. They lunge at every stupid squirrel, chipmunk, or leaf that sputtered across the road. Louise pulls on the leash almost the entire time and the more frustrated I get the farther forward she moves.

Finally, we get home and I proceed to emotionally explode. I rip off my sunglasses, throw their water bowl on the ground, and tell both of them that I don't even want to look at them. I am dripping with sweat. I tear my clothes off and get in my bathrobe. I hate my life.

I get in the shower. I sit on the floor of the shower. Sitting on the floor of the shower is the ultimate act of surrendering. It's where I go when I have been defeated. I think about nothing and everything at the same time. I stay there a while, just staring at my feet, feeling how when I lean forward, just a little, my belly can touch every part of my body.

I get out of the shower. Louise and Bug are lying in their bed. I turn to walk to the bedroom and there in the middle of the floor is a large pool of urine. I let my head drop.

I clean up the mess. I sit down and start to talk to them. I tell them that we still have to try. I know I'm not great at this, but we still have to try. A major realization hits me as I sit on the floor talking to Louise and Bug. Sometimes I reach a point, like on the walk, where I think my life is so unfair that there should be some magical divine intervention to help me. I should be able to go home, throw a fit, and after my shower, Louise and Bug should magically become Lassie and Old Yeller. But this doesn't happen. If fact, the pool of urine was an official announcement that this will probably never happen. I used to think that because of my tragic situation, everything else in life should somehow be easier for me. I used to think that I got a free pass, that I would never have to really work again, that someone should just send me money, and that if I ever needed anything, someone could get it for me. But with Louise and Bug I am constantly reminded that there is no easy way out.

Tonight I am taking a class through my hospital called Beginning to Breast-feed. It is, as it implies, a class designed to explain how to breast-feed, why to breast-feed, and to cover any problems that may arise while breast-feeding. The informational packet that was sent to my house encourages fathers to attend. I know that I will be one of the few single people in my class.

I walk down the halls of the building. The walls are lined with posters of moms and dads doing various parenting poses. One poster is about what the coach should do during childbirth. There is a picture of a husband holding his wife in various positions. Another poster reads INFANT SAFETY and includes pictures of a dad holding his baby supporting the head and neck. PARENTING A TODDLER is accompanied by a picture of mom, dad, and child all looking happy, the child with a cooperative smile on his face. DAD'S ROLE IN INFANT CARE depicts a man with a sleeping child nestled on his shoulder. I feel like walking down the hallway with both of my middle fingers exposed to both walls, which are suffocating me. Or maybe I should just periodically spit on some of them, the ones that I find most disturbing. I am annoyed with the assumption that all of us are here with a man. This is a ridiculous reason to be annoyed, I realize, and it is not the general pattern to be a widow at the age of twenty-four. But I still feel the burning desire to vandalize these posters, which are clearly mocking me.

Once I reach the classroom I walk into a room with six sets of moms and dads. I take the only table with one chair. A few moments later the instructor at the front of the room starts talking.

'Let's see,' she says. 'We are supposed to have

eight couples with us tonight.' The word *couples* pangs in my brain. 'Maybe we're not all couples!' I want to shout. 'What is this, 1956?' But I don't say anything.

'Yep, so we're just waiting on one more couple. Once the last couple gets here, we can get started.' How many times does she have to say that word? Is it really necessary? Do any of us need to know how many people are going to be here?

After the instructor, Kathie, goes through her introduction, we have to go around the room, introduce ourselves, and state our prenatal health care provider and our child health care provider. I know people always look at me and wonder. They see me without a wedding ring and think, *Oh, she must have gotten pregnant by accident. She's too young to be divorced.* Sometimes I think I should wear my wedding ring just to draw less attention to myself. But I don't like wearing it. It's like a big joke.

The class starts after the introductions and I am immersed in information about my own breasts that I never knew. It is pretty interesting, the fact that my body knows exactly what to manufacture, how to do it, and how often.

At eight o'clock, in the midst of a video with an incredible amount of footage of large, milk-bearing boobs, Kathie turns the lights on and we take a break. After returning from the bathroom I sit back down. The couple next to me does not speak to each other. The woman slowly eats Fritos

79

out of a small plastic bag from the vending machines.

'So how was your day?' she asks him, shoving a handful of Fritos into her mouth.

'Fine,' he replies, emotionless, looking forward at nothing. She reaches in the bag again. The crinkling of the wrapper is almost awkward. She looks at him out of the corner of her eyes, waiting to see if he was going to ask her about her day.

I want to start firing questions at them. I want to ask him, 'Why are you being such an asshole?' Or ask her, 'Why would you bring him if he's clearly not interested? Don't let him ruin this for you.' They annoy me, just sitting there not speaking to each other, not appreciating that they are physically sitting next to each other.

The class itself does not bother me as much as I expected. The hardest part is thinking about Josh in this class. He would have been making jokes and writing notes to me the whole time. Even as a twenty-seven-year-old, he would have thought a class about boobs was hilarious.

But then the class ends and I walk into the parking lot along with several other couples. With every single couple, the same thing happens. The husband gets into the driver's seat and the wife gets into the passenger's seat. Together they drive away. I get into the car and lose it. I start crying hysterically. The image of the car, the image of Josh always driving, and now the image of me always driving alone is completely overwhelming.

I had prepared myself for a class full of couples, but for some reason I didn't prepare myself for the parking lot. None of the couples realize how special this is, how special it is to have two people in the car, to fill the front seat with a mom and dad. And their children, everyone's child except mine, will grow up with this distinct image, the same image I have seen my whole life. Dad drives and mom sits next to him. But my son will always see me, alone in the front seat.

As it is for many couples, the car was always the place where Josh and I talked about everything. After we visited Margaret, Deedee, or my parents, we would always debrief about what happened. When we drove up north we had a mutual understanding that the drive itself was half the fun. Josh would drive and I would point out funny landmarks or we would discuss what it would be like to live in Standish or which gas station on I-75 was our favorite. But now my trips up north will be with my parents or Ashley or Deedee or Maggie, and it's not that I don't love these people, but they are not Josh. I will never get to carelessly climb into the passenger's seat as I did a few short months ago. I will always drive everywhere. I had never seriously thought about this concept until tonight.

The other morning on NPR was an interview with people in a small town in Alabama. The point of the story was to show how people feel about the

U.S. military in different parts of the country and why. In this small town in Alabama there was an undying devotion. At one point in the story the Stewarts, a couple who had an eighteen-year-old son who had volunteered to go to war after September 11, were interviewed. Their son was killed in Iraq. The mom started to cry when she talked about the three men in uniform who came to her door. More than three thousand people came to his funeral, and that night the towns-people had a walking vigil; they held candles and carried American flags. Obviously, not everyone who attended knew this young man, but to the town he had died an honorable death and he deserved to be commemorated.

At one point when the dad is telling the story about his son's death to the interviewer, he said that it was a Sunday afternoon and it didn't feel different from any other Sunday afternoon. Then the doorbell rang and three men in uniform were standing on his front porch with solemn looks on their faces.

'I had to change the ring on the doorbell,' the dad said, his voice breaking up. And right as I heard this, I started to nod my head. I completely under-stood. Anyone who has not lived through a day like his or mine would hear this statement and say, 'Well that's ridiculous. The doorbell had nothing to do with it.' But to us, the doorbell had everything to do with it. Thank God he changed the doorbell, I thought to myself. Thank God he and his wife never have to hear that doorbell again. I feel like Jay Gatsby and I are the only people who would find importance in that small detail.

When Josh called my phone, the phone erupted with his own unique ring tone. It wasn't anything special – I didn't download it or anything – it was just different from the one that everyone else in my phone got. It was called 'Latin Loop.' Ever since he died I haven't heard 'Latin Loop' and I hope I never do. One time I was in a coffee shop and I heard a phone ring that was just like the ring he had on his phone. I calmly stood up, got in my car, and cried until I could hardly breathe.

I look at pictures of him every day. I even watch videos of him. But for some reason, it's the other senses that rip the carpet out from under me. Right before Josh's accident we had gone to Costco together and bought this new detergent called Eco. Josh wanted it because it had something to do with being more environmentally friendly than our regular Tide. I remember the first time I did a load of laundry after Josh died. I took the clothes out of the dryer and I was relieved that they didn't smell like they did when he was here. I would have never washed clothes again. Thank God we'd bought this new detergent.

I don't know why this is, why my brain fears having those other senses register with the past. When I see something, I can rationalize it in my brain or at least can attempt to explain it to myself: *That's a picture of Josh at Christmas. That was his last Christmas. This year, he won't be at Christmas.* Sometimes it makes me upset, and other times I just keep walking down the hallway and try to let the words sink in. I feel like I try to explain to my brain what has happened. But with smells and sounds, my brain doesn't have time to react. There is no internal monologue to make things clear. My sense of smell and hearing don't quite know that Josh is dead. When I heard that phone ring, when I smelled his T-shirts, for a split second he wasn't gone. If his smells and sounds were still around, then he couldn't be gone. It just didn't make sense. He was so close. If I could smell him, he must be around here somewhere, right? Then I have to remind myself again, for the six thousandth time, that he's not here anymore. Every time that doorbell would ring, the Stewarts would have to remind themselves that one second before that doorbell rang they were normal people with normal lives whose son would be home in just a few short months. That doorbell was more than a doorbell now. It was a signal of their passage into the most difficult phase of life, the darkest phase they've ever had to face. It signals the moment their lives changed forever.

The dad on NPR isn't crazy. Gatsby isn't crazy. That's the word my students always use, *crazy*. They call Macbeth crazy, Lady Macbeth is crazy, Winston Smith is eventually crazy in *1984*. Any time they see a human outside of the normal range of emotion, they call them crazy. Gatsby just can't get it into his head that he can't go back. He's just like me and the Stewarts and so many other people.

Two years ago Ashley's live-in boyfriend abruptly moved out with little explanation. I remember her standing in our kitchen crying, going through her old text messages from him about how much he loved her, how he couldn't wait to marry her and have kids. She kept reading them, like little relics of a past life, and she didn't understand how she had crossed over into a new world of singleness. It was like she was arguing with the person who works at the ticket counter at the airport. 'No! I was scheduled for a wedding and pregnancy, but you've rerouted me to twenty-six and single!' And we all expect that some person behind a counter will just type a few buttons into their computer and hand us a new ticket. 'We're so sorry, ma'am.' And poof, we're back on track. But life can be so fucking absolute. It takes us a while to get that we will never be rerouted.

A few weeks ago I had lunch with a woman who had also lost her husband in an accident when she was pregnant with their first child. It was very nice of her to talk to me and I did find a lot of her words comforting, but the meeting did not leave me feeling particularly inspired. At one point in the conversation she said, 'You know, you just have to find your new normal.' I have heard this phrase before and I hate it. I want to wave my index finger at people and say, 'Don't put me in the same sentence as normal. I am not normal and I'm never going to be 'new normal,' so knock it off.'

Now that my due date is quickly approaching, I keep thinking more and more about being a mom and starting a family, a very abnormal family. How will my son develop knowing that he is different from the majority? My whole life I tried to put things together so it was completely normal – college, job, marriage, baby. But now, everything in my son's life will somehow remind him that most people are not like us. The language his teachers use at school will always include the phrase 'your mom and dad,' and he will know that it doesn't apply to him. Throughout his entire life people will constantly say stupid shit to him like 'Your dad must be so proud' or 'Did your dad take you to the Red Wings game?' And he will have to figure out how to deal with these stupid people. Sometimes he will have to say, 'I don't have a dad. My dad died before I was born.'

Then one day both of us will figure out that not being normal has its perks. Baby Taylor will have twenty-seven men he calls uncle and thirty-four women he calls aunt. 'Did your dad take you to the Red Wings game?' 'No,' he will reply. 'My grandpa took me and my uncle Toby and my uncle Brian and my uncle Chris and my uncle Adam.

I ate so much pizza and pop that I threw up on the way home. My uncle Chris threw up too, but he didn't eat any pizza.' While all of the other kids go on family vacations over spring break, Baby Taylor will travel to all sorts of different places. He'll go to Miami to visit his aunt Moo and uncle Dubs, he'll go to Los Angeles to visit his uncle Ads and aunt Ellie, he'll go to San Diego to go surfing with his uncle Pug, or maybe he'll even go hunting in the Rockies with his uncle Chris. Then during show-and-tell after spring break, all of the other fifth-graders will be showing pictures of their perfect families posing together at the top of a ski slope or sitting together in a giant teacup in Disney World. Baby Taylor will show his picture of him and an adult male both standing over a dead animal carcass in the middle of the mountains. 'This is my uncle Chris. We shot a buck together.' All of the girls will say, 'Eeeeeewwwwww,' and initially, Baby Taylor will wonder why his picture doesn't look like the rest of the students'. For a moment, for a fleeting moment, he may wish he were one of them. But then at lunch recess when all of the other boys are chasing him around asking him about shooting a gun and cutting the guts out of an animal, he will realize that being different is not always a bad thing. 'Is it hard to shoot a gun?' they will ask him, with their wide eyes and imagining the reaction of their own over-protective mothers. 'It's not *that* hard,' Baby Taylor will say, with his hands in his pockets, not knowing just how much of an enigma he is to his peers. 'It's a lot easier than shooting a bow and arrow,' he will say. 'You've shot a bow and arrow?' They will gasp in awe. 'My mom won't even let me watch movies that have guns in them, let alone shoot one,' says the boy from the teacup picture. Later that night Baby Taylor will call his uncle Chris and tell him all about show-and-tell and how all the other boys wished they had an uncle Chris who lived in the mountains and had guns.

In the next four weeks I am going to have a baby. That baby will know that his life is missing someone, someone very important. But Baby Taylor will always know that he can choose how to live. He can be brilliant or tragic. In having that choice, he will always know that there is only one choice he can make.

This positive sentiment feels good when it sits in my brain. I know my son will be okay. He'll be awesome. But for every inspirational flash, and they are merely flashes, I feel like I have a hundred dark moments to match. This is the craziest part about grief; it just swings you like hell from one end of the spectrum to the next. I try to savor my flashes of hope in regard to motherhood. I wish I could hang them on the refrigerator to remind myself of those moments on any given day when I am not scared to death of the future.

But always too soon, right after a fleeting moment of hope, the floor opens up and I sink to the bottom again. I'll think about Josh or I'll look at a picture I hadn't seen before and I'll think, I'll never be happy again. I'll never smile the way I did in that picture. I'll never see the world as I once saw it. No matter how much time goes by, no matter who comes into my life, I will never be as happy as I was before June 17, 2007. Even when I do buy my beautiful house, and even when Baby Taylor gets a full ride to Notre Dame on a soccer scholarship, and even when I somehow become famous and get to be on *Oprah*, and Victoria Beckham calls me and wants to be my best friend, even all of that won't do it. At the end of the day after Baby Taylor falls asleep, I'll still stand in the kitchen and cry over a bottle of wine and sing 'Didn't We Almost Have It All,' and my life will still feel just as pathetic and meaningless as it does right now.

Dr G. says that this is a place I am only 'visiting.' That my feelings of loneliness and emptiness are merely stops along the way of a very long journey. I believe her because she is a smart lady, but what if I never can smile again like I used to? What if I try everything and nothing seems to work. Then what do I do?

A couple of weeks ago I had to call Josh's dermatologist, Dr Samor, and leave a message explaining that Josh had died tragically in a horrible accident and that I wanted to pay off his account. I expected a return message saying, 'Sorry for your loss, you owe us fifty-three dollars.' Instead, I received a message from a woman named Suzanne. Suzanne works in the billing department. I had never met her or spoken to her before. Suzanne called me back and proceeded to tell me, all on my voice mail, that she was dreadfully sorry to hear my news. She could hardly speak, she was so broken up. She explained that a similar situation happened to her. Two weeks before her wedding her fiancé was killed in a motorcycle accident. She said she knew how I felt and she 'prayed that sunshine and rainbows find me down the road.' I don't know why, but her words sent me into a complete breakdown. When I first heard the message I was driving south on Adams Road back from Deedee's house. I was so upset that someone else had had to deal with this, that someone else had to feel the same way I did. I couldn't bear the thought that this had happened to another young woman, that this had happened to millions of people before me and would continue to blind-side completely happy people and ruin their lives forever. For a split second I wanted to swerve into the other lane and just get out of here. How ridiculous. I was so distraught by the idea of loss and death that I contemplated killing myself. I don't know how else to explain it, but I was painfully annoyed that this is what so many of us live with. Isn't that almost an oxymoron, living with the pain of death? But as Suzanne and I have come to realize, you can't really fully live with the pain of losing someone in your heart. I had spent the last three months feeling so irritated when people looked at me like I was half dead, but in listening to Suzanne's message, I realized I felt like I was half dead and so many other people had to feel the same way too. I'm half dead and I'm pregnant. How, as a twenty-four-year-old pregnant woman, am I supposed to compute all of this in my brain? Life sucks so much to the point that I don't even feel alive, and yet I am one month away from having a baby. So what do I do? I go through the motions of a day. I run errands, I write, I talk to Dr G., and I spend most of my time trying to convince myself that it will be okay.

When I was in college we read this Emily Dickinson poem. I have no idea what it was called or what it was about, but then again I never really know what any Emily Dickinson poem is about. All I remember is she used the phrase 'the Hour of Lead.' My professor mentioned that people who experience the death of a loved one have something similar to this. She said that while an hour is an arbitrary frame of time, the expression works. As I sit and look at pictures of Josh, as I think about my stupid, empty life, I consider this phrase. Yes, the expression works.

By the end of September, my eleventh-graders have finished *The Great Gatsby*. Or at least they were supposed to. I would be naive to think that all of them read it start to finish. But no matter how much they have or have not read, every student can participate in today's activity. At the beginning of the hour the white board instructs students to pick up the sheet of paper at the front of the room. Once the bell rings and everyone is seated, I tell students to quietly read the ten sentences on the sheet of paper. After reading the sheet they slowly look up from their desks. I tell them to silently go through each sentence and write one of two words beneath each phrase: agree or disagree. Do not explain your answer, do not say 'both,' do not look at what your neighbor wrote, just write one or the other. Students start to smile. They always like activities where they don't have to explain themselves in writing. Over the next two minutes students sit quietly and write in their answers. The statements are bold expressions that either directly relate to the text of *Gatsby* or a major theme: 'Daisy should have left Tom for Gatsby,' 'Money makes life easier,' 'Rich people get away with more than people who are not rich.' The most popular statement that always gets a rise out of teenagers is, 'If someone cheats on you, it's okay to cheat on them.'

On one side of the room there is a large sign that says AGREE. On the other side of the room there is a sign that says DISAGREE. Once students have their answers listed, I instruct them to stand up with their sheets. I explain that I will read a sentence out loud and they will walk to either side of the room. Once everyone is where they want to be, we discuss. The reason we move around is so that we can get a visual idea of the opinions of others; even if you do not participate in the discussion, we still know where you stand.

The activity works well. It isn't difficult to get teenagers to discuss such absolutes. The statement that intrigues me most is the one that reads 'It is possible to reinvent yourself.' The class is sincerely split on this statement. Immediately hands go up. Identity is a big deal to teenagers. Despite the fact that few of them have actually discovered who they really are, teenagers are incredibly astute when it comes to identifying 'phonies,' a term that all of them know from reading *Catcher in the Rye* last year.

We start off on the agree side. Lori Bingham goes first.

'People change,' she says confidently. 'I know a lot of people who I was close with in middle school and now we're not friends anymore. Sometimes people change for the better, sometimes for the worse.'

I call on Scott Sanders next. I know for a fact that he didn't finish the book, but I call on him so he can participate in at least one discussion. 'I got really bad grades in middle school,' he says. 'And then when I got to high school I just decided that grades were important. I'm a completely different student than I was in middle school.' I nod, trying not too hard to reveal my own opinion. A few more people speak on the agree side. It is obvious that like most of us, everyone claims that they have changed dramatically since middle school. I remind them that middle school is perhaps the most difficult stage of growing up and most of us are happy to shed that skin once we hit ninth grade. But then I ask them to push the statement a little further.

'But is wearing different clothes and getting your braces taken off a reinvention of yourself? Does that really change you? Can you ever really change?'

We bring the disagree side in. Morgan Palinksi is the first to speak. 'You can never change who you are. I mean, you can dye your hair and change your clothes, but you can never really get rid of the person inside.' Rachel Bearsley agrees. 'It's not that you aren't changing when you grow up. Obviously we're all different than we were in the first grade. We're just discovering more of ourselves as we get older.' *Quite reflective for a sixteen-year-old*, I think to myself.

We talk about the characters from the book for a while. Several students remark that no one is able to really move from one social sphere to another. None of the characters are able to change their identity.

'So what about us? What about Fitzgerald? What does he think?'

The conversation is interesting. The class has all sorts of different opinions and of course some students immediately bring up extremes. What about a prisoner who murdered someone when they were young? Have they changed after twenty-five years of being in jail? Can they shake the cloak of a murderer? Eventually we get back to us, everyday normal students. Can we change? Do people ever change?

Driving home from school, I think about Gatsby, Tom, Daisy, my students, and me. Can I reinvent myself? Before Josh died, I was the follower. He made all the decisions. He planned vacations, picked out paint colors, made plans for the weekend, figured out what we were having for dinner. He drove. He said yes or no to big purchases. He packed the car. He disciplined the dogs. I joked that when we built our dream house, he would plan the entire house. Blueprints to doorknobs, he would pick out everything and I would like whatever he picked out. He was the pack leader. But now he's gone and I have the dogs and the baby and the house and the bank accounts and now I have to drive the car. Can I successfully reinvent myself to be the pack leader or will I just bumble around unsuccessfully?

It's safe to say that none of us will be the same now that we have lived through the death of Josh. Right now I firmly believe I will never be as happy as I was. I will never exude that carefree smile I see on my face in my wedding pictures. Life will never look as bright, not simply because he's not here, but also because I now know that things aren't always fair in the world. But will I change? Will any of us change? Four months later, after vowing to live life differently, I wonder how much staying power those grief-stricken resolutions have. In the days following the funeral, Chris told Ashley that it was his job to make sure that the baby and I are always taken care of. But he's back in Denver hunting elk and sometimes forgets to return my phone calls. Deedee said she was finally going to start on the much-needed renovations of her house – Josh had always wanted her to fix it up. Months later she hasn't mentioned it again. I said I would never take a moment for granted. I would never get annoyed with stupid things like traffic or waiting in long lines at the post office, but I have gone back on those promises over and over. I said I would never reject an invitation to celebrate something, but months later I am already complaining about upcoming weddings and showers. So have we changed? Can I still change?

One of the few times I started crying uncontrollably in public was when I was at the checkout at Home Depot. I had to order carpeting for my bedroom and Mike, the carpet guy, had just asked me all these questions about my carpeting. What type of carpet pad did I want? Did I want the single layer or the water-resistant? Did I want the Stainmaster finish? Was I going to carpet the closet? Did I want a silver or gold runner? What day did I want it installed? Every time Mike looked up for an answer, my voice got shakier and shakier. 'I don't know!' I wanted to scream. 'I don't know! My husband knows! My husband is supposed to be here right now! Stop asking me! I don't know!'

By the time I got to the checkout counter, I was sobbing.

Can I do this? No, says Mike the carpet guy, you picked all the wrong answers. That gold runner is going to look ridiculous. No, says Louise, you'll never be able to walk us. Can I reinvent myself? I want to be able to. But what if I can't?

I want to be able to handle all of this. I want my dogs to respect me and listen to me when we go out for walks. I want my son to see me as a strong matriarch. Years from now I want him to say, 'When I was growing up, you didn't mess with my mom.' But can this happen? Can I be this person that I have never been before?

The Great Gatsby ends with 'So we beat on, boats against the current, borne back ceaselessly into the past.' Previous to this year I always asked myself, why does Fitzgerald use the word *we*, as if this is something we all do? This isn't something we all do. Not everyone wants to go back in time. Not everyone sees only the past as the happiest times of his or her life. And the word *we* almost sounds like it's Fitzgerald talking and not really the narrator at all.

When I read this now I know what he's talking about. This is my life. This line is my whole life, right now at this moment. A boat against the current of time. I know full well that I should be going in one direction, but subconsciously my mind is in the other. I come home from work, another day on the calendar, but all I can think about are the days of months before. I sit in the driver's seat and all I can think about is what my life was like when I was in the passenger's seat. I can't reinvent myself if all I want to do is go back. Unlike Gatsby, I know I can't repeat the past. But like the Stewarts, like Ashley, like Suzanne, like Gatsby, like so many other people, today, all I want to do is go back.

OCTOBER

> There is a property in the horizon which
> no man has but he whose eye can integrate
> all the parts, that is, the poet.
> —RALPH WALDO EMERSON, *NATURE*

Today in my ninth-grade English class we are practicing how to make an outline. I thought I would be on maternity leave by the time we got to the nonfiction unit, but here I am, nine months plus, getting my kids started on how to read informational texts and take quality notes. Because everyone is researching something different, I give them a sample set of notes that we can all use as a class. We read through the sample notes and talk about what common themes we see throughout the research. We have to think of three categories and we have to use ten facts from the notes for our outline.

The sample notes happen to be about how and why teens succeed (and don't succeed) in high school. These notes discuss how to be a successful high school student. In one part the researcher found an article about what holds students back from achievement. There are several lines about how low-income students are statistically low achievers because they get to school with a lower vocabulary than their higher-achieving, higher-income peers. Now let me remind you, it is eight o'clock in the morning. Hands usually don't go up this early. But this morning something has struck a chord in a few students.

'First of all,' I ask, forcing the class to be active readers, 'what does it mean to come from a "low-income" home?' Easy question, but I ask to make sure we are all on the same page. Matt Davis raises his hand. Matt did his summer reading project on a book called *The Cheat*, where a group of students try to cheat on a standardized test. During his presentation he said he did relate to the book because when he was in the second grade he cheated on a spelling test. He said that he used to think that all kids who wore glasses were smart, so he copied off of a kid who wore glasses. He got every word wrong. That was the last time he cheated.

'"Low income" means that the parents don't make a lot of money. It means that they can't afford certain things.' I nod. If we had more time, I would press his answer. I would ask, what does a lot of money get you, what things can a low-income person not afford that a high-income person can afford? But we don't go there for now.

'So,' I ask, 'these students who come from families who don't make a lot of money, they have lower vocabularies. Why do they have lower vocabularies? What do income and vocabulary have in common?'

Slowly we get to the part about how if neither parent is home, especially when children are building their vocabularies, it is difficult to acquire a large vocabulary. I tell them about all of the baby books I've read that say you're supposed to read to your baby as early as when he is in the womb. Once he comes home, you should talk to him in complete sentences, not baby talk. They think this is funny and interesting.

As a class we interpret the data and eventually the goal is for us to create an outline. But suddenly the class isn't interested in the outline. They want to go back to the part of the article that asserted that low-income students are not as likely to be high achievers. The same boys (and I don't know why, but they're all boys) continue to raise their hands and ask questions and tell me why the article is wrong. Just because your family doesn't make a lot of money doesn't mean you can't do well in school. To them, one thing has nothing to do with the other.

Daniel Stevenson is a short, slender African American boy with large glasses and a backpack that takes up half his body. He is a vocal student and has no missing assignments. His hand goes up as I attempt to move on to the next set of data.

'Wait a minute, Mrs Taylor. Are you trying to say that just because the *parents* don't make a lot of money, the *kid* doesn't do well in school?'

'Daniel, that is a great question. But let me remind you, *I'm* not saying anything. I'm reading the data from the article just like you are. The data suggest that students from low-income homes have a lower vocabulary, which hurts them when they get to school. You seem to have a different opinion.'

'Well, I'm just saying vocabulary is one thing, but what if that student works really hard in his classes? Why can't he be successful then?'

'Mrs Taylor.' Matt Davis's hand goes up before I can address Daniel's question. Matt always likes to tell me when his hand is up. Matt's mother e-mails me once a week to check on his progress.

I call on Matt. 'So what this article is saying is that if we come from a low-income home, we're already doomed from the beginning.'

'Do you think that's what it is saying?' I ask.

'Well, I don't think it's right, but that's what it says.' He throws his hand toward the overhead screen.

'But let me ask you this. This is a *statistic*. What does that mean anyway? What do we need to take into account when we look at a statistic?'

Several hands go up. The usual look of apathy has escaped their tired eyes. *How interesting*, I think to myself.

I call on Julia Scott. She is very bright and can

102

usually articulate ideas that the rest of the class struggles with. And we haven't heard from a girl in a while.

'It doesn't mean that that's what will happen to everyone. It just means that this author studied a group of low-income students and high-income students and that the low-income students had a harder time being successful in school.'

Daniel Stevenson's hand goes up again. He starts talking before I can call on him.

'What if you only have one parent? Then your family income is automatically lower than families with two parents.' He smiles a little as he says this. He wants to be discreet in asking the question, but if there is one thing that ninth-graders are completely incapable of, it is being discreet. I know that Daniel lives with his mother. His father is out of the picture, though I don't know why. Adam Dolman, who sits two rows in front of Daniel, lost his father two years ago when he was in the seventh grade; his mom told me about it at Meet the Teacher Night a few weeks ago. I am certain that there are other students in the room who come from truly single-parent homes. Not where there is a mom during the week and a dad during the weekend – although those students struggle for different reasons. But Daniel is certainly not the only boy in the room who is raised or will be raised exclusively by one parent.

I put the lid back on my overhead marker and stand up from the stool.

'Daniel, that's a great question. I think the answer is not so much to get an answer but to rethink the nature of our questions about statistics.' I cross my arms and take a moment to think about how I want to say this.

'First of all, the short answer to Daniel's question is yes. It's obvious. If you have one parent working and taking care of children, then there is less money than if there were two people – in most cases at least. And think of how this could affect these budding vocabularies. If only one parent works, then clearly he or she can't stay at home, so the child has to have some sort of alternative supervision, whether it is day care, a grandparent, or someone else. So arguably, these children who come from single-parent homes where the single parent doesn't make a lot of money might have quite a difficult time in school. Statistically the odds of them being high achievers is slim.' I wait a moment and look at the audience. Daniel's hand goes up again. I know what he's thinking. Adam Dolman gives me a perplexed stare. I motion for Daniel to put his hand down and I continue.

'But I'm going to be a single mom. My house will only have one income also. I don't know if my son and I will qualify as a low-income family, but I don't really care what we qualify as. And to be honest with you, I don't really care what the statistics say. I know that statistically things are not exactly in our favor. But because I am aware of the statistics, that means I will be even more conscious of how I raise him. We'll read a lot together in the evenings when I get home from work. I'll make sure he doesn't become a vegetable in front of the television and that he doesn't get addicted to video games. In the summer we'll spend a lot of time outdoors. I know that other parents won't have to work as hard as I will because there are two of them. And I know that he may not have it easy because he won't have a dad around. But that doesn't scare me and it certainly does not make me believe that my son will be a low achiever. I think statistics are just that – statistics. Numbers that represent a study that someone performed on a group of people. But they certainly are not my destiny, nor are they yours. So if you come from a low-income house and you look at this article and it makes you mad or it makes you think that you are going to prove it wrong, that's good. That's amazing, actually. That means that you are already a step ahead of the game and that you probably will be a high achiever, despite what this article says about you. Because, remember, it's not even talking about you, it's talking about people like you. Only you can decide what you're going to do.'

The room is quiet. For the first time all year I think every single ninth-grader in this room just heard what I said.

'Daniel, do you still have a comment?' He shakes his head. I can see him smiling just a little. He just wanted to make sure he could do it. He wanted to make sure I wasn't telling him that his dream of graduating from high school and college, maybe even his dream of becoming a doctor or an architect, wasn't as far off as he thought. It isn't.

It's odd how I connect with students now that I have this tragedy attached to me. Students just seem to be different around me than they were last year. Neil Michaels was in my ninthgrade English class two years ago. He was a mean kid. During our *Lord of the Flies* unit, I had to send him to the principal's office a few times for calling a chubby kid in class 'Piggy.' By the end of the first marking period, Neil had a 13 percent in the class.

During Neil's sophomore year he got himself into so many fights that he was kicked out of school. Shortly after that, his parents discovered that Neil, not even sixteen, was heavily into drugs and alcohol. They sent him away to a rehab facility for eight months.

For this school year, Berkley High School let him have another shot. On the second day of school Neil stopped by my room. He had a completely different temperament about him; I could notice a change just by watching him walk through the doorway.

He told me he heard about what happened to my husband this summer and he was so sorry. He asked about the baby and if I was nervous about being a single mom. He then told me all about rehab, the various problems he had along the way, and that he was so happy to be back at Berkley. He was relieved he'd been allowed back in. I told him it was good to see him and he nodded. He paused for a moment and I could tell he wanted to say something, maybe another comment about my situation or maybe an apology about being a jerk to me two years ago. But I cut him off. I didn't need to hear either comment from him. I knew he felt both.

'Neil, we all have something, ya know. We all have something we're trying to get through. It sounds like you're on your way to a better year. That's awesome.'

'Thanks,' he said quietly. 'I hope things turn out all right for you and your baby.'

'Thanks, Neil.' He waved and walked out the door.

Last year I had nothing in common with Neil Michaels and I had nothing of value to say to students from single-parent or low-income homes. Certainly I tried to motivate students who had challenges, but it was difficult for me to connect in a profound way with students whose lives were so drastically different from my own. I had a great life with no real obstacles ahead of me. Despite a few minor issues, my life was easy.

Four months after losing Josh, I know that my life will never be as easy as it was. I can't say that I've reached acceptance, but I understand the reality of what has happened to me. I know that there are people who have to deal with real issues, real problems that statistically set them behind or below others. I am now one of those people. And although I'd rather not be, although I would do anything and give up anything to go back to how it was, I know that I can't. So I'll do my best from down here. Daniel Stevenson, Adam Dolman, Neil Michaels, and I are going to do our best with what we have. The one comfort that all of us can take is that we are not the only people on the planet who have something to swim against. We are not alone in our battle to disprove a statistic.

One of the big things I've realized in the last four months is that I am unable to do anything without detaching it from the fact that I am a widow. I can't watch television, listen to a song, drive a car, see a movie, or do anything without having the death of my husband as the primary thought in my head.

For example, I just finished watching *Extreme Makeover: Home Edition*. I used to think that Ty Pennington was really the only man on the planet who could be compared to Josh. Ty seems like he could fix anything around the house, he knows how to build stuff, he has really good design ideas, and he looks like he is an incredibly generous and caring person. I always thought Josh could be the host of this TV show. He would be just as charismatic and energetic. At one point while job hunting, Josh and I actually discussed if we could somehow get him to be the next Ty Pennington. After Josh died, I had this vision that I would get Deedee's house on *Extreme Makeover*. They would just gut the hell out of it and turn it into a million-dollar home. While filming, Ty would see my selflessness in wanting the best for my mother-in-law and he would hear my story and be moved by my courage and strength as a mother. He would develop a secret love for me and in one of his confessionals on the camera, while he was making some sincere comment about the strength of the family – you know how he does that – he would say, 'And that Natalie. Wow, she sure is something.' Weeks later he would call me and say that he built a hand-crafted bassinet or something for the baby and the next thing you know we're on *Oprah* being interviewed about our relationship and Sears is remodeling our kitchen for free.

But tonight I realize two things while watching the Brown family run and scream through their new house.

1. Deedee could never be on *Extreme Makover*. The part where they let the families run through the house is really the best part of the show because we realize how grateful the family is. They cry and clap their hands and say endearing things like 'We've never had a *dishwasher* before!' The little girl who dreams of being a ballerina runs into her room and sees her new dance

studio and starts to cry and you really think, wow, these people really deserve this. And you're happy for them. At least I'm happy for them. But with Deedee, it would get to this part of the show and it would be a disaster. She would be doing the walk-through and she would get to the kitchen and she wouldn't be able to hide anything. She would say something like 'You know I really envisioned *oak* cabinets in here. I mean, I like the white. The white is nice. I had just *pictured* oak.' Then they would take her into the laundry room and she would have a whole new washer and dryer set, a beautiful storage system, closets for linens, and she would say, 'Oh.' Pause. 'Oh, you painted over my stencils on the wall. Okay.' Pause . . . pause (the pauses would really throw off the cameramen). Then: 'No, I like the lavender. It's just that, do you know when I painted those stencils? I was pregnant with Chris, right up until the day I went to the hospital, and I was on the ladder finishing those stencils.' And she would stare at the place in the wall where the stencils used to be. 'But the lavender looks fine. No really, it's fine.' The whole thing would be incredibly anticlimactic because with every room you would be able to feel her disappointment.

2. Ty Pennington uses too much hair

product for my liking. I am quite certain that he goes tanning on a consistent basis. I could never date a guy who uses too much hair gel or who goes tanning. It would never work out between us.

Every single thing I watch is like this – I can only view the world through my widow lens. I can no longer be entertained. I only think about how it compares to my loss and my current state of grief. For example, Halle Berry is on *Oprah*. She begins by talking about her pregnancy and her superhot model boyfriend. I immediately roll my eyes as Oprah inquires about their happy life together. I remember a week after Josh died I was watching *Oprah* and Faith Hill was on. It was absolutely the wrong thing for me to watch. Faith Hill went on and on about how amazing a husband Tim is, about how their sex life is great, about how beautiful their three daughters are. It was disgusting. There she was sitting on stage, tall, thin, talented, wealthy, married to an equally attractive, talented, wealthy man. And there I was, single, pregnant, and about to go from $1,130 every two weeks to $398.

Faith Hill smiled as she confirmed that Tim was everything he seemed to be – considerate, kind, a good father, and completely sexy. The audience gave their typical *Oprah* audience high-pitched scream and applause at any mention of their sex life. I've always found this to be totally bizarre, and if you're a regular *Oprah* watcher, you know that this happens often. When Halle Berry starts talking about 'trying' to get pregnant, the audience does the proverbial 'Whooooo!' and claps. How awkward that must be for Halle Berry, although Faith Hill did not seem to be bothered by it.

Halle Berry is on *Oprah* to promote her new movie called *The Things We Lost in the Fire*. The movie is about a woman who has two kids. Her husband dies and she finds strange comfort in her husband's best friend, whom she previously loathed. Basically it would be as if I lost Josh, and Doug Heinz, Josh's longtime neighborhood friend whom I have always suspected to have Asperger's syndrome, helped me raise my baby. What a horrible, horrible idea.

The interview is a little frustrating because Oprah, of course, is asking Halle about what it was like to *play* a woman who had experienced so much. I am annoyed by this. This is where I go from liking Halle Berry to becoming frustrated with all that she is associated with: 'Oh, Halle, tell us what it was like to *act like* you were a woman who lost her husband. What was it like to play *pretend* widow and then go home to your gorgeous boyfriend? Oh, Halle, that must have been so difficult, I mean to play dress-up for a whole day, to actually convince other people that you had lost your husband and get paid millions of dollars for it and then go home to a beautiful man who loves and adores you. What a challenge. Was it difficult to balance the emotional burden of playing a widow and then go home and have sex all the time with your supermodel boyfriend? [Audience screams and claps]. Well, I think we know what the *audience* wants to talk about!' Blah, blah, blah.

I felt the same way when I saw pictures of Angelina Jolie in magazines and write-ups about her 'stunning performance' in *A Mighty Heart*. 'Oh, Angelina, you did such a wonderful job at acting like your new soon-to-be-father of a husband was kidnapped and killed. Let's talk to Angelina about what it was like to *imitate* a woman who had actually lived through the worst situation imaginable. Angelina, tell us what that was like for you.'

So annoying. Why are these people more popular than Marianne Pearl? Why don't we interview Marianne Pearl? (I know, I know, Oprah did interview Marianne Pearl, which is why we never judge Oprah). Still, so sickening. So frustrating. I just feel like I am the one who should be rich and famous, not them. I am going through this horrible fucking situation; doesn't the universe *owe* me something? Don't *I* get to be on *Oprah*?

But I don't. I'm not. I'm sitting on my couch with an eight-pound baby sitting on my sciatic nerve taking my hormonal aggression out on famous people who don't even know me.

Right now I am reading a book called *Goodnight Nobody* by Jennifer Weiner. I read her first novel,

Good in Bed, which was pretty funny as I remember it. But when I read *Good in Bed*, I was in college, perhaps even single, so I thought reading chick lit about some woman who was 'trying to find herself' through a series of screwed-up relationships was quite entertaining. But *Goodnight Nobody* irritates me every time I open it. It's about this woman named Kate who lives in an extremely affluent suburb in New Jersey and is married to a very wealthy guy. Despite her three beautiful children and rich husband, she is supremely unhappy because she feels like she's lost herself. Give me a break.

First of all, I probably shouldn't be reading this book. I am fully aware that there is an entite population of mothers who live a daily life of complete malcontents because their identities have been 'reduced' to driving children around in a minivan, grocery shopping, and doing laundry. I know that these are the women who end up snorting crystal meth or resorting to alcohol or who yell at their kids in that tone that just screams 'I am a bitter human being.' They watch *Oprah*, they think about having affairs (some probably do), and all of this in their minds is justified by the idea that they've been 'suppressing' their real selves their entire life. Tragic. So sad I could cry. These are women who make choices their entire lives – they choose to be married, they choose to have children, they choose to not go back to work – and get everything they want only to one day wake up and say,

'I am horribly unhappy.' If I could personally punch all of these women in the face, I would.

In a world where *Desperate Housewives* has come to describe more than just the four women on a prime-time television show, I find myself increasingly frustrated by this genre of women. Dr Joy Browne gets callers like this all the time. Yesterday I was listening to her, and a woman named Donna called in. Donna's problem was that she was obsessing over the fact that her husband constantly pointed out other attractive women in public. Donna was annoyed by this in part because she had struggled to lose her postbaby weight. Dr Joy Browne of course immediately asked how often they were having sex. (DJB *always* asks this question). Dr Joy told Donna that she shouldn't let it get to her. It is natural for all of us to look at the opposite sex, but she needed to explain to her husband that he doesn't have to make a comment every time, and if she trusts him and she knows he isn't cheating, then it's not really that big of a deal. Before Donna hung up, Dr Joy asked a series of interesting, clearly relevant questions.

'Donna, how many children do you have?'

'Three.'

'How old are they?'

'Five years, three years, and sixteen months.'

'Donna, do you get out much?'

Pause. 'No, I don't actually.' She started to cry right there on the phone. 'I feel tired all the time.

I feel insecure and overweight all the time. So when my husband says these things, it just . . .' She could hardly talk. 'It just really hurts.'

At this point Dr Joy obviously realized that this woman has a lot more going on than just her husband. She attempted to explain the importance of taking time for yourself.

'You know, Donna, assuming you can afford to get a baby-sitter a few times a week, it is really important that you get out by yourself a little. Join a women's group, take a yoga class, take an aerobics class. But your confidence cannot be defined by your husband and his stupid remarks. Do something that makes you happy and that leaves you feeling refreshed. I think you'll find that that makes a big difference.'

'Thank you, Dr Joy,' she said as if she had been blessed by the pope.

It's not that I don't feel any sympathy for people like Donna, but I don't feel a lot of sympathy. I get frustrated when people get themselves into situations that make them unhappy and then instead of attempting to get themselves out of the situation or just deal with it, they turn into complaining machines.

I personally think I would make a fantastic psychologist. Women would walk into my office and tell me, 'My husband doesn't pay enough attention to me. What should I do?' I would reply, 'Leave your husband.' My patient would get a little flustered and probably a little defensive and maybe even a little annoyed that I didn't let her talk about herself more. I would lean back in my chair and sip on my Starbucks, looking completely comfortable with the fact that I told this woman to get a divorce. The rest of the session would consist of her trying to explain to me that her life is shitty but not shitty enough for her to do anything about it, just shitty enough so that she complains about it constantly to her girlfriends and spends thousands of dollars on a therapist. The rest of the conversation would proceed like this:

STRESSED-OUT MOM (LET'S CALL HER DEBBIE; DEBBIE IS A TOTAL MOM NAME): What do you mean? I mean, he doesn't pay a lot of attention to me and our sex life is mediocre, but he is a good dad. The kids love him. You really think I should just divorce him?

ME: You really need to ask yourself how much your husband sucks on a scale of one to ten. I don't know how much your husband sucks because I'm not you. But you have two choices. If he really sucks – I mean if every day all you can think about is how pathetic and horrible your life is because your husband no longer makes eye contact with you when he speaks to you, or because you take all the time in the world to cook a thoughtful dinner and he says nothing and you truly believe that your marriage is setting a horrible example for your children and your daughter will think that being a wife means being a doormat – then divorce him, or separate at least. But if it's really not all that bad, if it's really more you just trying to find something to complain about because you're bored out of your mind as a stay-at-home mom, then deal with it. Talk to your husband, maybe go get some couples' counseling. But honestly, the bottom line: quit your bitchin', sister, and do something about your crappy life. Take the bull by the horns and work for a positive marriage or leave his sorry ass. But don't sit around and complain about a situation that you have control over. It's just obnoxious.

DEBBIE: But you're my therapist. Aren't I allowed to complain to you? Isn't that the point? You're not allowed to say that my complaints are obnoxious.

ME: Uh, yeah, Debbie, I am allowed to call you obnoxious. [I say this with wide eyes as if she is the moron in the room. I put my hands behind my head, casually, and put my feet up on the center table.] Look, Deb, you need to *do* something. That's the operative word here. Stop sitting on your ass in the pity pool feeling sorry for yourself. Let me ask you a question, just out of curiosity: What else do you find 'wrong' with your life?

DEBBIE: Well, I've gained fifteen pounds in the last six months. I have a hard time finding time for myself during the day. And I'm tired all the time. [All the women who call Dr Joy Browne say this.]

ME: And I bet if I gave you the next thirty minutes, you would find a way to blame all of this on your husband.

DEBBIE: It's not that I'm blaming him. I really think that it is his fault that—

ME: Stop right there, Deb. Stop right there. It may be his fault, but you have the power to change all of that. But nothing is going to change if all you do is complain. You need to get the gears in motion.

DEBBIE: I just don't think it's that simple. I mean—

ME: No, Deb, it is. [I get up and walk over to my desk to schedule our next appointment.]

DEBBIE: I just don't feel like you're listening to me. I keep trying to say—

ME: Deb, the problem here is that you're not listening to *me*. I'm telling you what you don't want to hear because the next step in your life is a scary one. You need to confront the problems of your marriage head-on or you need to throw your hands in the air and say, 'I've tried, and it's not working.' Both are difficult options. Both require more time, effort, and thoughtfulness than sitting at Starbucks with your bffs and bitching about your crappy husbands. If you want to continue to sit at Starbucks and bitch about your husband, go right ahead. We don't need to schedule another appointment. But if you want to be happy, all the time, not just for select moments, then you'll come see me again.

DEBBIE: But I think it's more than—

ME: How's next Wednesday at four?
DEBBIE: Sounds good.

Debbie walks out of my office feeling confused but eventually she figures out that I am the smartest person she has ever met in her entire life.

But back to *Goodnight Nobody*. I have two major problems with this book.

1. There is a scene in which the main character's three kids are in the bath splashing water everywhere and fighting over plastic toys, and her sleeves are sopped with water. Her husband comes home and stands in the doorway of the bathroom and asks, 'What's for dinner?' The narrator gives some ridiculous inner-monologue rant about wow, doesn't this suck that this is what my life has come to? I used to be a single working woman in New York City, wearing fancy clothes and dining with clients in nice restaurants, and now here I am, up to my elbows in bubble bath, my shirt soaked with water and serving as a cook for my husband. But she is too stupid to realize that she is a fortunate, fortunate woman to have three healthy children and a husband who comes into the bathroom to chat with her after work. There are thousands of women who cannot conceive children, who try for decades and cannot have kids. There are

thousands of parents who have lost their children, who never got the chance to hang out with them in the bubble bath. But does our narrator see any of this? No, she doesn't. In doing so she encourages other women to ignore the positive parts of their lives. Make sure you constantly express how annoying and frustrating your children are, make sure you constantly consider the life you wish you had. Doesn't it suck to be home with your children all day? Don't you just go fucking crazy in your million-dollar house with your SUV and your unlimited credit card? What a shitty fucking life. It's so fucking horrible that you should write a book about it. Your kids will never notice how much you hate being a mother. They will never absorb your sense of discontent.

2. I can't remember number 2. I got so worked up with number 1, I forgot. What is wrong with me? Why do I think everyone in the world – Halle Berry, Angelina Jolie, Jennifer Weiner, fictional protagonists, Ty Pennington (who has anything bad to say about Ty Pennington?) – is stupid: What am I turning into? Why am I so mean to people in my brain? I don't know. I feel so imbalanced. Physically and mentally, I am completely imbalanced. I need to have this baby already.

Days pass after my due date. Then a week. People call me every day, all day, and ask the dumbest questions.

'Do you feel anything?'

'Oh, you mean like the strain of my uterus contracting? No, I don't, ya jackass.' I start going to my obstetrician every day. Finally Dr Wiermiller says she can't stand to see me go through any more agony. She's inducing me tomorrow. I go home. Moo, who arrived a few days ago, spends the night with me. Not surprisingly, I can't quite get settled. What kind of pillow-think do you have the night before you are induced? I know I won't go into labor tonight. It's October 17, the four-month mark of Josh's death. I know Baby Taylor won't be born on the seventeenth. Every day since October 1, I woke up thinking, *Maybe today*. But on the seventeenth, I know he won't come. He knows what day it is too.

But tomorrow for sure he will be here. On October 18 at 7:00 a.m. I am going to be induced. This is my last night as a pregnant woman. Tomorrow is my first night as a mother. A real mother, not an expectant mother.

At first I thought it would be great because if I have the baby, I can stop worrying. I won't have to continue to count fetal movements, think about what I'm eating, if he's positioned right, if he is growing properly.

But the whole thing is a little odd. Four months ago today I had a life-altering event descend upon me. There was no warning. There was no preparation. It was a complete and total surprise. Tomorrow I have a life-altering event that I have been thinking about for nine months and I know when it is going to happen down to the hour. I don't know which one is worse or better. Then I think that I must have an easy labor because I deserve it. Someone, some spirit of Mother Nature, some angel, some saint in charge of women going into delivery, has to be watching over me tomorrow. Nothing bad can happen to me or the baby – it's simply not allowed. I have earned an easy labor. Don't they know that?

But the reality, which I can't say I've completely accepted, is that life, health, living into my nineties, having a 'normal' baby, is no more or less guaranteed than it was before Josh died. Something bad could happen. If not tomorrow, sometime in his life something could go wrong. My co-worker Don Williams had a baby boy, Eric, who stopped breathing in the middle of the night when he was two years old. Aunt Hettie and Uncle Jim's son Aaron was diagnosed with an advanced form of cancer at sixteen and died within two months of the diagnosis. Lauren Keller, a girl I went to school with, died at twelve from leukemia. Alley Oberlein has a brain tumor. Conner Dembs is autistic. Dan O'Brien is a delinquent who has almost gotten himself killed on several occasions because he's such an asshole. My child could be born with a severe physical disability, a harrowing mental condition, an emotional disorder. He could be the kid who wears a trench coat to high school and everyone thinks he's going to bring a gun to school. He could be completely healthy but a total asshole or a big crybaby. The odds are he'll be none of these things and he'll be fine. But four months ago today I stopped playing the odds.

So tomorrow the worrying doesn't stop. It only starts. Does he have a fever? Does his breathing sound funny? Is he too hot? Too cold? Is he eating enough? Is he eating too much? Are his toes supposed to look like that? Is his skin supposed to be yellow? I will worry for the rest of my life. I don't know how to make sense of any of this.

The only reassuring fact, as dark and dismal as it may sound, is that everything is uncertain and worrying doesn't make anything more certain. I remember when Josh was still here every night I locked the doors. I locked the doors because I worried that someone would break in. Every night I locked those doors. I applied heavy amounts of sunscreen because I worried about getting skin cancer. I worried about my dad getting skin cancer because he never wears sunscreen. I worried about a massive earthquake hitting Los Angeles and never hearing from Moo or Ads again. Then Moo moved to Miami and I started worrying about hurricanes. I worried about losing the baby once I got pregnant. I worried about everything. And then my husband was killed in a freak accident – an accident that involved an activity that I never worried about him doing. How ridiculous. How fucking ridiculous. So what's the lesson? What do I take away from all of this? What conclusion do I come to on my last night of being a nonmother? What do I tell myself? What's my mantra? Shit happens? Don't sweat the small stuff? Bad things *do* happen to good people and they *do* happen more than once so don't get too comfy? Lightning *can* strike the same place twice? Sometimes I think that I never worried about Josh and that was the problem. Maybe if I worried about him *more often*, he would still be alive. I don't know the answer.

My mom calls me and tells me to make sure I go to bed early. She is nervous I won't be able to fall asleep. Deedee calls me with the same concern. 'You'll need a good night's sleep,' they say. But I know they may need one even more. After all, they are already moms. They know what lies ahead of me and so they won't be able to sleep. I have no idea what my life will be like tomorrow or the next day. My ignorance is my Ambien tonight and I'm okay with that. As I go through my hospital bag over and over again, I think about how not every woman in the world gets to pack her hospital bag in preparation for childbirth. Not every woman gets to watch her body transform over the course of forty weeks and create new life. I remind myself not to overlook that fact. No matter what happens tomorrow, no matter how hard my labor is, no matter what challenges lie in front of Baby Taylor and me, we get to be here. Four months ago I saw my husband lying in a coffin. Tomorrow I get to hold my baby boy in my arms for the first time. All I can do is savor the fact that I am still here and that he is about to be here. My son will take his first breath four months and one day after his dad took his last. He gets a chance. I get a chance to be there for him. There is something beautiful in that.

Just after 1 a.m. I go into labor. At 5:30 I wake Moo up. At 6:00 we call my parents. They pick up the dogs and drop them off at the boarding place. By 6:30 we're at the hospital. I'm in a birthing room for a while with my family. By 9:00 I kick everyone out. At 11:00 I get an epidural. A little after 11:00, Dr Wiermiller says I have to have a cesarean, but I've had an epidural so I don't really care what they do to me.

Moo comes with me into surgery. They numb my body and pull up a blue sheet. It feels like someone is tugging at my stomach. I stare at the ceiling for a while and all I can think is, *I just want to hear him cry.* Everyone is quiet. The doctors are all focused and working away. Where is he? Shouldn't they have gotten him by now? Why can't I hear him? Moo holds my hand. Where is he? Where *is* he? All of the sudden, I feel a very strange sensation. I feel like the air is being pulled out of my body through my stomach. My breath is taken away. And then I hear the greatest sound in the entire history of the world. He cries. I make Moo tell me everything she sees. I feel a tear roll down my cheek.

On October 18, 2007, at 12:10 p.m. Kai Joshua Taylor is born. Eight pounds, one ounce. His mother's exact birth weight. Completely healthy. More than healthy. Madly healthy.

There is no literary connection for the birth of my son. No author has done justice to this miracle. There aren't words to describe this day or the magic and power that surround the moment a baby is born. Emerson claims the only eye who can truly observe the beauty of a natural landscape is the poet. And while the natural world may hold its mysteries and miracles, it pales in comparison to the incredible experience of childbirth and the natural landscape of the human body. The best way I can say it is that when a baby is born, the ghosts of the world's greatest poets stand and listen to the cry of a life that just took its first breath and even they can't find the words.

After Kai and I make it safely into our recovery room and he gets his tests and first bath, we begin to enjoy our first calm moments together. Our family quietly files in, some in tears. Suddenly Ashley bursts in and announces in a very loud voice, 'Oh *my* God, that is the cutest *fucking* baby I have ever seen!' I picture Emerson's ghost, in his nicely tailored 1836 suit, jolting at the use of such an obscenity and quietly saying, 'Oh my,' and stepping out of the room.

Everyone comes to see me. Flowers fill the room. Flowers, bright yellow trucks, cards, presents, food, everything. Everyone holds Kai. He sleeps in the arms of everyone.

At night everyone goes home. I sleep while Kai sleeps. For the last four months I've been mad at the universe. I've been standing in line with a lot of other very unhappy people waiting to yell at someone about how unfair my life is. I've been mad and angry with everything. But when I lie in my room and I see Kai's chest go up and down, I decide I don't want to stand in this line anymore. 'We're just gonna,' I say, quietly stepping toward the exit sign, 'no really, just forget about it, no big deal, just tell the Wizard of Oz, or God, or whoever is answering grievances up there that I'm not . . . we're not . . . we're okay. We're going to be okay.'

Then Kai and I come home. It is a beautiful fall day. Mid-sixties, sunshine. We come home to our house.

NOVEMBER

It is chilling to know that some accepted ways of being with children can leave them vulnerable to suffering from anxiety, depression, or rage in later life. The statistics are alarming: about 2 in every 100 children in the US are taking antidepressants, and the World Health Organization reports that depression in adults will soon reach epidemic proportions. More than half of all children have experienced bullying at school, and 3,080,000 children in the US are excluded from school each year for bad behavior.

—MARGOT SUNDERLAND, *THE SCIENCE OF PARENTING*

In the corner of my bedroom there is a stack of books. Throughout the school year and summer, the stack consists of mostly fiction. Some of the books are work-related, others are my own personal endeavors. Ever since Kai was born, however, the stack of books has changed completely. All of the fiction paperbacks have been shoved into the closet; I don't have time to read them. The only thing I make time for are books about babies.

The Science of Parenting, The Ultimate Breastfeeding Book of Answers, Babywise, Your Child's Health, Girlfriend's Guide to the First Year, What to Expect: The First Year, Healthy Sleep Habits Happy Child, Your Baby's First Year, Secrets of the Baby Whisperer. This is my list so far. Some of these have been given to me and others I've bought on my own. People always say, 'Babies don't come with a manual.' They do, actually. There are thousands of them, each with their own catchy title and slick cover. I've spent hundreds of dollars on manuals.

As a first-time mom with no husband and too much stubborn pride to ask other people for help, I turn to these books for advice. I read passages over and over again, like I'm trying to perfect a recipe. (A recipe! What a ridiculous metaphor for caring for a newborn.) And every decision, no matter how minute it may seem on the surface, is a major decision.

The biggest issue is whether or not to feed on demand or develop a schedule. This is basically the Republicans and Democrats of baby maintenance; you can't find two groups who disagree more on a topic. *Babywise* claims that babies on a schedule surpass nonscheduled babies on a variety of levels. The text states that scheduled babies are 'characterized by contentment, healthy growth, and optimal alertness. People on the street will remark on a *Babywise* baby's happiness.' People on the street will remark? How can I turn down that selling point? On the other hand, *The Ultimate Breastfeeding Book of Answers* argues that a schedule is ridiculous. 'An emphasis on timing of feedings is an unfortunate legacy from a decade when babies' lives were rigidly scheduled, even though those schedules frequently led to breast-feeding failure.' Unfortunate legacy? Breastfeeding failure! So what am I to do? Two credible author-ities completely disagree. One recipe says add a stick of butter. The other says, for the love of God whatever you do, *don't* add a stick of butter.

The problem with all of these decisions is that everyone in my life wants to weigh in on the debate. 'You're *waking him up* to feed him? [pause while question asker gives me a judgmental look] Hmm. That's interesting. When I had [insert name of child here] they told us *never* to wake a sleeping baby. *Never.*' Questions about scheduling specifi-cally piss me off because I am truly insecure about what I am doing. When people ask questions about it, I feel guilty and inept.

'Well, *I* never used a schedule,' Deedee tells me. 'I mean, I'm not saying it's *bad*, I'm just saying that I think it's appropriate to feed a child when he is hungry.' She makes these narrow eyes when she says this. I am also annoyed because the women who tell me these things are usually in their fifties, which means they had children twenty-five years ago when the world had just discovered that smoking and drinking were bad for pregnant women. I know that my mother-in-law is a wise woman, but I am confident that the field of prenatal medicine and infant development has come a long way in twenty-five years.

One thing that I cover with my students during our nonfiction research unit is how to assess a source. I ask them, how is this person qualified to speak on the subject? Does she have a degree? Does he have firsthand experience? Where was the article published? I take into consideration these same questions when reading my baby books. *The Ultimate Breastfeeding Book of Answers*, for example, is written by a man, and although he is a doctor and has had decades of experience, he has never breastfed. I read his book because I know he's a fantastic doctor, but I also know that he's never walked into the bank and realized he has leaked all over his shirt or felt the pain associated with full breasts and no takers on milk. Ashley, however, isn't a doctor and she has never had kids, but she still declares herself the Fountain of All Knowledge on all things baby.

In the last four weeks Ashley has made all sorts of suggestions about how I can and should improve on my care of Kai. Kai has developed scaly dry skin on his head. In the midst of showing it to my mom, she jumps in. 'It's called cradle cap. A lot of babies get it.' She rifles through his drawers and holds up outfits she bought over the summer. 'Hey, Nat?' I hear her say from the nursery. I walk in to see her holding up a blue zip-up top from Old Navy. 'Has he worn this yet?' I tell her no. She says she'll put it on top – he'll be too big for it soon. She buys me a car seat cover from Home Goods even though I already have one. Mine is a hand-me-down from a co-worker. 'I'm not saying yours is bad,' she says. 'It's just that this one looked a lot warmer.' By 'a lot warmer' she means not a hand-me-down.

Recently we had a conversation that went something like this:

ASHLEY: Hey, Nat, what kind of passie is he using? [her word for pacifier].

ME: Oh, I just took the ones from the hospital. He seemed to like those, so I kept them. [Pause]

ASHLEY: Oh, okay. Well, if you're interested, when I had the triplets I used the Avent passie with all three girls and they *loved* it. I remember Gracie was three before she gave it up.

ME: Cool.

ASHLEY: Do you want me to get you some? I can pick them up tomorrow after work. It's really not a problem.

ME: No, I like the ones from the hospital. You can see through them, so I can tell how he is sucking and where his tongue is when he sucks.

ASHLEY: Yeah, that's cool. Just so you know, the Avent is see-through too. It's clear all around the sides and in the middle.

ME: Great.

ASHLEY: Yeah, it's not a big deal, I can pick some up for you.

ME: No, thanks. I think we'll just stick to the ones from the hospital.

ASHLEY: It's really not a big deal.

ME: No, we're good with the ones we have.

ASHLEY: Okay.

With every conversation her subtext is, 'I know what I am doing and you don't, so let me help you. Aren't I *so* generous?' My inner monologue always seems to be, *Are you fucking kidding me?*

Everyone wants to tell me how to do things. In part, I need to listen because I really don't know how to do anything. But it is hard to admit that I am a mom and I don't know anything about how to take care of my own baby.

I wish I had some sort of fairy godmother. I think everyone who is suddenly dropped into an unlikely change of circumstance should get his or her own version of a fairy godmother. There could be the Fairy Breakup Godmother, the Fairy Divorcée Godmother, and the Fairy Over Forty Godmother. Or wouldn't it be great if we had a fairy godmother for even basic transitions? I could've really used a fairy godmother in middle school.

But what I really need now is a fairy godmother for moms. Like every other fairy godmother, she would visit me when my life is fraught with confusion and frustration. Through her gentle guidance, she would help me see the truth. But she wouldn't look like your average fairy godmother. She wouldn't bear the angelic exterior with the flowing dress and neatly tied hair, and her language wouldn't be fluffy or full of false praise. She wouldn't be the fairy-tale type, because she would be a woman who has gone through the challenges of child rearing, so she would know this job is no fairy tale. My fairy godmother would wear her hair in a banana clip with strands sticking out everywhere. She would dress in an oversized T-shirt covered in spit-up stains, faded black stretch pants, worn-out running shoes, and one ankle sock and one tube sock. She would be the fairy godmother for new moms. Every now and then she would appear and guide me in my journey, but she would advise me honestly, without the veil of what things are supposed to look like. She would sit slumped in the glider and talk about what it was really like to be a mom. She would answer all of my questions in a plain and direct way with no subtext attached. She would be my Fairy Mom Godmother.

'Fairy Mom Godmother, everything I've read says not to put the baby in bed with you, but it would be so much easier for me if I didn't have to get up every time I heard him cry.'

'Ignore everything you've read. Everything. If it's easier for you to have the baby in bed, put him there and don't be an idiot. You need to make things easier on yourself if you don't want to go completely insane. And you can go insane doing this – I've seen it happen plenty of times.'

Much like the other fairy godmothers, no one else could see her except me, which would come in really handy when I'm trying to figure out how to deal with Ashley or other people who try to tell me how to be a mom. Because as any mom knows, being a mom isn't just about taking care of a baby, it's about dealing with the crazy aunties, the lazy uncles, the grandmas who want to do everything their way. Maybe she could even wander in and out of important conversations between Ashley and me to help me gauge how to stay calm. When Ashley goes through Kai's closet and pulls out the cute jacket he hasn't worn yet, Fairy Mom Godmother would just lean against the changing table, watching her.

'Hey, Nat,' Ashley would say from the closet. I walk in and see both of them standing there. 'Has he worn this yet?' Ashley hands me the corduroy jacket and goes back to flipping through hangers.

'Um.' I take the jacket and look at it. It has hardly been touched. Kai has absolutely not worn it yet. I consider telling Ashley my own personal opinion about how ridiculous it is to buy a jacket for an infant who doesn't even leave the house. My Fairy Mom Godmother looks at me and, reading my mind, shakes her head. I follow her lead. 'Yeah, he's worn it. We wore it last week when we went to dinner at my parents' house.' Fairy Mom Godmother gives me the thumbs-up.

'That's weird,' Ashley says, 'Why is there a tag still on it?' With a quick sleight of hand, my Fairy Mom Godmother swipes the jacket, pulls off the tag, and throws it back at me just as Ashley peeks her head out of the closet again.

I show her the coat. 'No tag, see?' Ashley flips the coat over and scrunches up her nose.

'Oh, I could have sworn I just saw it.' She hangs it back up and closes the closet. She tells me she's glad we like the coat. 'We love that coat!' I say as Ashley walks out. My Fairy Mom Godmother makes a face in Ashley's direction and spins her index finger next to her head as if to say, 'What a wacko.' We exchange a high-five.

The one way we quiet Kai down when he gets fussy is we wrap him tightly in a fleece blanket, hold him as close to our bodies as we can, turn on music, and dance around with him. This strategy has yet to fail. When I dance with Kai, I like to listen to Abba, Alison Krauss, and Jack Johnson. (Vito was a little disturbed to hear that Kai was being rocked to 'Dancing Queen.') Chris plays Bob Marley. Deedee can't figure out how to work the iPod, so she sings to him. My dad sings to Kai also, but he only knows the words to three songs: 'Amazing Grace,' 'The Star-Spangled Banner,' and 'O Canada' (from watching thousands of hockey games). Whenever my mom walks in and a song is playing that she doesn't know, she'll say, 'Okay, Kai, let's change it. I know, I don't like this song either.' When Kai is at her house she puts on Johnny Mathis's 'Chances Are' and announces, 'This is his favorite.'

I love this. I love that everyone in my family has their songs for Kai and their moments with him. He has bonded with everyone and he's hardly one month old. But at the same time, I see him passed around from person to person and I can't help but think that Josh is the only one who doesn't get to hold him.

I've told myself over and over that I won't be a sad mom. I remember when I was eight months pregnant, Toby was over with a few other people and we were all chatting about how excited we were for Baby Taylor to arrive. Toby remarked how seeing the baby would make him so happy, but he knew he would have to go in the other room and cry at the same time. I sat there, stoic, with my large pregnant belly, and said, 'Don't be surprised when I *don't* do the same thing.' I was convinced that motherhood would make me stronger in my battle against my grief. I would show Kai a life filled with laughter and love and I would not concede to revealing my long journey with darkness. He would never see me sad. He would never hear me cry. But Kai has been here for two weeks and I have found that my grief has sort of started all over again. It is as if I just found out that I don't have a husband. My reflections of Josh are more frequent than they were in the weeks before Kai's birth. In many ways they are more profound. I think about Josh a lot when I nurse Kai. I know for some that may seem a little perverse, but for any mother who has nursed her child, she knows exactly why I would find this moment a moment of deep reflection. I don't just think about losing Josh, I find myself remembering small details about him that I hadn't thought about since he died. I think about how he wore his watch so that the face of it was on the inside of his wrist. I think about how initially he didn't want to wear his wedding ring because he had never worn jewelry before, and then without me nagging him at all, once we were married he never took it off. I remember odd memories that have no significance whatsoever except for the fact that we were together. I remember standing in line at the Denver airport on our way home from rafting. He was wearing a gray T-shirt and his blue Salmon River Experience visor. I remember taking Louise for walks through the park in our neighborhood when she was a puppy. I remember how he sang songs in the car. How he would play the same verses over and over because he knew all the words. I remember we had this sort of dance to the song 'Gloria' by Van Morrison. He would mouth the lyrics into his fake microphone and I would do this sassy hand motion like a background singer and we thought it was hilarious. Just the two of us, singing 'Gloria' over and over again in the car. These are the things I remember suddenly. I am happy they are so vivid. But they bring me immense pain at the same time. All of these glimpses of our life together flash in front of me all the time.

Last night Kai and I slept at my house, just the two of us, and we did fine. Technically, this was our first night alone together. Chris had been here since he was born, but I never woke up Chris in the middle of the night. Ashley, Maggie, and my mom keep insisting that someone stay with me, at least until after his midnight feeding. But I keep insisting that no one should be here. We need to learn how to do this by ourselves.

This morning after I feed Kai, I decide that I want to take a shower. Prior to this morning, I only took showers if there was someone else here to watch Kai. But this morning I figure we need to learn how to do another thing on our own. I lay Kai's changing pad on the floor of the bathroom and lay him on the pad. He is always content on his changing pad. I get in the shower and talk to him the whole time so he doesn't think I've left him. I take a nice shower. I get out, get dressed, put on lotion, and Kai never cries once. This is a huge accomplishment for us. The fact that I can resume a normal daily activity with Kai and no one else is a very big deal.

When Kai and I walk back to my bedroom to put the dirty clothes in the hamper, I look at the computer and see a picture of Josh on the screen saver. It is a picture of him and me standing in the streets of Denver at night. He's looking right at the camera and I'm laughing at something else, looking off to the side. I look at the picture, and without even thinking, a flash of emotion runs through my body. I don't know what word best describes it. It's like I suddenly said, 'Yeah, that's right, we can do this.' It isn't anger or frustration; it is more of a pompous emotion. A confident, edgy streak that comes into my eyes as I look at him.

I have vivid memories of last spring when I was coaching and teaching and Josh was looking for a new job. The dogs were crazy, I was pregnant, and we felt like our lives were incredibly hectic. I can remember feeling completely overwhelmed, and then I would settle myself down by thinking, *As long as I have Josh, I can handle this*. I vividly remember saying that to myself. Now the one person that I convinced myself I couldn't live without is gone. For weeks after his funeral I remember looking at my stomach or staring out the window, thinking, *How am I going to do this? How the hell am I going to do this?* Then I went back to work in the fall, and then Kai was born, and this morning I took a shower all by myself. Now I look at his picture and I want to yell, 'Yep! This is me, doing this! I am making this happen without you!' I know there are setbacks to come, and in five minutes or five hours I could feel sad and frustrated again. But just give me this one second with this very small moment of triumph.

Tonight, Friday night, a bunch of my friends stop by my house a few hours before going out.

141

Toby, Nikki (Toby's fiancée), my friend Becky, Mathews, and Elliott. Everyone is dressed in bar clothes. Mathews is wearing black slacks with a baby blue button-down shirt. Elliott has his leather jacket on. Toby is wearing cuff links. Becky has straightened her hair and is wearing makeup. This is not the first time my friends stopped by my house before going out for the night. My friends do a really good job of including me in their social schedule. They usually plan on meeting at my house so they can spend some time with me before they leave. Instead of going to dinner, sometimes they bring over carry-out so I can be included. They are amazing people. But it always feels a little strange seeing them leave. I feel like I'm their grandma. They come over, help me around the house, bring me food, see how I'm doing, and then after a little bit of time they get in their cars and drive away to do things that young people do.

It's not that I want to be one of them. It's not that I want to be a young, single, twenty-something who can go out and get drunk and sleep until eleven the next morning. I want to be a mom. I want to stay home with Kai. But turning to an empty house after everyone leaves is not the way I envisioned things. Obviously Josh should be here. Obviously I wanted to be a mother with a husband. Every weekend Josh and I would have stayed home in our pajamas, talked about Kai's latest developments, and watched him fall asleep. But now I sit in my bedroom alone, wait for Kai to wake up, type on my computer, and listen to my podcasts. No one's voice fills the room except Kai's quiet squawks as he rustles around in his bassinet. At this moment I am not unhappy, but it feels a little odd as I watch my friends pile into their cars. Part of me would like to go with them, but I know full well once I got to the bar I would just want to go home.

The problem, the root of the problem, is that I don't fit anywhere. I am a huge paradox. If Josh were here, I would fit here. It would be normal to stay at home with my husband and my son. We would be a family together. But now I am single. And single women in their twenties go to the bar, perhaps not even to meet someone, but that's just what they do. But I am also a mom, and moms stay home with their children. And I don't even fit into the category of single mom because single moms do go to the bar on occasion. And some single moms do go out to the bar to meet people. But I am a single mom who is a widow in my midtwenties, and I have no idea what the rules are for me, but at this point I am in no way prepared for or interested in going to the bar or meeting people.

One of the best things Dr G. told me was that I didn't have to judge every new situation I encountered. Living alone, for example. She said I didn't have to say living alone was good or bad, I could just live alone and not make a judgment on it. I know this moment is the same situation.

I stay at home on weekends because I am a single mother and even when I do go out, it will not be to meet people, and I don't have to say that any of those things are good or bad. They can just exist. Still, tonight feels different. I don't know why. It's not even that I want to be at the bar. It's just that I feel so out of place. I look out my front window and I think, I am the only single widowed mother in her midtwenties on this planet. The only one. There is something a bit isolating about that.

On a side note, today Amy Grant and Vince Gill were on *Oprah*. In the middle of their interview, Oprah pulled out Amy Grant's book *Mosaic*. As Oprah explained, *Mosiac* is general musings about Amy Grant's own life authored by Amy Grant. It's about her life as an artist, a mom, a wife, raising her children and Vince's children and their children together. The excerpt that Oprah read out loud was about when Amy was telling Vince something and she said his response really showed her that he 'understood.' Then he said to her that he may not always understand her, but he 'welcomes her and everything she brings to the table.' As you can imagine, this only spurred a deep-seated hate for Amy Grant that I never knew I had. Instantly I became furious. I was furious that she had published a book about her life, her life with twenty Grammys and her huge house and how she 'struggled' and blah, blah, blah. I was pissed that Amy Grant was wildly successful and made it look so effortless. And that scene that

Oprah read, how lame. I was so mad at Vince Gill and Amy Grant because they looked like they really did love each other, and their perfect kids from their perfect two-parent home, and everything seems to fit so well together.

I have to stop getting angry at celebrities I've never met. It's not healthy.

My Fairy Mom Godmother lies next to me on my bed. I say all of this to her. She has her back to me as I relay the details of this *Oprah* episode, but once I finish she turns so she stares at the ceiling with me. She is in her pajamas, which consist of an extra-large T-shirt that says RACHEL'S NIGHT UNDER THE STARS, NOV. 3, 1988, from one of her kid's friend's bar mitzvahs, and a large pair of sweatpants. She yawns widely and says, 'If you find yourself yelling at random famous people on television, that's okay. They don't care that you suddenly hate them. And you only hate them because they have something you want. In fact, everyone has something you want. So go ahead, yell at the television. It's only because you don't have anyone else to yell at.' She rolls back over. She isn't the type that is interested in long, drawn-out, touchy-feely conversations. I stare at the ceiling, considering her advice.

'And besides,' she says, looking up from her pillow, 'other than that Christmas album, what is that woman really good for anyway?'

I look at the clock and turn out the light.

★   ★   ★

145

Recently I have been leaving the house more and more during the day. Sometimes I take Kai with me, and sometimes Maggie will come over and watch Kai and I'll go solo. My outings have included Kroger, Target, and the mall. As a postpartum mom, I am not quite back into my prepregnancy jeans ('not quite back' is a gross understatement of the truth), and I don't wear fitted shirts because my stomach still has a little bulge to it. So I leave the house in the same thing that I wear around the house – black stretch pants, running shoes or slip-ons, a sweatshirt or some sort of baggy pullover top. Everywhere I go during the day I see women wearing almost the exact same outfit as me. The black stretch pants, the running shoes, the messy hair tied back. All of us look as if we have just come from the gym, but none of us has actually come from the gym because none of us has had time to go to the gym. We all look like this because we are all aware that there is only a small window of time to go to the grocery store, the post office, the bank, and so on, before our children completely flip out. There is no time to brush hair, put together an outfit, put on makeup, or any of these other commodities that we used to take for granted. The other day I saw a woman walking her two Labradors with a baby in her Baby-Björn strapped to the front of her in forty-degree weather. I said something about how she looked like she had a lot to handle. She shrugged and said, 'You do what you need to do to make it work.'

The more contact I make with other mothers, the more I realize I'm not the only one who is trying to balance something unbalanceable. The challenges of my days seem monstrous. Getting a baby and two dogs loaded into the car, remembering the leashes, the food, the collars, the stroller, the extra outfits, the diaper bag, my purse, cell phone, and car keys all while the dogs bark and Kai screams and I try to carry three other bags out the door – all this just for one night at my parents' house. Or in the middle of the night, nursing Kai, then rocking him to sleep, then an hour later he finally nods off and then poops, which goes through his diaper, pajamas, blanket, bassinet mattress cover, all the way through to the plastic bassinet mattress. I only sleep in three-hour increments max, and usually when he sleeps during the day I have to do things like empty the dishwasher, throw in a load of laundry, shower, urinate, put on deodorant, get dressed, or clean up the kitchen. All of this, however, is strikingly similar to the lives of women everywhere – only many of those women do what I do with two, three, four, or five children. 'One kid and two dogs,' I can hear a stressed-out housewife say. 'Gimme a break. I could do that in my sleep.' And it's true.

Now I am a part of this club of motherhood. I know what it feels like to wear the same outfit for three days straight. I know what it feels like to not run a brush through my hair for an entire week. A few days ago around five o'clock in the afternoon, I realized I hadn't brushed my teeth all day and I couldn't remember if I had brushed them the night before. But as my tongue grazed across my bumpy front teeth, I realized I really didn't care. I was completely indifferent to my own personal hygiene. But this is not a unique feeling. I am not different from the average mother because I do not have a husband.

You do what you have to do to make it work. That's the anthem. The weeks before Kai was born I panicked about having the dogs and a newborn. How would I make all of this work? How would I be able to handle the dogs and all of their demands and take care of a baby who couldn't possibly come in second? But now that we're all here, somehow we make it happen. My friends and family come over all the time to hold Kai while I walk Louise and Bug, and although we're still not perfect, we still try as often as we can. It's not always pretty, but we try to make it work.

'You're going to surprise yourself,' my Fairy Mom Godmother says from across the room. She is slouched in the rocking chair with one foot on the ottoman and one foot on the floor. 'You'll figure out ways to do things that you never thought possible.' I can only hope she is right.

Everyone comes to town for Thanksgiving. My parents, Hales, Deedee, Ashley, Chris, Ads and

Ellie, Moo and Dubs. We call David 'Dubs' because when Moo was in college, before she started dating him, she had a crush on him and referred to him as 'D.W.' (his initials) to her friends. After they had been dating a while, she confessed that she had a code name for him and she sort of resurrected D.W. We (my brother mostly) shortened it to D-Dubs and then just Dubs. The nickname fits him perfectly. He's a tall guy with broad shoulders and red hair. He's from Canada and he's Jewish, so as a red-headed Jewish Canadian, he's pretty unique. 'David' just doesn't suit him. Also, Dubs is kind of an oaf. He can be clumsy and sometimes he says the wrong things without thinking. The best part about Dubs is that he thinks he is hilarious. He is always telling us about the latest 'bit' he's been working on. Recently he told us aboot (about, Canadian style) his theory that only when people are flying on airplanes do they enjoy tomato juice and Sudoku, but never when they're on the ground. 'I mean, right, nobody ever orders tomato juice in a restaurant or a bar. But on planes it's so popular!' Dubs is a good person to have around during potentially painful holidays. He either makes us laugh because he tries to lighten the mood, or he tries to be serious and say something sentimental, which usually comes out wrong, which makes us laugh harder.

This is my first major holiday without Josh. I am relieved my family is all here, but surprisingly the day itself hasn't seemed to stress me out. Something else, however, has been sitting like a rock in my stomach. I've been consumed in thinking about one teeny-tiny moment that may rip me to pieces: saying grace.

Every Thanksgiving since the history of our family, my dad has said grace. We are not a grace or prayer-at-dinnertime family throughout the year, but we always say it at Thanksgiving. My dad always says it. I don't know how it started that he was the grace-sayer, but in previous years, it has always been him. He usually says something short but very touching. Something like 'Dear Lord, thank you for this beautiful table of food, but thank you more for the people surrounding it. Bless those who are not here to join us. Amen.' While he says it we all bow our heads, and although I don't know this for a fact, I bet everyone in my family closes their eyes. We have never been a very religious family. Our church experience mostly consisted of playing tic-tac-toe and hangman on the Steeple Notes during the service. Traditional prayers have never really been our thing. But when my dad bows his head at Thanksgiving dinner, we stop and listen. That's the kind of grace it is; even if you don't believe in anything, you close your eyes during my dad's grace. Most times my dad gets choked up after saying grace. Although we never press him on it, we all know why. He cries because he really is thankful for the people at the table. As a dad, there is nothing, literally *nothing*, in the world as wonderful as having all four of his adult children in the same place.

But this year I can't imagine hearing my dad say grace. I've worried about it for weeks. I know he won't be able to get through it. I can't imagine what he would say. What kind of thanking can you do when your daughter has been turned widow and mother in a few short months? There is a newborn baby and lost husband. How can you articulate a Thanksgiving prayer around that?

The other element is, it is so hard to watch my dad struggle. All my life, my dad has been the strongest, toughest, smartest guy in the world. He has two artificial hips and plays hockey three times a week. At fifty, he took up the hobby of wind-surfing on Lake Michigan. He always knows the answer to every question. All of the children in our family know this. If your car doesn't start, you call dad. If your check bounces, you call dad. If you're stuck in traffic on I-75 and you don't have a map of the back roads (even though Dad told you to put one in your car), you can call him and he'll safely guide you home.

He has spent thirty years doing everything in his power to protect his children from the torturous forces of the world. He has done every-thing to give us a happy and healthy life. He has done things I'll never even know. But tonight, he can't say grace because it will remind him that he, my father, is not enough to protect his children.

Now he has to look at me and admit he has no answers. He can't make a phone call, he can't pay a bill, and he can't wrestle anyone to the ground. So no, he can't say grace. Because for the first time in his life he doesn't know what to say to one of his children.

We all sit down at the table. As everyone sits down, it starts to get quiet. Minutes before, there had been three different conversations going on, but when we pull our seats out from the table the air in the room seems to deaden the chatter. Suddenly we have nothing to say, we're all just waiting to get through the moment. In the awkward silence I have a flash that I should've just talked to my dad about it earlier, but I knew a conversation about it would be worse than enduring it. So I don't say anything. My dad doesn't make a move. My mom says something like 'Everything looks great, guys,' but no one picks up their fork. I can feel my throat tighten. I can sense everyone else's throat tighten too.

Finally, someone says through a mumble, 'Should we say a prayer?' and at the same time someone wants to refill her glass with water and the pitcher is sitting by Dubs, so she says, 'Can someone pass the water? Dubs, hey Dubs . . .' Dubs, however, hears these two lines at the same time and thinks he is being asked to say the prayer, in response to which he puts his head down and turns bright red. After figuring out that he is not being asked to say the prayer, we all burst into laughter at the thought of Dubs, the Canadian Jew, saying a prayer at Thanksgiving. And then Dubs of course grabs the awkward moment and turns it into comedy. He launches into an amalgamation of all of the prayers that he would have said. 'Oh, baby Jesus,' he begins. 'Thank you, God, for the food, the baby Jesus.' We eat.

Later that night some time after eleven o'clock, I have another strange experience. I have just put Kai down after his last feeding. I am the only one awake and the whole house is dark. I go into the bathroom (which I only do twice a day), and on my way out, I go to turn the light out. I pull the switch down, but only one light goes out and the second light stays on. I turn it on and off again. Same thing. One light stays on. Immediately, an odd person zips into my brain.

When Josh's grandma Margaret was at home with hospice in February, there was a nurse named Nancy who was there most of the time. Nancy the nurse never really did anything medical – there was another nurse who was in charge of that stuff. Nancy would just float around the house and talk to people and tell her stories. I found Nancy to be incredibly irritating. I know it sounds horrible that I would find a hospice nurse irritating, but the woman drove me nuts. She basically made herself a self-proclaimed member of Margaret's family. Once she found out I was pregnant, she told everyone about it. I remember Josh calling me from Margaret's house and telling me that Nancy the nurse told Mrs Mansfield – the neighborhood mom who is basically the walking version of *Us Weekly* for southeastern Michigan – that I was pregnant. When Margaret passed, I remember we all stood around her in a circle and held hands while her minister said a prayer. It was me, Ashley, Deedee, Mary (Deedee's sister), Mary's sons David and Scott, Chris, the minister, and Nancy the nurse. Nancy was sobbing.

In the aftermath of Margaret's death, I knew that I could always make Josh laugh by bringing up my annoyance with Nancy the nurse. He thought it was hilarious that I became so fed up with her. 'The burial plot looks really nice, Josh,' I said to him on the ride home from the cemetery. A few of us had stayed to watch Margaret's casket placed. It was a gray February day. 'Yeah,' he said quietly, staring at the road. I could tell he was having a rough time. 'I just wish Nancy the nurse could have been there,' I said. I saw a smile creep across his face.

But on Thanksgiving night Nancy the nurse floats into my brain for a very different reason. Nancy the nurse, as you would expect, had been in the presence of death too many times to count. She often shared her experiences with us. She told us stories in a soft, serious voice about connecting with spirits, and I would sit on the couch and think to myself, *Don't they screen people before hiring for this kind of work?* She told me that she had several experiences where a spirit or soul of someone who has passed away sort of 'comes to' the family. She said the spirit almost always came in the form of a light of some sort. One time she remembered a family lost their daughter, a woman in her twenties with a little boy, to cancer. Shortly after she passed, Nancy saw a blue light stream through the house. *Right*, I thought. *Do you believe in vampires too, Nancy?*

On Thanksgiving night, however, Nancy's ridiculous, unscientific observation comes back to me. I remember right after Josh died I was at my parents' house and the same thing happened with the light. I hit the switch and it didn't go off. Immediately, I thought it was Josh just saying, 'I'm here. I'm right here.' I asked my mom about the light (obviously not telling her my theory about how it was my dead husband reincarnated into electricity) and she just said, 'Yeah, sometimes that light does that.' Sure enough, every now and then the light will stay on. It hasn't done this in a long time. I can't even remember the last time it stayed on, but on the night of Thanksgiving that light stays on. I know how ridiculous I sound. I sound as ridiculous as Nancy did. But that light makes me feel a little better. I really think it's not just an electrical quirk. I think it's a little reminder that he's not as far away as I think. Weird. The bathroom light. Who knew.

DECEMBER

Sleep that knits up the raveled sleeve of care,
The death of each day's life, sore labour's bath,
Balm of hurt minds, great Nature's second
  course,
Chief nourisher in life's feast.
> —MACBETH IN WILLIAM SHAKESPEARE,
> *MACBETH*

Even though I'm on maternity leave, I still think about my students and my job. I think about how they are treating my sub. I wonder if they're still trying hard or if they're having more fun without me. Right now they are starting Shakespeare's *Macbeth*. *Macbeth* takes place in eleventh-century Scotland. It's a fictional story, but historians say that Shakespeare got his idea for the play because he had done some research on that period in Scotland's history and found that it was an incredibly violent and ruthless time and place – perfect for a dramatic storyline. *Macbeth* is about a guy (Macbeth) who starts off noble and then after getting a taste of

156

power (he gets promoted to Thane of Glamis), he gets hungry for more. He ends up killing his king (Duncan) and his bff (Banquo) and a list of others. The body count is pretty high by the end of the play. There are a lot of factors that push Macbeth to turn to the dark side; three witches give him these prophecies of his future, and his wife is out for blood before Macbeth even starts to think about killing anyone. By the end of act I, Macbeth and his wife have set out to murder in their hunt for the throne.

But Shakespeare is tricky. Macbeth and Lady Macbeth engage in some pretty horrific foul play. If you know anything about Shakespeare's tragedies, then you know that the main characters always end up dead in act V. But for Macbeth and Lady Macbeth, their real torture happens long before they die.

Right after Macbeth kills his sleeping king, he claims he hears a voice. He runs out of King Duncan's bedchamber, and says, 'Methought I heard a voice cry 'Sleep no more! / Macbeth does murder sleep,' the innocent sleep.' And there we have the ultimate tool of torture for Macbeth and eventually his wife. They can't sleep. If you think Shakespeare is going easy on these two, then you've obviously never been sleep-deprived for an extended period of time. Because Shakespeare knows that if you really want someone to lose their fucking mind, you take away sleep.

In act V, Lady Macbeth starts to sleepwalk. While

wandering around at night, her servants hear her confess all of her crimes. I always picture her bumping into furniture, walking around with the cartoon swirls in her eyes. I used to think she lost her mind because of her guilt, but now I realize that's not it. Girlfriend can't sleep. Everything I do on a daily basis is from this same Lady Macbeth sleep-deprived state. It's not just that I'm tired. We're not just tired. We are coming completely unraveled.

For example, everywhere I go I see the same set of snowmen. In the aisles of Target, in the pages of Garnet Hill, in the Pottery Barn window, on television, in advertisements, it's the same three snowmen. There's the dad, the mom, and the little baby snowman. Everywhere, it's the perfect little snowman family. Mom, dad, and baby. They terrorize me. One day at the mall, I am going to go nuts on the three-snowmen display. One of these days, I am going to be walking through the mall, with all of the parents and their kids standing in line to see Santa, and I'll hear some kid say, 'Mom! Look at the cute snowmen. It's just like our family, you, me, and dad,' and something will come over me. Weeks of staring at this perfect little snowman family, weeks of being mocked by this snowman family will get to me, and all of the sudden I will lash out at the snowman family right in the middle of the mall. I will start punching the big dad snowman, but not any normal punch, more of a frantic, almost deranged swing. Instead of my arm coming through the middle of my body, like you would see a boxer throw a punch, my fist comes over the top of my head, like a crazed stage mom. I swing at the daddy snowman in an unco-ordinated manner; first I knock off his black top hat and then on my second swing I miss and throw myself off balance and fall onto the mommy snowman. Then, in a rage of frustration, at myself and the snowmen, I start thrashing my body in all directions, hoping to take out all three at once. Think Orson Welles in *Citizen Kane* when he trashes Susan Alexander's room at Xanadu after she walks out. He tears the place down, but he's so old he can hardly pull the shelves off of the wall. You kind of feel bad for the guy, but at the same time you know he's losing it big-time. That's me, only with three oversized snowmen. 'Mommy,' the little boy says as he tugs at his mother's coat sleeve outside of Rocky Mountain Chocolate Factory, 'why is that crazy lady hurting the cute snowman family?' The Somerset mall guards drag me away as I kick and scream.

The best part would be they would haul me off and throw me into some holding tank where they keep the mall perpetrators until the cops arrive. Some small cell with one plastic bench and a gross tile floor that never gets cleaned. But by the time the cops get there, I'd be asleep. Not even on the bench. I'd be asleep on the floor. Some cop would roll his eyes and say, 'All right, ma'am, you can go. Your family is outside waiting for you.' And I would wave my hand and in a groggy voice say, 'Ten more minutes, jus' gimme ten more minutes.'

At Dr G.'s today, I feel inclined to discuss how angry I am. I leave out the part about the snowmen. This is the first time I've seen her since Kai was born.

In the midst of our conversation, she says something about bitterness.

'I think I'm bitter,' I say.

'You do?' she asks, with this weird look on her face. 'Who are you bitter toward?'

I think about this. I am not really bitter toward anyone specifically. Battersby recently got engaged to her boyfriend, Paul, and I am actually very happy for her. I found myself being able to participate in conversations about weddings much easier than two months ago. Everyone around me is getting married – my friend Janna from college, Battersby, Terrah, Toby and Nikki, but I don't feel bitter toward any of them. I am bitter toward the idea of romance. I am bitter at the couples in the mall who are Christmas shopping at Gymboree. 'Oh, honey, look at this, isn't this adorable? We should get it for Nolan. He would just love it,' the mom says, full of Christmas cheer. I want to shove these people and say, 'Ya know, some of us are trying to grieve around here! Would you mind keeping your happiness to yourself?' Finally, I figure out who exactly I am most bitter toward. Everything can be summed up in two words.

'Diamond commercials,' I say. 'Diamond

commercials make me furious.' Of course, anyone who watches television knows exactly what I am talking about. These stupid fucking diamond commercials where some handsome guy and his pretty, unassuming wife are driving along together, the snow is falling just slightly outside, the street is lined with Christmas lights, the couple is holding hands, and then suddenly, magically, he slips a diamond necklace into her hand and then they exchange this picture-perfect kiss at the stop-light. Or the one where the woman is asleep and her husband slips a diamond necklace on in the middle of the night and she wakes up and he pretends to be sleeping – this one is the worst! Or the one where the guy unhooks the diamond gift bag from the snowman's hand. There are a million of them. A million too many and all of them make me want to throw my shoe at the television.

'Ugh.' Dr G. rolls her eyes. Obviously, she has seen them too. 'Just turn the television off,' she tells me.

'Told you,' my FMG remarks from the other end of the couch. (FMG is short for Fairy Mom Godmother. Now that she's part of my family, she wanted a nickname like everyone else.)

'Why are the holidays like this?' I ask. 'Why are they so hard?' Dr G. nods along with my question and scoots forward in her big chair.

'You know, I was at a convention with a group of other psychologists and we all concluded that this is our busiest time. This week and next week

I have more appointments than at any other time of year.'

'Seriously? Why is that? Why do the holidays make us feel this way?'

'Because,' she starts, then thinks about her answer for a moment. This is another reason why I like Dr G. She thinks about the things that come out of her mouth. 'People know that they are going to be disappointed. The media, the stores, the catalogs – they all make us feel like something amazing should happen, and then it doesn't.' I lean my head back at the thought of this. Yes, I agree. For example, no woman in America will get a diamond like the women in those commercials. All that will happen is millions of women will watch those commercials and think, *Wouldn't that be nice. Wouldn't that be nice if he just completely splurged on me? Even though we said we wouldn't spend much on each other, wouldn't it be nice if he completely broke the rule.* And then on Christmas morning, that woman will unwrap a DustBuster and she will scold herself for being so hopeful. And her husband will see the look on her face and say, 'But remember, honey, we said we wouldn't spend a lot.'

'Don't even get me started on the holidays.' My Fairy Mom Godmother holds her right hand out like a stop sign, like she's telling the holidays to talk to the hand.

'I could *kill* the person who invented so many holidays,' she says.

Compounding the problem of sleep, grief, and the holiday stress is that the dogs are still out of control. Kai's sleep is totally irregular, but the dogs have to come out of their crate at a certain time in the morning. Even if I haven't slept since four in the morning, they still need to go outside and eat by seven. When Kai sleeps I can't go back to bed because they are always going in and out, getting into things, demanding more time and attention than what I am capable of. Some days I can't make arrangements for people to come over while I walk them, so they just end up getting all riled up from staying inside all day. When Louise misses a walk, she sits with her front paws on the windowsill, her body completely erect, trembling at the sight of a squirrel. She makes this horrible noise that sounds like a tea-kettle and I can't get her to stop. I can only put her in her crate, but she just barks until I let her out. Walks are torturous for all three of us. Both dogs are now completely unmanageable. They are sad and angry and acting out, and so am I.

I envision punching inanimate objects, I'm mad at commercial America, and I can't seem to feel anything toward my own pets except extreme frustration. On top of everything, I don't sleep. Sleep is like the little Jenga block at the bottom of my already shaky tower. The longer I go without sleep, the more I feel like I'm going to collapse into a million pieces.

Right after Macbeth tells his wife that he heard

a voice curse his sleep, he reflects for a moment about the importance of sleep. He says, 'Sleep that knits up the ravell'd sleeve of care, / The death of each day's life, sore labour's bath, / Balm of hurt minds, great nature's second course, / Chief nourisher in life's feast.' This quote says it all. What wonderfully comforting words: a bath, balm for a hurt mind, a second course. But all of these things have left me. My chief nourisher is gone. My mind and my body don't seem to get any rest. One time I read something that said some historians suspect that Shakespeare was a woman. But every time I read this quote, every time I think about his amazing understanding of the importance of sleep, I think about how he wasn't just a woman, he must have been a baby-mama too.

Tonight is my first parenting group session. Beaumont Hospital arranges parenting groups for all new mothers. It's free and anyone can sign up. I called Beaumont earlier this week to see when the parenting group met. The woman on the phone told me that my group would start after the holidays.

At the end of the conversation she said, 'And you want to be in the couples group, right?'

'Ugh . . . no, actually, now that you mention it, I don't.' Well, lucky for me, there is a single moms' group that meets once a week for six months and it was about to start in a few days.

'Where does the group meet?' I asked, hoping I wouldn't have to drive too far.

'The group meets at Embury Methodist Church, right at the corner of Fourteen Mile and Woodward.' My heart sunk. Two years ago this December, eleven days from today, Josh and I were married at Embury Methodist Church at the corner of Fourteen Mile and Woodward. The last time I was there I was wearing a wedding dress. Now I'm going for a single moms' group.

'Do you know where that is?' she asked me.

'Yes.' I took a deep breath. 'Yes, I know exactly where that is.'

Now, I walk into the small room off to the side of the sanctuary, the same room where the brides-maids and grandparents waited until it was time to walk down the aisle. Fortunately, the room is very different from how I remember it. It looks much duller tonight. There aren't as many lights on. The Christmas decorations aren't glowing like they did the night of our wedding. The first girl I see is a tiny brunette. She sits on the floor with her head down over a little baby girl. I look over at the woman who I assume is the facilitator. She welcomes me and we take care of introductions; her name is Janet. I sit down next to the brunette with a ponytail. 'Oh, he is adorable,' she says, smiling at Kai. She has braces. She looks like she is fourteen.

Next to me on the floor another girl sits with another baby girl. This mom is wearing a sweat suit. She has long brown hair also; it is pulled back in a messy ponytail. This girl looks older, but not by much. Across the room, a blond girl sits with a baby on her lap. She is wearing a Notre Dame sweatshirt and jeans with a hole in the knee. In the midst of getting myself settled, a fourth woman walks in. She wears a green knit hat and carries a Starbucks cup. Finally, the last woman comes in. She hurries in and says something about being late. She says a few words to the facilitator and it is obvious that English is not her first language. Her hair is black with orange highlights at the end. Her nails are painted a bright red.

Within minutes, I have judged all five women. Without hearing from any of them, I conclude that they are all under twenty-five, and perhaps a few of them are under twenty-one. None of them have a bachelor's degree, and a few may not even have a high school diploma. Their income is less than eight hundred dollars a month. All of them got pregnant unexpectedly with men who are either their ex-boyfriends or will be their ex-boyfriends before their child celebrates his or her first birthday. *I have nothing in common with these women*, I think to myself. *We have nothing to talk about.* I should have just joined the couples' group and gone alone. I should have just been the odd man out, but at least I would be dealing with people who have a life more similar to mine. These girls probably use double negatives and watch *A Shot at Love with Tila Tequila* with their babies instead of reading Eric Carle. I realize this is a horrifically judgmental conclusion. I am certain it stems from the fact that I just feel like a total couples' group reject and now, here I am with the other societal rejects. None of us got invited to the cool kids' party. So yes, I am bringing down others to make myself feel better, which isn't right or very mature, but I can't help it. I even feel guilty that I think these things, but I still can't help it.

At first, everyone just chats. Nisi, the woman with the green hat and Starbucks cup, is half Moroccan and half Israeli. She sits with her little boy, Roger, who looks *nothing* like her. Nisi is very vocal. She talks the most. Next to her on the couch is Galina, the girl with black hair and orange highlights. Galina speaks broken English. She is from Russia. Her son's name is Tasha. I eavesdrop on Nisi and Galina's conversation. Nisi, who is hardly listening to Galina, thinks that Tasha is a girl. In her broken English and soft voice, Galina tries twice to clear things up, but Nisi is not listening, she is busy trying to think of the American celebrity with a name like 'Tasha.' Finally, Janet says, '*No*, Tasha is a *boy*!' 'Oh!' says Nisi. She stops talking long enough to hear Galina say that in America Tasha is a girl's name, but in Russia it's a boy's name. Nisi nods.

Finally, Janet and Heidi, the two facilitators, start the meeting and explain that every Wednesday we will meet here at the church. Tonight we will just get to know each other, but usually there will be someone who will talk to us about a specific topic such as infant massage, CPR, starting foods, and so on. To get the conversation going tonight, Heidi invites all of us to tell our birthing story. I go first. My birthing story is short and nondramatic. I do not mention that I am a widow. I say nothing about Kai's dad.

Laura, the brunette without the braces, goes next. Her daughter Megan is four months old. Megan is completely bald except for the base of her head. It looks like a little brown dust ruffle. It goes from ear to ear, no higher than an inch. Laura was in labor for seventeen hours and then had a C-section. Ellen, the girl with the braces, is Laura's friend. Ellen actually babysits for Laura when she goes to work. Laura works at a church day care. Ellen's daughter's name is Rose. She said she was so 'drugged up' she hardly remembers her delivery. I wonder if the conception was a similar experience.

Kat, the blonde with the hole in her jeans, tells her birthing story with Maya asleep on her lap. Kat is very loud and boisterous. She uses the phrase 'pissed me off' about three times when describing the nurses. When she describes her obstetrician, she declares, 'She was a total *bitch*.'

Nisi had a long labor followed by an episiotomy and the use of suction. Gross. That poor woman. Roger was almost nine pounds. Nisi seems to have three different accents going on. She wants all of us to be 'girlfriends' and suggests each week we should bring a dish to pass, 'maybe something that reflects our culture'!

Galina goes last. She speaks slowly as Tasha awkwardly moves around in her arms. She seems uncomfortable holding him and a little frustrated that he is being squeamish. She labored for ten hours and she said it was frustrating because the nurses did not understand her very well when she tried to ask questions and talk to them. Galina lives with her parents in Southfield. Galina, Kat, Laura, and Nisi have returned to work full-time.

After that, we talk casually. Everyone slowly reveals the relationship they currently have with their baby's father. Kat lives with her boyfriend, Randy. Laura is still living with Tony, but things aren't going well. The same for Ellen and Pete. Galina, who was quiet for most of the meeting, ends up explaining her 'baby daddy' situation. (Heidi initiates the use of this phrase. No one seems to mind.) Galina had been dating a man for seven months. He proposed, they planned the wedding, she got pregnant, he left her. She said her pregnancy was difficult because she was so emotional over the breakup. (*Oh really, Galina? Welcome to my world*, I think to myself.) She talks for a while about how hard it was. She had to go on bed rest at six months. The fiancé said he wanted nothing to do with her or the baby. All of us are on pins and needles as she gets though her story. 'How does it end?' Kat asks as Galina takes a break to put Tasha into burping position. Kat sounds like she's watching a soap opera. 'Did he ever contact you?' Galina explains that she ran into him at a restaurant and he walked past her as if he didn't even know her. She looks incredibly sad as she says this. It suddenly occurs to me that death is not the only thing in this universe that causes pain.

'He deed not eeven luk at me,' she adds.

'Is he paying child support?' Kat asks, eagerly. 'Take that jackass for all he's got,' she adds. Galina says yes, he is paying child support.

Kat moves to change Maya. It is obvious that I am the only one who has not revealed my baby daddy story. Kat goes for it.

'So, Natalie, do you keep in touch with Kai's father?' Everyone looks at me. I am surprised that my throat tightens up. I am annoyed and surprised that my throat tightens.

'I'm a widow.' The room goes silent. Of course it does. Who is a widow with a newborn baby at age twenty-five? Nobody. Nobody on the entire planet except me.

There is a long silence and then someone says that she is so sorry to hear that. I don't know who it is. I focus all of my energy on not crying. I have gone so long without crying in front of people.

Someone asks me how. Shit. I explain in as few words as possible. They can hear me, they can hear my throat, I don't cry, but they know I am struggling to get through my sentences. I am so angry that they can sense my weak voice. I don't know why, don't ask me why it is so important to me to always be the toughest person in the room, but it is. The room goes quiet again. Everyone is staring at me. I glance over at Galina, who looks like she's going to throw up. I can read her mind. She wants to say sorry for her whole story. I just stare at Kai, I literally stare at Kai as everyone stares at me. He is asleep. I can't speak or else I'll fall apart like a house of cards. I thought I was past this stage. I thought I was past the falling apart like a house of cards stage. Apparently I'm not. I feel pressure to say something.

'It's okay,' I say (what a stupid thing to say). 'It's okay, we're okay. Kai and I live by ourselves and my family is close and my husband's family is close and we get a lot of help.' But that's not enough for them. They keep staring. They feel so horrible. They feel so horrible they can't even speak. 'It's okay,' I mutter again. 'You know, we're all single moms,' I say, trying to put them at ease, because this is how it always goes: I have to put other people at ease. I have to explain to other people that this world is not cruel and there is a reason to get out of bed in the morning. 'We all have something that . . . We all have things in our life that . . . We all have something. Mine is just a little different.' I look back at Kai. He is still asleep.

'Well.' Janet breaks the awkward pause. 'We're just going to help you be the best mom you can be.' Everyone tells me how beautiful he is, how long his hair is, how great I look for just having a baby.

Then mercifully the meeting ends. Janet walks me out. 'We are so happy you're with us, Natalie,' she says as she walks me down the hallway. 'We are here for you.'

A number of different conclusions run through my brain. I am out of place everywhere. I need to join a support group for women my age who have lost their husbands. Kai and I are lucky: I get to stay home with him twice a week. Kai and I are unlucky: We should be in the couples' group. For a moment, I wonder if I can switch groups. I had planned on being married – doesn't that count for something? I have more in common with married people . . . I am a single mom. I am a single mom. This is my group.

A few weeks into December, I decide to clean out my bedroom closet a bit. In late August I took all of Josh's clothes to the basement storage room except his bathrobes and his shoes. I have no logic in keeping his bathrobes and shoes in my own closet, but I did. I guess I felt like his suits never were really a part of him, his job was never a huge part of his identity, but his shoes and his bathrobes were. I can still picture him wandering around the house in his bathrobe on Sunday morning. I could tell you exactly where his hair stuck up when he got out of bed. As for his shoes, he had a couple pairs of soccer cleats and a few pairs of New

Balance tennis shoes. He only wore New Balance shoes because his feet were so wide. I remember one summer evening he went for a run in his new gray New Balance running shoes. When he got back I was in the driveway and he said, out of breath but with a little alarm in his voice, 'Hey, Nat, can you check the backs of my shoes?'

'Yeah, why? Did you step in something?'

He replied, 'No, I think there are rockets on them.'

I decide to move the shoes to the basement. I don't know why, but I just know I can't continue to see his shoes in our closet anymore. On the way down the steps I catch a glimpse of the bottoms of his brown New Balance shoes, the ones he always wore for yard work and mowing the lawn. There is still grass embedded in the bottom. The sight of that grass and dirt hits me like a punch in the stomach. I have this moment where I realize that grass can only get in the shoe if there is someone walking around in them, and there had been someone walking around in them not too long ago. The next time the weather is warm enough to see the grass and do yard work, these shoes will still be sitting in the house. The grass, I don't know why that grass is so poetic. But it is. So I just sit there on the steps holding his shoes, staring at the worn-out bottoms, crying.

I don't know why I moved his shoes today. I put them on a shelf in the basement and think, *Will I ever have to throw these away?* As if some grief overseer is going to come to my door in five years and say, 'Okay, Natalie, today is the day, it's all got to go.' Then I think, *No, I will never throw these away.*

Today is my two-year wedding anniversary. I almost forgot about it. A few days ago I was talking to my mom about Josh's birthday. I told her about how on the twenty-first (Josh's twenty-eighth birthday) I wanted all of us to go to dinner at Peabody's. A few minutes later my mom asked, 'Nat, what about the sixteenth?' I had no idea what she was talking about. 'What's the sixteenth?' She gave me a sad look, like she didn't want to be the one to remind me. 'It's your wedding anniversary.' It hadn't even occurred to me. I felt so guilty. But I know why I forgot about it. For the last six months I've been trying to get it through my head that I'm not married anymore. I go to a single moms' group. I tell people I'm a widow. I don't wear my wedding ring. People who don't have husbands don't have wedding anniversaries. But once my mom reminded me, I knew exactly how I wanted to spend December sixteenth. I just wanted to be alone. I wanted to take an hour or so by myself and go through pictures of my wedding and talk to Josh and cry and that's it. I don't want to talk about it or cry with anyone else. I just want to be alone.

The day is intense from the very beginning, from the middle of the night. Kai wakes up at 2:00

a.m., then 4:00 a.m., then 5:00 a.m. Every time he wakes up, he isn't hungry or wet, he just wants to be held and rocked, but he will only stop crying if I am standing up. Once I sit down, he starts crying again. I am so tired. My body literally hurts as I stand in the middle of my bedroom. My feet hurt. My shoulders ache. By 4:00 a.m. I can feel my eyes hurt.

As he dozes off in my arms, I just start talking. I tell Kai about the day I was married. I tell him it was a snowy, beautiful day. The snow had fallen the night before, so all the roads were clear. Terrah and Angela picked me up in the morning and we went to McDonald's to get hash browns and orange juice for breakfast. Terrah did my makeup. Toby was late to the church because he forgot his dress shoes. The church was adorable with all of the Christmas lights. The ceremony was brief. We had an awkward kiss, which was completely my fault, and then Mathews drove us to the reception. The reception was perfect. Everyone we loved was in the same room. The one thing I will never forget about that night was that everyone was so happy.

I tell Kai all of this. Then, after he falls asleep, I start talking to Josh. I say, 'Can you see me? Can you see me now?' I have a little edge in my voice as I speak because I am frustrated. 'I'm the only one here. I'm the only one to wake up with him in the morning. I'm the only body that can rock him back to sleep. Can you see me, standing alone in our bedroom, rocking our son by myself? The bedroom shouldn't even look like this. We should still be arguing about paint colors and closet doors.'

Standing there at 4:00 a.m., looking at the dimly lit bedroom, thinking about what my life should be like, I realize what today is supposed to be like. A day where I can be free to wallow. Every other day I use all of my energy to convince myself, either through thought or action, that I can do this. I can take on this new life. I can be the single supermom and my son will be fantastically successful. I make myself think about all the things I have to be thankful for, all the people I have to love. But days like anniversaries and birthdays, these are the days where I can sit back, let go of my effort to appear normal, and say, 'Life is not fair. I'm not supposed to be a single mom. I was robbed.' For a few hours, maybe not even that long, I can revel in the fact that Josh was unfairly taken from me and that sometimes my life sucks more than I ever imagined it could. Although I try to be noble and courageous, today for a few short hours I get to be sad. Nothing but sad. Not just stare-out-the-window-and-shed-a-little-tear sad. I'm talking curl-up-in-the-fetal-position-and-cry-into-Josh's-bike-jerseys sad.

I finally put Kai down and I get back into bed. Literally, seconds after I close my eyes I see, through my eyelids, a giant flash of light. I fly up and hear a huge rumble outside my bedroom window. I walk over to the window, pull down the shades, and realize it is thundering and lightning in the midst of the snowstorm. I've never seen this happen before. Two more flashes of lightning follow. I feel like Josh is talking back. Or maybe he knows it's our anniversary too, and he is sitting up in heaven, angry and sad like me, and out of nowhere he tackled St Peter or God or whomever right to the ground. The thunder and lightning was Josh, rolling around on the floor, with some saint, using his best wrestling moves from high school. He is mad. He probably pinned God and started yelling, 'Why am I here? Why is my wife alone?' Then quickly, God's security guards come running in and drag Josh off.

In just a few hours there are about five inches of snow on the ground. My dad comes over to clear my driveway and sidewalk. I watch him through the kitchen window. My dad looks old. I can see the creases in his skin from where I stand. He looks tired. The wind blows his brown wispy hair around. But he clears the driveway. I know he feels like this is the least he can do. When my dad gets sad, he has to translate his emotions into some sort of physical work. This is his grief this morning.

A little after one o'clock in the afternoon, I get Kai and the dogs settled at my parents' house. I get back in the car and put on Bob Seger. Josh and I loved listening to the *Greatest Hits* album on the way up north. We would make up our own

177

lyrics to the song 'Night Moves.' Now the sound of Bob Seger's voice is like pitocin for my tear ducts. Every time I hear the song 'Night Moves,' I just lose it. Today I want to lose it.

When I get home, I clear off the dining room table. It is important that there is nothing on the table. I even spray it with Mrs Meyer's countertop spray to make it look clean. Then I set out two candles. Each candle sits on top of a glass container. The containers hold dried flower petals from Josh's funeral. One of my students, Brad, lost his dad in an accident right before he started his freshman year. I had Brad in class for a few years and I got to know his mom fairly well. Right after Josh's accident, she told me about drying the funeral flowers and saving them. The piece of advice seemed so odd, a strange logistical detail from the *Widows' Underground Handbook*, but I did it. I did it because she told me to and I knew that she knew more than anyone else at that moment in time. On the day of my wedding anniversary, I clean the dining room table off and light the candles. Even before I take off my coat, I clear the table, set up the candles, and light them. For some reason, I couldn't do anything else until I lit the candles.

I go downstairs. The minute I walk into the storage room, I start crying. I cry so hard I am hunched over, my knees bent, my hand over my mouth. I heave air in and out. Snot comes pouring out of my nose. My vision is blurry with tears. I haven't cried like this since the summer. I look at all of his bike jerseys, his old button-down shirts, his shoes. I look at the bookshelf and all of his old books. *The Greatest Fly Fishing Worldwide, The Power of One, The Red Badge of Courage, Trout Bum, The Climb, A Short History of Nearly Everything.* I look through his CDs and old pictures. Then I come upstairs and boot up his computer. I go through his pictures. I go through all of his work résumés and saved work documents. I just want to find things that he wrote, that he had typed into the keyboard. I go on the Internet and look through the search history. I try to find things I haven't seen before.

I go into his gear closet and go through his old backpacks. I just look for stuff that hasn't been cleaned out yet. I want to find something that had been last touched by him. I just want some evidence that he had been here, that he was a part of this house once. His body, his hands, his feet had been in shoes, his chest had filled these empty jackets.

I go into our bedroom and go through the stack of pictures I kept from the funeral. I love those pictures. It's the same stack of pictures I looked at every day during the summer. I go through his wallet. He has a Moomers ice cream card (his all-time favorite ice-cream store in Traverse City) with three holes punched through it, a Jet's Pizza card with one hole punched through it, his medical alert paper, his REI membership card, his

179

Manchester United Club membership card, a gift card to Best Buy, and three ticket stubs from *Spider-Man*. It's like walking through a museum. I am certain that I will keep everything in the same order it was in on the day that someone handed me that wallet.

Finally, at 3:07, I blow out the candles. I can't say that I feel better. I don't think I'll ever be able to say I feel better. All I know is it feels good to cry that hard. It's like cleaning the leaves out from the gutters. If the leaves sit there too long, they weigh on the metal and hurt the house. But it doesn't bring him back. Someday I'll realize that nothing will bring him back.

Kai and I spend Christmas morning at my parents' house, then around noon go to Deedee's house. To my utter delight, Ashley bought me the one thing I really wanted. Extra-large Hanes men's sweatpants. Two pairs, actually. One light gray and one dark gray.

'Yes!' I exclaim as I open the box. 'I am so happy you took me seriously when I asked for these!' She looks at me a little perplexed. She still doesn't understand why a twenty-five-year-old female would want two pairs of men's XL sweats. I spend 90 percent of my day wishing I could go back to bed, but I can't go back to bed, so I'm just trying to wear my bed on my body. I wear my blue bathrobe all the time, but the sweatpants really complete the outfit.

Later in the evening Mathews comes over to my parents' house. He sets down a beautifully wrapped rectangular-shaped present. I speculate that it's a picture of Josh, him, and me. I didn't expect something sentimental, but how nice of him.

It's not a picture frame. It's a book, *The Science of Breath: A Practical Guide to Controlling the Breath, Mind, and Body*. I give him an evil look. He starts laughing hysterically.

'What the hell is this supposed to mean?' I ask, smiling. He tells me he thinks maybe I could use a little help in keeping calm and staying centered. I throw the book at him. 'I don't have time for staying centered,' I yell at him. He tells me that's the whole point.

The day after Christmas is also a big tradition in Josh's family. Ever since I started dating Josh, I've gone to Cousin Shannon's house the day after Christmas. I can never remember how exactly they are related, but nobody really seems to care. This is obviously my first year going to Shannon's without Josh. I am fearful because I know it will be hard and I don't want to bring down the festive spirit. But there is one key motivating factor in going to Shannon's. Her son, Spencer.

Spencer is five. Last year we went to Shannon's house and Josh and Spencer spent a lot of time together. They lay together on Spencer's beanbag chair and just talked. I remember Josh telling me that they talked about how Spencer liked juice and race car games. Josh was so impressed that a four-year-old could sit and talk to an adult for that long. During the beanbag talk, Spencer asked Josh if he could come out to our house and spend the night. Josh agreed instantly. Unlike many adults who throw out promises to kids only to promptly forget them, Josh made sure Spencer came over for his sleepover. It was hilarious. At ten o'clock at night they went to Meijer and Josh bought Spencer any cereal he wanted. They came back and sat on the couch and ate Cap'n Crunch and watched the movie *Cars*. They both had a blast. After Josh died, Shannon told me how mature and understanding Spencer had been about Josh's death. Shortly after the funeral, Spencer asked Shannon if they could print out some pictures of Josh so he could have them in his room. They picked out the picture of Spencer and Josh together on the beanbag chair and they printed out a picture of Josh and me at our wedding.

About halfway through the party, I quietly ask Spencer to show me his pictures of Josh. I know I will cry, but I feel like I owe it to Spencer to see his pictures. He takes me up to his room and points to the shelf above his bed. Shannon said that Spencer had asked her to put them above his bed.

As usual, whenever I see a picture of Josh that I haven't seen before, I start to cry. At first I try to distract myself by averting my eyes to other things on his shelf, but deep down I know that Spencer is okay with seeing me cry. He knows. He knows how to do this better than most adults.

At the beginning of December, I looked at the calendar and saw a lot of scary dates. My anniversary, Josh's birthday, Chris's birthday, Christmas. Everyone worried about me on those dates. Today is New Year's Eve, which for me is perhaps a worse day than any other holiday. New Year's Eve was the night that Josh and I first kissed. It was our first kiss and then a new year. It was a new beginning for both of us. That night changed my life.

In the afternoon, I am at Potbelly Sandwich Shop, picking up a sandwich for Chris who is still in town for the holidays. It's the first time in a few days where I have been out by myself, where I've had a moment to myself to just think. While I wait for Chris's order, I think about how sad this day is. A secret-sad day. A new year. New Year's is a stupid holiday to begin with, but this year obviously, it's a lot worse.

Last year on this day I was sitting in my basement with Josh and all of my friends. I was a little drunk and Josh and I were laughing as I wrote down in a random notebook all of the events that had occurred in our lives throughout the year. But now, I can't write in that journal. What would I possibly write? 'Josh died.' How ridiculous. I am sad as I walk out of Potbelly, I would even venture to say I am feeling sorry for myself. All of the sudden I hear a voice say, 'Excuse me.' I turn around and there is a woman driving a large rusted-over blue van. She has brown hair to her shoulders and big round glasses.

I turn around and look at her and she doesn't say anything. She sits there, staring at me, scratching the top of her hand. She looks uncomfortable, like she has a stomachache. She stares at me for a couple of seconds, so long that I think this is not the woman who had said 'excuse me.' Finally she says, 'Can you help me get some food for my kids?' I glance in the rear windows and see at least two tiny heads bopping around in the backseat. I look at her and say, 'I'm sorry,' and I keep walking.

I get into my car and instantly feel horrible. I suddenly realize I made the wrong choice. I said no because I was afraid that she wasn't being honest with me or she would follow me home or something else. But in my heart I know none of those are true. She was just a woman with children and they wanted something to eat. And now she is gone.

I drive home and relay everything to Chris. I am ashamed of myself for not helping. I can tell he wishes he could've been with me because he would've done something. He tells me next time I should go in and buy the person food. It suddenly occurs to me that she didn't ask for money, she asked for food, which only makes me feel worse. I spend so much time thinking about myself and my own problems and the one shot I had to come up for air and think about someone else for one second – someone who was really in need – I turned my back. I turned my back on a mom with hungry children. I feel so guilty for not doing anything.

I look at Kai asleep in Chris's arms. Kai is so fat. Part of the reason we love fat babies is because we know that they are full. Full of food, full of love, full of everything we can possibly give them. Shame on me for sitting around on New Year's Eve thinking of all of the things I don't have. Yes, I understand I have room to grieve and be sad about losing Josh. And maybe even that shouldn't take up so much space.

Josh always said that he never wanted his parents' divorce to interfere with his personal success. 'I don't wear my situation on my sleeve.' He said that to me once, before we were dating. I was a sophomore and he was a junior. He was an RA in my building. We were talking about how some people have the need to explain their personal baggage to anyone who will listen and he wasn't one of them. He mentioned that his family had problems too, but he never let it affect how he lived or how he built successful relation-ships. He didn't use those words, but that's what he meant. He told this to me in a private conver-sation and I never heard him talk about his parents' divorce again until months into our romantic relationship, which was years later. He never let his crappy situation get in his way of being happy. I know for a fact that he would want his son to be the same way.

Josh would not want me to be sad on New Year's Eve. And I shouldn't be. I may be sad, I may be exhausted beyond repair, and yet I am extremely fortunate. I have a warm home. I have food to eat. I have friends and family. But most important, more important than anything else on the entire planet, I have a fat baby.

JANUARY

He too was completely covered with dust; he dragged around with him on his back and along his sides fluff and hairs and scraps of food; his indifference to everything was much too deep for him to have gotten on his back and scrubbed himself clean against the carpet.

—FRANZ KAFKA, *THE METAMORPHOSIS*

Even though I'm not back at school, I know exactly where my students are in the semester. Right now my eleventh-graders are reading *The Metamorphosis*. One day Gregor, the main character, wakes up to find he is a giant bug with no identity. I am a giant bug in a blue bathrobe and extra-large sweatpants – who breast-feeds – with no identity. My FMG tells me this is a normal feeling. She says it may last for the next eighteen years, except the breast-feeding part, of course. 'The milk becomes a metaphor,' she says as she yawns. 'Didn't you ever read *The Giving Tree?*'

Ads writes me an e-mail asking me something along the lines of 'How are things going?' Hmmm . . . This is my response:

I write these lines in a hurry. I have just set Kai down in our fourth attempt for a nap since he awoke at eight this morning. He is already stirring again. I did not take my bathrobe off until noon today even though I am well aware that the bathrobe is not an option for the answer to the question 'What should I wear today?' I am fully aware that the bathrobe is simply an article of clothing that was designed to get one from the bathroom to the bedroom without the hassle of clothing but with more coverage than a towel. However, this morning I literally did not have the three minutes it takes to get dressed. Between the dogs and Kai, all I had time for was to make a cup of coffee, and in my world of four hours of sleep a night, coffee trumps everything. So, around noon I set Kai down for a nap and I take off all of my clothes, so there I am, in my bra and underwear, standing in front of the closet, looking at what to wear. Before I can open the drawer and pull out a pair of black 'yoga' pants from my stockpile of 'yoga' pants (I tell myself they are yoga pants because I can't handle the fact that I wear stretch pants

188

every day. I told myself I wouldn't be the mom who wears stretch pants every day . . . but I do wear them every day, so I call them 'yoga' pants even though I have never worn them to do yoga. Actually, I have never even done yoga). So before I can even put my yoga pants on, Kai starts to cry. He wakes up within one minute of being set down. So I pick him up in my bra and underwear and start to rock him. And by rock him I mean I start doing squats in my bedroom. Next thing I know, Louise is barking insanely at the front window. She does not stop. Finally, I go out and see the Consumers Energy truck and the Consumers Energy guy looks up and gets the surprise of his life with me in my bra and underwear. I yell at Louise. She ignores me. Kai is still crying. Finally, I bark at the girls to get into their crate. I squat for another twenty minutes (for some reason this is the only way I can get Kai to fall asleep) – which doesn't seem like a lot when you read it, but go try and squat for twenty minutes. Go and try it, and I'll even be generous with you and you can hold a ten-pound weight, even though Kai is probably more like fourteen. Finally, he falls asleep. I get dressed. I put on black yoga pants, a fleece sweatshirt, and my slippers. Is this any better than a bathrobe? This is my life and there was a time when I would have thought this was a crazy person's life.

I remember a time period when I judged moms. I was annoyed at moms who complained. Remember how I cursed that book I was reading about a stay-at-home mom who dared to whine about her stay-at-home-mom life? Now, as a mom who doesn't sleep or get dressed on a consistent basis because I don't have the time or energy, I am in awe that there was once a point in my life when I could actually read a book. More important, I am sorry I said those things and thought those things. I didn't know. I wasn't a part of the club yet. I just want to take a moment to say I'm sorry. At the time I cursed all of you, I wasn't a mom. Now that I am one, I know all the secrets. I am now one of you and this job is not easy. I didn't mean it.

I remember last January, when I didn't know I was pregnant yet, I returned to work after our two-week winter break. I asked my co-worker, Susan, how her vacation was. Susan has three children: four years, two years, and nine months. '*Vaca*tion?' she said. 'I didn't get a *vacation*.' She said that every minute of her time away from work was taken up with fulfilling the requests of someone else: her children, her husband, her in-laws, and her parents. She went on to explain that Christmas Eve was the worst. She didn't want to go to church. The kids were tired, she was tired, and she still had presents to wrap. But her husband insisted that they go as a family. So the five of them went to a full Catholic Christmas Eve service. 'I sat in the pew thinking, *This is why Gregor turned into a bug.*' She ended by saying that she was overjoyed to come back to work.

At the time, I thought Susan was being a little dramatic. Now, as I run around the house with *one* child, I get it. I am turning into a bug at an alarming rate. I feel like my brain is diminishing. My memory, my patience, my ability to put logical thoughts in order – everything is slowly leaking out.

At the same time, however, even in the midst of this sleepdeprived, emotionally unstable place, there are certain parts of me that have sharpened immensely. *Sharpened* doesn't even quite capture my capabilities. On one hand, I can't even get myself dressed, and on the other hand I'm suddenly superhuman.

For example, you could take any object in the house and give it to the dogs and have them slap it against the hardwood floor and from two rooms away I could tell you what object they had in their mouths. Thus far I have been able to identify Kai's pacifiers, their sea-ray chew toy, my slipper, a diaper, one of Kai's socks, one of my socks (Bug treats them very differently), my flip-flops, and dozens of other items. Honestly, you could blind-fold me and sit me in the bedroom and let them roam free and the second they had something they weren't supposed to have, I would know.

The other day I was rocking Kai in my bedroom (which is at the back of the house), and while we were watching *American Idol*, I heard a noise that was not in my registry of normal house noises. I walked to the front of the house, suspecting that the humidifier might be malfunctioning or perhaps a toilet was running. I walked to the bay windows and discovered the source. My neighbor, on the other side of the street and two houses down, was snowblowing his sidewalk. Kai and I returned to my bedroom. Noise identified. Classification: harmless.

In addition to improving my auditory identification skills, I have also developed strange talents that I did not have as a non-mother. They are as follows: (1) When Kai wakes up in the middle of the night, I know what time it is without looking at the clock, and he wakes up at a different time every night. (2) Without looking at the humidifiers (there are two in the house), I can *sense* when they need to be refilled. (3) If someone (say, my overbearing sister-in-law) changes the thermostat by *one* degree, I know in an instant. (4) If you handed me an empty container of any depth, width, or shape, I could pour you eight ounces of water almost on the dot. (5) I can tell snot color, quantity, and consistency just by the sound Kai makes when he sneezes.

Now that I'm a mom, I'm some weird spawn

of a human. Franz Kafka, you think you know what a metamorphosis looks like? I got news for you. You don't.

Ashley is going through the guest bedroom on her continual quest to identify baby clothes and products that I haven't used yet. There is a stack of clothes on top of the Boppy swing. I walk in to see what she is doing. She holds up my purple sweat-shirt revealing the buried Boppy swing and says, 'Did you know this was in here?' (Subtext: 'It's a good thing you have me to go rifling through piles of shit in your house or else you may lose track of things.' Dialogue she will later have with Deedee: 'I mean, Mom, have you *seen* her house? She's got stacks of clothes in every room and she doesn't even know they're there.' They'll have a long talk about how disorganized I am and how badly they just want to come in and rearrange things themselves. If I don't watch myself, this will actually happen someday.) I take the sweatshirt and say, 'Yeah, thanks.' She picks up the Boppy swing. The following conversation takes place:

ME: Ash, what are you doing?
ASH: Well, I was just looking for this Boppy swing because you know how he likes the big movement of you rocking him, and I am wondering if this will help him go to sleep.
ME: Yeah.

ASH: Does it help him fall asleep?

ME: It did a couple times.

ASH: Then why is it in here under a pile of clothes?

ME: I tried the swing a couple of times, but then it broke.

(What I want to say:) Ashley! Do you *really* think that if I found the secret trick to helping my son sleep – remember, I am completely sleep-deprived on a daily basis – I would put it in the guest room under a pile of clothes? All this time I've been looking for something to help Kai sleep and *here it is*! The magic swing is sitting right here in the guest bedroom! Holy shit, you've solved the fucking puzzle to it all! *This is it!* This is the *answer*! This is fucking Rosebud right here under our noses! I am so stupid! We might as well get the adoption papers ready because clearly you are the smarter mother (even though you're *not* a mother)!

ASH: What do you mean? (Her tone clearly says she thinks I simply do not know how to use the Boppy swing. She begins to fiddle with it as if I am not intelligent enough to operate the swing. She thinks she can fix it.) What happened to it?

(SIDE NOTE: The Boppy swing runs on three C batteries, but the contraption itself is a piece of shit. It's difficult to get the battery pack in and out of its holder. After a few uses, the swing stopped working. I tried putting in new batteries, but nothing happened. After wrestling with the battery pack four or five times I decided that the Boppy swing would not get the best of me, so I put it in the guest room. Ashley, who clearly assumes that I haven't spent hours trying to fix the fucking Boppy swing already, continues to mess with it.)

ME: It wouldn't go. It started making this weird noise, like the motor wasn't working, and it stopped swinging on its own.

I then see Ashley discover a small plastic knob on the right side of the swing. Underneath the knob is a lock icon, the same icon you would see on a keyless entry of a car. Obviously, this plastic knob locks the swing in place so it won't move. I had put the lock on when I put the swing away. That way I could stack stuff on top of the swing, like my purple sweatshirt, and not worry about things toppling over. Ashley pulls the plastic knob out and the swing moves freely. She then says (get ready for it): 'It wasn't just locked?'

ME: No. It wasn't just locked. (What I want to say:) Are you fucking kidding me? Are you *fucking* kidding me? Do you seriously think that I didn't check to see if the Boppy swing was *locked?* Do you honestly think I am that stupid? No wonder you come over all the time. You must think your nephew is in danger living with a person who is too stupid to check to see if the Boppy swing was locked!

I walk out of the room. I cannot handle this conversation anymore. The Boppy swing has already stolen enough minutes from my life. I let her mess with it. She is still clearly not convinced that the swing is truly broken. I go into my bedroom to dig up *The Science of Breath*. My FMG is rummaging through my sock drawer. I ask her what she's doing.

'Just seeing if we have any STFU cards left.'

I am standing in Kai's bedroom. All of the lights are off, all I can hear is the noise of the fan and the humidifier. As I rock Kai to sleep, I feel my breath shorten. I can feel myself getting upset. I don't even know why. There is no trigger, no picture, no smell or sound, it just happens. It's been happening all the time lately.

I want to tell you that I have made progress, capital *P* Progress. I want to tell you I am better. I am great. I smile. I take care of my baby. I enjoy my life. I like waking up in the morning. But I don't know if that's true. I think I am only starting to admit that my journey through grief is going to be a lot longer than I ever imagined. Sometimes I think I'll be grieving for the rest of my life.

After I put Kai in his crib, I look through a stack of pictures of Josh. I find one of me lying on the dog bed with Louise and Bug and I have my arms around Louise. My eyes are closed and there is this soft glow from the lights of the Christmas tree. Josh took this picture. I look so happy. The dogs look so relaxed. You can feel the love when you look at this picture. We look so balanced, the three of us. Now, it's still the three of us, and we are completely unstable.

Sometimes I feel like I cannot survive with the dogs in this house. It is just too much. But when I look at this picture, it rips through my heart because I know there was a day when I loved Louise and Bug and they loved me back. Now they destroy everything. They jump on the beds. They know that I can't handle them. They're mad. I'm mad. I feel such a huge loss when I look at this picture because I know that I didn't just lose Josh, I lost my life that I had with him.

I've hit a snag. I feel more depressed than I have in the last two months. It is as if someone has put a light behind all of the pictures in the house with Josh in them. They are illuminated. I can't make it down the hallway without getting choked up. I miss him more today than I did during the holidays. I am regressing. Fuck.

Ashley stops by tonight for a little while after Kai goes to bed. We talk about everything. We talk about *The Biggest Loser* and how much we love the pink team. We talk about sperm banks (for her, not me) and being single moms. We talk about being single for the rest of our lives, about how we'll just live for our kids and be happy. We talk about my parents, Deedee, Josh, Chris, Drew, Margaret and Ray, Kai, me, and her. She says that she's always so impressed with my dad, with how kind and considerate he is. He always knows what to do and how to help. She says she still feels guilty and regretful about her relationship with Josh. We both cry. We cry for Josh, Margaret and Ray, and we cry for the rest of us who have to deal with all of it.

After Ashley leaves I think about how I have nothing negative to say about her visit. I am not filing a complaint. I am really happy she is in my life. I am fortunate she is here to talk to me, to entertain me, to help me, to love me.

Before I go to bed, I put on my headphones to listen to Dr Joy Browne as I pick up around the house. Her opening anecdote is about how it is important to be thankful, even when times are bad, because if anything is certain, it is that time passes and things change. She says that sometimes they go from bad to worse and sometimes they go from bad back to good. But at any point, we should be thankful. We should be thankful that we had good times when they were here and we can be thankful that they will come again. Despite my state of regression, Dr Joy's words are a tremendous comfort to me. I'm not mad or angry at her wisdom, which has been my usual reaction when someone tries to reassure me that it's going to be okay. Here it goes again, this bizarre side effect of grief; I am completely manic-depressive. I go from the darkest place in the world to being inspired by a radio psychologist. But she is right.

I need to be more thankful even when I hit a bad patch.

My quiet house, for example: I can honestly say that I am getting used to the peace and quiet. I even savor it a little. I like spending the evenings with Ira Glass and Dr Joy Browne. If I do watch TV, I just quietly sit and rock Kai and watch *Dog Whisperer*. I have become so accustomed to these people that I can picture them sitting in my living room.

I feel like I know Ira Glass. I feel like after dinner, it's just me, Ira Glass, Dr Joy Browne, and Cesar Millan, just sitting around and chatting. I know what all of them would say. Ira would do a lot of listening, make an occasional witty comment, and ask poignant questions.

'I know Ashley drives you crazy,' he would say in his distinct voice, 'but have you ever thought about what your life would be like *without* her?' His tone isn't abrasive or judgmental; it's just a question. Dr Joy Browne would do the most talking. She would have strong opinions and try to get me to not be so hard on people. She would force me to see things from other people's points of view, which would initially frustrate me. 'I mean, Natalie,' she would say, in her direct, somewhat harsh tone, 'you really just need to think about how Deedee feels.' I would sit and listen and sigh. 'You need to start being more polite on the phone. Tell her a nice story about Kai when she calls. I mean, you don't think it's killing her to be away from her grandson? I've got news for you, Cookie, she's not calling to hear about you, she's calling to hear about *him*. So get over yourself and fill her in a little bit more.' Cesar would describe things in a straightforward, honest fashion, just as he does on his show. He would never accuse me of being too aggressive or short with people, but he also would never blame outsiders for their behavior. 'Natalie, you have to have rules, boundaries and limitations. Humans are a lot like animals: they will follow rules, but you have to give them rules to follow.' The whole time Cesar talks, he would be on his knees playing with Louise and Bug with his perfect posture. I would vent to Cesar about how my dad is always trying to give me advice on how to get through to the dogs. Cesar would add his insight. 'You can't get frustrated when your dad talks about the dogs all the time, because your dad doesn't know that talking about the dogs is against the rules, because you haven't *set* the rules.' In his calm, assertive voice he would give me some direction. 'Next time you talk to your dad just say, 'Dad, the rule is no talking about the dogs until *I* bring it up.' Then, he will know how to behave because you have drawn the line for him.'

Sometimes we don't talk about me, sometimes we talk about other things like the latest political news or the weather or who Ira has interviewed lately. It's quite a panel when you think about it.

Three people who know how to ask questions and solve problems. Every now and then Ira comes over with his friend David Sedaris, who wanders in and out of conversations and picks up on strange details that no one else has noticed. 'Kai,' he would say in his dry voice as he looks at Kai's big blue eyes, 'do you think it's frustrating when people shake things in your face all the time?'

'That's how babies *develop*,' Dr Joy Browne would snap back. 'Research proves their eyesight improves if they look at contrasting colors.'

'I'm not arguing the *research*,' he would say. 'I'm just saying it certainly would frustrate me.'

This is what I picture. I know if my parents knew my evenings were filled with podcasts and odd journeys of my imagination, they probably wouldn't leave me by myself so often. But I'm okay with it. This is good for now. Maybe someday I'll have the desire to share my space with someone again, but certainly not now or anytime soon. Kai and I are quite content being all alone. It's all a part of this strange metamorphosis.

The dogs are getting worse. They are bad on the walk, and then when we come back to the house, they are horrible. Louise whines all afternoon. Bug barks incessantly in the backyard. Every time I yell at Louise, Bug gets scared and runs to her crate, but it doesn't faze Louise. In the middle of feeding Kai, Louise starts barking in an incredibly loud alarming bark at a squirrel out the front window. I cannot get them to calm down. I am losing it. I can't do this.

In the middle of all of this, my mom comes over. She can tell I am frustrated. She offers to take the dogs for the night and bring them back in the morning.

While she is over, I take a shower and have a curl-up-in-fetal-position-on-the-shower-floor moment. As the water steams around me, I stare at the handles. The hot and cold are completely in line with each other and the shower handle is sticking straight up. I feel like saying a prayer, but I am too angry for a prayer. I have been praying a lot lately, although I still am not quite sure about God or prayers. When I pray at night, I don't fold my hands or even close my eyes. I don't even address anyone, because I am never quite sure to whom I am talking or if anyone is even listening at all. But everyone is praying for me, so the least I could do is pray for other people.

So there I am sitting in the shower, staring at the handles, but instead of bowing my head (which I never do anyway), I just start talking to the handles. They look like little messengers. The middle handle, pointing straight up, a microphone to the heavens.

'This is not a request,' I start off saying. 'This isn't a question or a favor. This is a statement. I need someone to take those dogs. I can no longer provide them with a good home. It's hurting me, it's hurting them, and anything that hurts me hurts Kai.'

I pause for a moment, as if the bathtub handles are conferencing about my request. I look up at them again.

'You know, I've never said this, but I think I deserve this one. I think I've had a hard enough time. I think you can do this for me.' I pause and then make serious eye contact with the middle shower handle. 'You will do this for me.' I get out of the shower and call Jason the dog trainer. Over a voice mail, I tell him I need some help.

That night, I have a dream. In my dream I am sitting up in bed feeding Kai. It was the same pose I had held an hour earlier with Kai before I fell asleep. It was the same scene, but in the dream I am looking at our reflection, Kai and myself, in the opposing window. When I am awake rocking Kai in my bedroom, sometimes I look at my reflection in my window. I always look a little ghostly. I sometimes think that if I look hard enough, I can see Josh's face, just looking at me through the window.

In the dream I can see my reflection in the window from my bed while I hold Kai. And then, just as I had pictured it in real life, I see the image of Josh in the window sort of come out from behind me. In the dream, all I can see is the reflection. I have no sense to look next to me to see if he is there. He appears and he doesn't float like a ghost. The picture of him is not incredibly clear.

For a brief moment, he appears. He doesn't say anything, he just does this one swift movement. He takes his right arm and raises it above his head and sort of flexes it, his hand is balled in a fist. I know exactly what this movement means. Anyone who knew Josh, if they could see it, they would know what it meant. It was the same motion he made when Pavel Datsyuk scored a goal for the Detroit Red Wings or when he watched the Glasgow Rangers or Manchester United. I can see him doing it right now. It's his gesture for cheering someone on. I know what he is saying, but doing this motion, this one sweep with his arm, is more effective than talking to me. This is all he has to do, and I know what he means.

I wake up. You'd think I would wake up out of breath, amazed, unable to fall back asleep. But I don't. At first I hardly remember what happened. Once I realize the dream, I just feel calm and confident. I check on Kai, his sleeping angel face, and I fall back asleep.

The next day Jason calls me back. We have a long talk. He says that he will do anything to help me, it is the least he could do. He doesn't think it will be hard to find a new home for the dogs, especially somewhere in a more rural area. He says he'll be downstate next week and can pick them up then.

I don't think Josh is running around answering my prayers. Although, if he could, if there was any way he could intervene with my life, he would.

Maybe he did. But I am still too skeptical to admit that Josh heard me and helped me.

All I know is that yesterday I came close to losing my mind. I know that a lot of women with children say this, but I mean it. I came close (I'm still close) to going crazy. Right at the moment where I wanted to give up, to call my parents and say, 'Come take care of me and my son because I can't,' just when I thought no one could help me with my dogs, I had this dream. It doesn't matter if Josh actually tried to send me a message or if my own subconscious saved me. All I can see is his face and his arm and his closed fist. He's not sad or mad or angry. He's just looking at me and rooting for me like I'm about to win the Stanley Cup. Like he's proud of me. He's proud to wear my jersey, even at my worst moment. He's elbowing the guy next to him. 'That's my wife,' he says. I'm his wife and he knows I can do this.

In the 'King's Cross' chapter in *Harry Potter and the Deathly Hallows*, after Harry has his long conversation with Albus Dumbledore, Harry looks at Dumbledore's twinkling blue eyes and says, 'Tell me one last thing. Is this real? Or has this been happening inside my head?' Dumbledore says, 'Of course it is happening inside your head, Harry, but why on earth should that mean that it is not real?'

I feel like I read that chapter six months ago to prepare me for the dream I had last night. I can't quite say if Josh and J. K. Rowling and Albus

Dumbledore and the handles on my shower and me are all spiritually connected. I do know that this morning I worke up and I did not feel the need to sit on the floor of the shower again.

A week later Jason comes over and picks up the dogs. Part of me feels hugely disappointed in myself. They have to leave because I am making them, and I am making them leave because I couldn't pull it together. Growing up, if there was one thing my dad never allowed us to do, it was back out of a commitment. Joining the softball team, playing the flute, writing for the yearbook staff. I vividly remember wanting to quit all of these things and being told I couldn't. I had to stick with it until the end. But here I am quitting. I am giving up. I am ashamed of this. This goes against how I was raised to resolve problems. But even with that sense of shame, I am hugely relieved in their departure. I hate to say that even more. I am ashamed that I gave up on something and I am more ashamed that giving up is going to make my life easier. But I can't put this back together the way it was. I can't make this work.

While out shoveling the driveway I slip on some ice. For a second, I think I am going to fall, but then I catch myself. How horrible, I think, if I fell and hit my head and died, just like Josh. Then my mind starts to wander about what would happen when I got to heaven.

Shortly after Josh died, I had a lot of moments

in which I didn't want to be alive. I was never suicidal, and it wasn't even that I wanted to leave my family or friends, but I just wanted so badly to be with Josh. I even thought about it in my head as a sense of sympathy I had developed for Romeo and Juliet. I was going to write about how I felt for them. It's not that I wanted to die, but I just suddenly knew where they were coming from. That's how badly they wanted to be together.

But as I catch myself from falling, I realize that I feel totally different from the days of sympathy for Romeo and Juliet. It is because of Kai. I don't want to die solely because I cannot leave my son. The thought of having to be without my son is more immense and powerful than I ever imagined.

If I hit my head today, I would get to the gates of heaven and go insane. I would trash the place in a screaming fury. I would throw chairs through glass doors. I would knock the clipboard out of the receptionist's hand. I would take every pile of papers and splatter them across the room. 'I don't belong here, you fucking assholes!' I would yell as I kicked over desks and smashed harps. I would destroy the place. Not out of anger, but out of pure desperation to get back to my son. 'You screwed up again! I DON'T BELONG HERE!' I would scream. 'What kind of *fucking morons* do you have running this place! SEND ME HOME!' I would look crazy. My hair would be everywhere. I would be doused in sweat. Then they would bring Josh out and they would say, 'But he's here. Didn't you say you wanted to be with him? Didn't you say you wanted to be where he was?' I would look Josh straight in the face, I mean a real solid stare, and without hesitation I would say, 'No. I don't want to be here.' The words would sit in the empty space like a heavy load, like a punch in the face. Josh would just stare back, not knowing how to respond. 'Now send me home.' They would look at each other, and they would check their files and ask me again, 'Now, ma'am, you're sure. You're sure you don't want to be with him. You can. He's right here. You can stay. We'd like you to stay.' And the whole time they were talking, Josh and I would be staring at each other. But he would hardly recognize me. My chest would be heaving from the destructive rage. I would be taller than he had remembered. I would look more confident, stronger than when he had left me. I would be looking at him with angry eyes. He would be looking at me, trying to figure out what was going on. 'Yes, I am sure,' I would say slowly, so everyone knew I was certain. 'I do not want to stay here with him. Send me back to my son.' They would shrug at each other. 'Okay, you heard the lady. You're free to go.' Without another word, I would turn and march out. On my way out I would shove little old St Peter right in the chest, a onehanded, fuck-you-asshole shove. And Josh would stand there, completely bewildered. The guys working in the office would say, 'Sorry, man,

208

we didn't mean to set you up to hurt your feelings.' Josh would stare off to where I had just
stood, and finally it would hit him. 'No,' he would
say, 'that's why I married her.'

I am taking stock right now at this moment. I
do feel better and I know exactly when it
happened. When my son smiled at me, when he
was able to communicate his approval and love,
that's when something fused in my brain. At that
moment, motherhood body-slammed wifehood
and deemed herself to be bigger, stronger, and
downright more important. My FMG sits on the
stoop of my house in her puffy winter coat and
nods in approval. She doesn't judge me for imagining myself pummeling a religious figure in
defense of my son. She shrugs her shoulders and
explains it's a primal instinct. 'And,' she adds,
'motherhood is all primal instinct.'

I am catching up on my podcasts of *This American
Life*. The episode from the end of December is
titled 'Home Alone.' The last story, the most
intriguing story, was about a woman who was held
hostage in her own home with her two children.
For a while I've been thinking about the idea of
a new year. Who was I last year? At one point I
was married, then I was married and pregnant,
then I was widowed and pregnant, and then I was
a widowed mother. I can't help but be a little
nervous as I wind up to face another year. All
throughout January, part of me has been thinking,

God, I wonder what horrible things will happen this year. 'Home Alone' comes at me at just the right time.

Ira Glass introduces the last story as 'when the scariest thing possible actually happens.' Of course, I find this intriguing. I thought that was my situation.

A young mom named Ezra had married a man named Raymond. They lived in a two-bedroom apartment in New Jersey. When they got married, Raymond was earning an honest living selling jewelry. Years later, a family member got him involved in dealing cocaine. The job change had affected their relationship for obvious reasons. Ezra and her daughter, who at the time was in kindergarten, tell the story. Raymond had been gone for several days, but the daughter remembers nothing about her parents having a damaged relationship, nor did she ever suspect her father was a dealer. One day a man came to the door asking for Raymond. Ezra said he wasn't home and she had no idea when he would be back. The man said Raymond owed him money and he was not leaving until Raymond showed up. He then showed her his gun. After a phone call to his 'boss' in Florida, the man told her that she and her children would be killed if Raymond didn't show up.

Ezra tells the story confidently, although she reveals that at the time she was scared to death. But she did not show one hint of fear to the gunman or to her children. She told her children

210

that their dad's friend was staying with them for a few days. The kids didn't think anything of it. After a few days of fearing for her life, Ezra realized she had to come up with a plan. Ezra started dropping hints to the gunman that she had connections with the mafia and the police force. Both were lies, but the gunman bought it. She overheard him on the phone with his boss saying he didn't feel safe. She had the upper hand. Finally, Raymond came home and settled up with the gunman. Before leaving, the gunman profusely apologized to Ezra and begged that she didn't send her 'family' after him. Ezra said this was the moment when she thought, *Damn I'm good*.

Ezra admitted that this event changed her. Nothing fazed her after this. She became fearless when confronted with all situations. Her daughter tells another story that took place after Ezra's metamorphosis. Ezra, who was five foot two, worked as an insurance agent. One day an angry client stormed in and started yelling at Ezra. He became so enraged that he threatened bodily harm to her. In response, Ezra calmly stepped out from behind her desk and said, 'Well . . . have at it.' The man left and never bothered her again.

I am inspired by this story, obviously. Who wouldn't be? Another mom going into survival mode and coming out victorious. I always think that I've got the worst situation on the planet, but I don't. And who cares about who has it worse?

The best part of the story is how Ezra, despite her stress, fear, and angst, was able to convince her children that everything was okay. Day in and day out she went on as if everything was normal and in doing so she protected her children from a horrifying situation. Every day they went off to school laughing and playing and never suspected that their lives were in danger. A situation that could have landed them in therapy for years was averted because their mother made a choice to handle it. That's how I want to be. I want to be Ezra.

With all of this in mind, I consider how I want to live this year. In this past month I've confronted the new year tired with bags under my eyes, my shoulders hunched forward. I've crossed the threshold of the new year wearing my blue bathrobe, my sweatpants, my slippers, my hair a mess, my eyes watery, my arms and legs weak. I hold Kai, cradled in my arms, but I am hardly able to lift him anymore. My motto: 'I can't take another day, let alone another year.'

But I don't have to be Gregor Samsa. Gregor woke up one morning and found himself a bug. Something happened to him and he had no control over the results. Something happened to me too, but that doesn't mean I have to lose my identity. I can control my metamorphosis.

After listening to Ezra, I have a new image. It's the image I want to take on this year. I see myself with war paint on my face, my hair tied back in a tight ponytail. I am wearing a camouflage Under Armour sports bra as my muscles bulge from underneath. Kai is thrown over my shoulder and he laughs at the chaos that surrounds us. I have a machete between my teeth, and a pack on my back that holds a bow and arrow, a Buck knife, wipes and diapers. I look determined, strong, bold, and fearless. My motto: 'Well . . . have at it.'

FEBRUARY

Picnic, Lightning
Billy Collins

'My very photogenic mother died in a
freak accident (picnic, lightning) when
I was three.'   *—LOLITA*

It is possible to be struck by a meteor
or a single-engine plane
while reading in a chair at home. Pedestrians
are flattened by safes falling from
rooftops mostly within the panels of
the comics, but still, we know it is
possible, as well as the flash of
summer lightning, the thermos toppling
over, spilling out on the grass.
And we know the message can be
delivered from within. The heart, no
valentine, decides to quit after
lunch, the power shut off like a
switch, or a tiny dark ship is

unmoored into the flow of the body's
rivers, the brain a monastery,
defenseless on the shore.

This is
what I think about when I shovel
compost into a wheelbarrow, and when
I fill the long flower boxes, then
press into rows the limp roots of red
impatiens – the instant hand of Death
always ready to burst forth from the
sleeve of his voluminous cloak. Then
the soil is full of marvels, bits of
leaf like flakes off a fresco,
red-brown pine needles, a beetle quick
to burrow back under the loam.

Then
the wheelbarrow is a wilder blue, the
clouds a brighter white, and all I
hear is the rasp of the steel edge
against a round stone, the small
plants singing with lifted faces, and
the click of the sundial as one hour
sweeps into the next.

As I rush from Kai's bedroom to heat up a
bottle, I catch a glimpse of a splotch of
jelly on the floor. The splotch is about the

size of a quarter. It's been there for a few days, I can't quite remember how long. I know how it got there because the other night I was eating a peanut butter and jelly sandwich for dinner while I was holding Kai and I spilled this little bit on the way to his room. I've been meaning to clean it up, but I just haven't gotten to it. It sounds ridiculous when I say this. How have I not had the three minutes it takes to clean up this jelly? Clearly, I've had three minutes in two days, but it's still there. When I do find three minutes, I don't rush to clean it up. I don't really care that there's dried jelly on the hardwood floor. Just like I don't really care that I pull my hair back in a sloppy ponytail every day and hardly brush it. Why clean it up? Why use a hairdryer? I have half a mind to buzz my hair. My FMG tells me I'm not allowed to shave my head. She says she needs to see a signed note from my therapist first.

The jelly on the floor is my whole life. Everything is a giant mess. My house is the metaphorical representation of the inside of my brain. There are laundry bins throwing up everywhere. The refrigerator hasn't been cleaned out in a century. But I'm so tired, I can't get caught up. And sometimes, even when I do have some time, I just need to lie down, clear my head, and spend some time with my grief. I feel adrift. I had such a good few weeks, and now I feel exhausted and completely uninspired. My Ezra moment has vanished.

Sometimes I think my grief is like a physical

injury – every day there's a little more range of motion. But that doesn't work because some days it feels like the pain is getting worse instead of better. The range of motion becomes more limited. When I look at that dried jelly and the laundry bins, I think grief is a really sloppy roommate who just leaves his shit lying around everywhere. Lately, things feel more like grief is having one arm cut off. Some days are good and I think, wow, I can really do this with one arm, look at me, making it work with one arm, and I never knew how useful each finger was, and even each toe! But then other days when I haven't had a lot of sleep and I feel sadness pull at me like a giant magnet, I look at that little splotch of jelly and think how this life is just really fucking hard with only one arm.

The bottle is warm. I see the jelly on the way back to Kai's room. I let it sit. I'll get to it eventually.

I'm certain that part of this shift of dealing with a messy house and messy brain comes as a result of going back to work after maternity leave. There is just less time to get things done and a lot more to think about. There is no doubt, however, that it is good to have a place to go and be forced to think about the needs of my students over the needs of myself. Grief seems to be a completely egocentric emotion, but teenagers even have me beat when it comes to being the center of the universe.

Right now in eleventh-grade Honors English we

are reading *No Exit* by John-Paul Sartre. Sartre was a French existentialist philosopher and writer. Existentialism is an incredibly complicated philosophy. The one basic component that we consider is Sartre's idea that 'your existence precedes your essence,' meaning you are not what you believe you are; you are a product of your actions. There's a lot more to it than that, but that's about as far as we get in eleventh grade. Anyway, in the play *No Exit* there are three characters: Garcin, Inez, and Estelle. All three have landed themselves in hell for sinning in various ways and they are there to torture each other. The play does a lot of interesting things, but one of the main things we talk about is how it exposes this philosophy of what you are over what you say you are. We start off at the basic level.

'Raise your hand and give me an example of when a person – do not name names – says they are something, but their actions prove them to be something completely different.' The room is silent. I already know how this will go. They'll be silent and then they'll get into it when they see what we're getting at. Finally, after waiting for a little bit (not long enough, that's always been one of my problems), I say, 'Have you ever heard someone say, 'Yeah, I know, aren't I *such* a good friend.' [I do a really good imitation of a snotty high school girl. It's not a Valley girl, which is what you're probably thinking; it's more entitled white girl. It's killer.] But really that person is a horrible friend. She talks about other people behind her back, she never asks questions about other people or sounds interested, and if a cooler crowd were to come along, she'd be gone in seconds.' I see heads nodding.

'Popular,' Leah Simon says from the front row.

'Excuse me?' I'm not quite sure how this connects to my imitation.

'People would call themselves popular, but they're really not.' I turn and write *popular* under the heading 'Essence.' This conversation is a total Leah Simon topic. On most days, Leah wears a worn-out green army jacket, baggy pants, and her black Doc Martens. She has long black hair that is usually tied back in a messy bun. She is incredibly bright but prefers to show people how sassy she is over how bright she is, though sometimes she can hit them both with the same chord and it's awesome. Other times, she just sounds impolite. One time before class, Leah picked up my picture of Kai and said, 'Your baby looks creepy in this picture.' I had absolutely no idea what to say. I just had to initiate an inner chant in my head that said something like, 'Don't swear, don't swear.' I told her to set my baby's picture down and find her seat. I really hope one day she realizes how she can be wickedly intelligent in a way that would make her incredibly successful.

'What word can be put under the heading 'Existence' for popular people?' I ask. I look around the room to let the class know that Leah doesn't have to answer this. She does anyway.

'Well, they suck, mostly.' The class laughs and luckily Leah's poignant observation of high school social hierarchy catapults us into a rich conversation. *Leader, good sport, honor student* (I love that that phrase made the board!) – all of these words are our essence, but what about our action? We talk about whether 'honor' students actually behave in an honorable manner. There is a lot of snickering from Ryan Dannerman and Doug Treen. For one of their group projects earlier in the year, Ryan and Doug somehow incorporated the two of them playing Guitar Hero in front of the entire class for five whole minutes.

By the end of the discussion, they're beginning to get it. I assign the entire play for the weekend. When I sit down to reread *No Exit*, as with everything else in my life, I think about Josh. Garcin, the only man in the play, worked for a pacifist newspaper when he was alive. When war broke out, he fled. Garcin is convinced that he is not a coward and all he wants is for Inez, another character, to validate the fact that running away from his ideals does not make him a coward. She will not admit this. In the midst of their argument, Garcin gets frustrated and says that his life ended too soon, and that if only he'd been given a little more time, he could have proved that he was the hero that he had dreamed himself to be. He could have proven that he was a real man. He asks Inez, 'Can one judge a life by a single action?' Of course, the audience knows that this is Garcin's main problem. The existentialist would say, yes, you can judge a life based on one single act.

Josh died too young, but he didn't wait around for anything. He didn't wait around to prove he was a real man. If you went back in time to any moment of Josh's life, you could judge his life in any act you found him doing. He biked across the country. He traveled the world. He loved his friends unconditionally. He was compassionate toward children. He worked for charities. He took time to have fun. He lived. He never complained. He cooked delicious meals. He kissed the women he loved. He soaked up as much of Michigan summers as he possibly could. He did not wait for anything. Maybe somewhere he knew it would end quickly.

I won't share any of this with my students. I'm there to teach a play, not to exercise my grief-stricken brain in front of them. Besides, *No Exit* is a short unit. Before I know it, we're on to poetry.

I never really think about how an upcoming novel will impact me before I read it. It just happens. So far this year, I have done an astounding job at keeping my act together at school. I've only been back for four weeks, and I've put all of my energy into staying focused on work while I'm at school and not letting my mind wander off into the land of emotions without any reins. But I worry about poetry.

I think of Dennis, who also teaches eleventh-grade Honors English. In February of last year,

Dennis's mom passed away. She was the mother of thirteen children. Before we go any further, did you hear that number? *Thirteen.* Double digits of children.

A few weeks later, after the funeral, he was back at school in the middle of the poetry unit with his eleventh-grade class. One of the poems that his students had read for homework was 'Do Not Go Gentle into That Good Night' by Dylan Thomas. One interpretation of the poem is that the speaker is pleading with his father not to die. The last stanza of the poem reads:

And you, my father, there on the sad height,
Curse, bless me now with your fierce tears, I pray.
Do not go gentle into that good night.
Rage, rage against the dying of the light.

They were planning on discussing it in class. When they got to that poem in class, Dennis stopped his students and said, 'I'm sorry, but we will not be discussing this poem.' He explained that his mom had just passed away and this poem was too hard to read right now. The students were shocked. Mr McDavid was a tall, stern man; he was notorious for being a tough paper grader and a teacher with high standards who did not tolerate misbehavior. And here he was, tearing up from behind his glasses saying he couldn't read a poem.

Now that poetry is in the wheelhouse, I think specifically about Dennis, his mom, and Thomas's poem. I think maybe I will have a hard time with 'Do Not Go Gentle into That Good Night,' but I read it, we read it in class, and I'm fine. I take a deep breath before I read 'Death Be Not Proud,' but it doesn't faze me. None of the death poems get to me. But then today I am sitting in my empty room on my planning period and I begin to read 'Picnic, Lightning' by Billy Collins. All of the sudden, my throat dries up and I can feel my body start to shake.

Out of nowhere, the poem crushes me. I move to the corner of my classroom where no one can see me from the hallway. I cry and shake. I have worked so damn hard since returning from maternity leave to not cry at work. I am so mad at myself. I had no idea it would be 'Picnic, Lightning' that would get to me. I was completely unprepared for it. But it just hit a certain nerve, a nerve that I wasn't sure even existed, about the uncertainty of life that I will never be able to escape. Sayings like 'It could never happen to me' or 'What are the odds?' no longer supply me with any comfort. Most humans say these things to themselves in order to mask or ignore the truth that none of us, not our loved ones or ourselves, are promised to be here for any length of time. 'Picnic, Lightning' comes at me like a nightmare. 'Remember me?' it says. 'I'm that little reminder that someone is here one second and then – *boom!* – they're gone.' Senseless, undeserving, unjust, untimely death is a rare occurrence, but

'Picnic, Lightning' affirms that no matter how rare it is, it is always close enough to strike.

I turn off the lights in my classroom. I sit on the floor and take deep breaths through my tears. I keep looking up at the clock. I know I have to get myself under control in forty minutes. Not just under control. There must be absolutely no evidence of crying. There can be no puffy eyes, no plugged-up nostrils, no red face. As I cry, I continually wipe under my eyes to make sure my mascara isn't smearing. Thirty-five minutes, *shit*. Finally, with about fifteen minutes to spare, I open my door and walk down to the bathroom. I check my face, get a drink of water, and go back to my room. Without thinking, I get my white boards ready for class. 'Take out your h.w. and something to write with!' it says at the top. I list our agenda underneath.

I've had days like this before. I feel like I take a step up, right to the edge of the earth, and look over the cliff. On these days, I don't want to hand Kai to anyone else. I want my sisters and my brother to move home. I don't want to go to work. If it could end in one flash of a moment, then why on earth would I spend my time at work? But I can't operate normally with this mindset. I hate these days. Picnic, Lightning days.

Valentine's Day falls in the middle of the poetry unit. You'd think I'd create a lesson plan around some love poems to honor the holiday, but I don't. I'm not into love poems right now and I'm certainly not interested in discussing them with teenagers. Overall, I have a general feeling of resentment toward this holiday. One year ago today, Josh and I drove over to my parents' house and told them we were pregnant. We called Moo, Ads, and Hales from my parents' house. All night we laughed and relived everyone's reaction. I remember my brother kept saying, 'I just need to sit down for a minute.' I could hear him smiling through the phone. I can vividly remember standing in my parents' kitchen with Josh. All of us were smiling, crying with happiness.

So this morning I wake up and of course all I can think about is how stupid Valentine's Day is. As if most of us don't get the crap beaten out of us by Christmas, now we have another holiday to remind us about the lack of love in our lives.

Most of these negative thoughts leave me by the time I get to school. Once I get to the classroom, I focus on tasks at hand; copies for first block, checking in homework, updating my gradebook, getting my lesson plans together.

In the middle of first hour, nine upperclassmen dressed in white button-down collars and pressed black pants show up at my classroom. First block is ninth-grade English and all of us, my ninth-graders and I, know what is going on. For the past two weeks the Berkley A Cappella Choir has been advertising Valentine's Day serenades. There were posters all over the hall-ways and announcements right before lunch. You pay two dollars and this small group of choir students will come to your first hour and completely embarrass someone on your behalf.

They come to my room. I smile as I see them walk in. I wonder which one of my students is in for the surprise. Maybe an older sister ordered a serenade to torture a little brother (that happened last year), or maybe a ninth-grade boy actually had the guts to send a girl a Valentine's Day song.

'Hi, Mrs Taylor!' Erin Gilson walks in first. I had Erin in my eleventh-grade class last year. I remember she came to the funeral home during Josh's viewing. So many of my students came to the funeral home. Erin came with a few other students from our English class. I remember them staring at me, not in a bad way, just looking at me with sad and wondrous eyes. That image unconsciously flashes in front of me when she walks in. I dismiss it quickly, knowing I can't think about that day or that place while I'm at work.

Tim Argbaum holds the harmonica. They don't have any music sheets. They take their places in front of my class. I wait to hear the name of one of my students. Erin looks at me and says, 'We're here for you, Mrs Taylor.' Then, before I even have time to think or mentally prepare myself, Tim blows into his harmonica for the first note and they all start in. They sing the first verse and one chorus to the song 'Lean on Me.' They sing 'Lean on Me' to me on Valentine's Day.

Once they are done, I stand there frozen.

Somehow I say thank you and they file out as quickly as they came in.

I will never forget that moment as long as I live. There were so many gripping elements of it, I can't quite bottle it up. Their thoughtfulness, the way they said something without making a big deal out of it, walking out without analyzing my reaction or asking for a follow-up conversation. But also it was just the pure sound of their voices. It was a cappella, so there wasn't a sound in the room expect for these eight students singing. There is rarely a time in our lives anymore where we sit and intensely focus on one single sound. Their voices were so strong and so real. For the rest of my life, every time I hear a rendition of that song, I'll smile and think that no one will ever do it as well as the Berkley High School A Cappella Choir. On my next Picnic, Lightning day, I'll close my eyes and think of their voices.

On Friday after school, Deedee picks up Kai and tells me to take a few hours to myself. I decide to wander through Borders bookstore for a while. I find a book called *Not Quite What I Was Planning*. *Smith* magazine invited its subscribers to submit their own six-word memoirs. The book was inspired by an Ernest Hemingway line: 'Baby shoes: for sale, never worn.' Hemingway proved that an entire story could be told in six words. The book is amazing. It's funny and sad. I want to meet all of the people behind the quips. 'I'm ten and have an attitude.' 'I still make coffee for

227

two.' 'Accidentally killed cat. Fear anything delicate.' One of my personal favorites: 'Birth, childhood, adolescence, adolescence, adolescence, adolescence.'

Of course I think about my life in six words. What would it be? What six words would summarize the insanity of the last year of my life, let alone the first twenty-four? What first comes to mind is 'Single widowed mother trying to recover.' But then, I reason, if I only had six words, would I choose the word *widow*? Would I allow that word to make up my identity? Just a half-dozen words to describe everything I've been through – would *widow* make the team? If I wanted to be as descriptive as possible, then certainly *widow* does explain a lot. I am a widow, at least in title. But after reading through some more six-word memoirs, I decide that if I only had six words, I wouldn't take *widow*. 'The female version of Indiana Jones.' That's not mine, that's an entry on page 29. It's brilliant. I want to be friends with that girl. Maybe she's a widow too and she just decided that her adventurous spirit was more important than her marital status.

A few days ago I was in the book room at school, which is a creepy room to begin with. It's dark with only a small window. The metal bookshelves take up the majority of the room – and it isn't really a room, either, it's more like a large walk-in closet. Dust lines the black and maroon tiled floor and there is a very odd smell. It's the smell of stale books. I had to go in the book room to get sixty copies of *Lord of the Flies*; my ninth-grade class starts it next week. The book room holds all of the books we currently teach along with all of the books that we used to teach. As I walked through to find the Everbind stack of *Lord of the Flies*, I saw the stack of Nathaniel Hawthorne's classic, *The Scarlet Letter*. I read *The Scarlet Letter* in Mrs Madison's class in tenth-grade English. But now, as a single mom myself, I feel a new connection to *The Scarlet Letter*.

The plot of *The Scarlet Letter* revolves around this woman, Hester Prynne, who has an illegitimate baby. Hester Prynne sleeps with this guy in town and we're in Puritan America, so the town is really pissed at her. She has to serve a prison sentence while pregnant, and then after the baby is born she has to stand on a scaffold for a while with her infant. (Gotta love the Puritans.) Finally she is made to wear the letter *A* across her chest, which is meant to stand for adultress. First of all, this book is about a baby-mama. Hester never confesses who the father is, although the blood-sucking psycho residents of mid-seventeenth-century Massachusetts really want to know.

Even though the book was a tough read for me in the tenth grade, there was one part of it I remember enjoying. At one point Hawthorne describes how Hester no longer thought of her *A* as standing for adultress but rather for *able*. That's all I remember, the word *able*. I like these moments. These are the moments that I really enjoy as a reader. It's like in *The Color Purple* when Sofia tells Celie that if Harpo (Sofia's husband, technically Celie's son-in-law) beats Sofia again, she's going to kill him. ('Now you want a dead son-in-law, Mrs Celie? You just keep on advising him like you doing.') Suddenly, literature turns into a good movie and you're standing up in your seat, smiling and clapping in your head. You wish at some point in your life you get to tell someone how you really feel about them. It makes you wish that you had the courage to redefine what your letter stood for. So, looking at the gray, beaten copies of *The Scarlet Letter*, I started to think about myself. I have a big *W* sewed across myself. I am a widow. My title is Widow. Not Mrs or Miss, but Widow. Not married or divorced, but Widow. But what else could my *W* stand for? Wise? Not quite. Wonderful? Once in a while. Willing? I think about this. What's my new *W* word? What's my nonwidow six-word memoir?

My FMG sits in one of the big comfy leather chairs at Borders. Her eyes are closed and her head is tilted back. She's wearing a big black puffy coat and sweatpants. I ask her what her six-word memoir was when she was raising her children. Without even taking a moment to think or use her fingers to count out words, she says with her eyes closed, 'Leave me alone for five minutes.'

MARCH

George's hands stopped working the cards. His voice was growing warmer. 'An' we could have a few pigs. I could build a smoke house like the one gran'pa had, an' when we kill a pig we can smoke the bacon and the hams, and make sausage an' all like that. An' when the salmon run up river we could catch a hundred of 'em an' salt 'em down and smoke 'em. We could have them for breakfast. They ain't nothing so nice as smoked salmon. When the fruit come in we could can it – and tomatoes, they're easy to can. Ever' Sunday we'd kill a chicken or a rabbit. Maybe we'd have a cow or a goat, and the cream is so God damn thick you got to cut it with a knife and take it out with a spoon.' Lennie watched him with wide eyes, and old Candy watched him too. Lennie said softly, 'We could live offa the fatta the lan'.'

—JOHN STEINBECK, *OF MICE AND MEN*

*O*f *Mice and Men* is set in rural California in the midst of the Great Depression. George and Lennie are two migrant farmers who are wandering around looking for work. Lennie, a massive human being with tremendous physical strength, is mentally handicapped. Although Steinbeck never gives a diagnosis, we don't need one. Lennie doesn't understand certain things. He doesn't understand certain rules of social settings, and George has to explain things to him over and over. George is his primary caretaker; we quickly learn that Lennie cannot survive on his own. Lennie likes to touch soft things, but he is unaware of his own strength. At one point in the book, he is petting a puppy and accidentally kills it. He has the mind of a four-year-old but the body of a Cyclops.

George and Lennie are always on the move. Lennie continuously gets them intro trouble and George has to find a way out. Steinbeck has a lot of big ideas in this book, but one thing that we talk about in class is how all of the characters are powerless. Steinbeck is interested in our surroundings and how those surroundings affect us. In literature, this is referred to as naturalism. It's kind of like the opposite of existentialism. While Sartre argues that the individual is ultimately responsible, Steinbeck counters that no matter how hard we try, we cannot outwit the circumstances into which we are placed. Lennie, for example, must live the way he does because of his mental disability. Another character, Crooks, is a black stable hand. He has to live in a bunkhouse separate from all the other guys because of his skin color. Crooks has a crooked spine as a result of being kicked by a horse. So sure, he can make choices. But he's a black man living in America in the 1930s and he is physically handicapped, so Crooks doesn't have a whole lot of options.

Throughout the book, George and Lennie have this dream. They dream that one day, despite the economic climate, they can earn enough money to buy their own plot of land. They don't want a lot of it, just a little slice. As long as it's theirs, as long as there is no boss, that's all they care about. This would be an amazing feat for this unlikely duo – not only to survive the financial black hole of the twentieth century but actually to beat it. The two of them are so committed and so hard-working, we (or at least I) are led to believe that they may actually pull it off. But the one important detail about the dream is that they can only survive together. George needs Lennie's size and strength. And Lennie obviously can't do anything without George.

At the end of the book, George is forced to make an important choice about Lennie's life. Lennie accidentally killed the landowner's wife and now Curley (the landowner) is out to kill him. But Lennie didn't mean it. He isn't a murderer. So George takes Lennie by the river. Lennie anxiously asks what he did wrong. George calms him down and tells Lennie to talk about the dream – the rabbits, the smoked ham. George hears the sound of the mob approaching, and he holds a pistol to the back of Lennie's head. Right before the mob arrives, George pulls the trigger.

In the end, George makes a choice. But the biggest question is, did he really have any choice at all? And the other question is, was there ever any hope in fulfilling the dream, or did the economic climate and Lennie's disability mean that failure was the only outcome? We talk about this in class. We talk about the notion of being a victim and being a product of your surroundings.

Not surprisingly, teenagers are incredibly reluctant to admit or to consider that they are a result of anything except their own efforts and ideas. They don't want their parents or their homes taking credit for their good or bad qualities. And of course I have to ask myself this question. Am I powerless? Will I turn into a different mother because I am a single widow? Will I be more short-tempered because I do this on my own? Will I be more frustrated and tired? Will that affect my ability to parent? Will that affect the boy and man that Kai becomes? Steinbeck would say yes. Or at least he would say it's worth thinking about.

The word *victim*, obviously, has some connotations. It evokes a sense of pity, not a proud pity, but an overdue, almost unearned pity. Nobody likes to be pitied. It also triggers this sense that the victim is choosing not to do anything and may be evoking his or her own sense of victimhood. But at the end of *Of Mice and Men*, the reader gets this sense that this is the only way it can be in life. Everybody has to be where they are and no one can escape. I don't want to be a victim, but sometimes I can't help but feel that way. I can't help but feel that I have no control over my surroundings.

Every now and then in eleventh-grade Honors English, we ask students to write something about themselves in connection to literature. But every time I ask my students to make a connection with a character or a problem from an assigned text, no one ever chooses to connect to naturalism. I've only had one student choose to write about *Of Mice and Men*. Last year, Sam Baker wrote about how he is like George and his girlfriend is like Lennie. She's not mentally handicapped, but she relies on him for everything. He makes all of the plans, he drives everywhere, he always has to tell her how pretty she looks. He is constantly comforting and reassuring her. Sam expressed in his essay that this was a tiring position to have in a relationship and as much as he adores her, he really wishes she were more independent. I made as couple of formatting and structural notes on Sam's paper, but at the end of my comments I said, 'Sam, above all, the most important message to take from me is, whatever you do, under no circumstances do you show this essay to your girl-friend.'

Teenagers want to feel like they are in control. We all do. I thought I was in control until Josh died and then it hit me that I'm not in control and I never will be.

I think about Steinbeck when I go to my single moms' parenting meetings. I love going to group. I look forward to it all week long. When someone is absent because of the flu or something, I get sad. I love seeing all of the girls and hearing about their lives. In the middle of teaching *Of Mice and Men*, I can't help but look at them and think about how much power we don't have in the world. At the same time, it never seems to faze us.

A few weeks ago, my single moms' group gained a new member. Miranda is short with long dark hair. She wears a brown puffy coat with a fake-fur-lined hood. On the back in gold embroidery it reads APPLE BOTTOM JEANS. Her son, Alex, is the oldest in the group. He has large brown eyes and curly black hair. He rivals Kai for cutest baby boy ever. Miranda is attending alternative high school. She is seventeen.

Last week we didn't have a speaker, so Janet and Heidi had us do an exercise about thinking about our goals for the future. They had us write down what we wanted for ourselves in the future. When Janet asked if any of us would like to read our goals out loud, Miranda raised her hand. She said that her goal is to be completely independent. She told us about her sister-in-law who buys Alex tons of clothes and gives her all sorts of hand-me-downs. Miranda added that of course she is grateful, but she feels like her sister-in-law's charity project. 'I'm not your *Oprah* episode,' she said, moving her head back and forth. 'That's what I want to say to her. It's like she doesn't think I can buy clothes for myself.' Miranda started to cry. In the spring she is going to Oakland Community College and then on to earn her bachelor's degree. She said her goal is to become a pharmacist. Not a pharmacy technician, a pharmacist. She said that someday she'll make more money than her sister-in-law. She said this and smiled and wiped her tears away. I wanted to hug Miranda. I want to tackle her to the ground and tell her that she can do it, that if anyone can do it, she can. Can't she? Why shouldn't she be able to do this?

This week, Miranda tells us about her current battle in trying to figure out her health insurance. She is unemployed, under eighteen with a baby, and she said she's not sure what to sign up for. No one is very helpful in explaining things to her and everything she reads is confusing and everyone she calls is standoffish or rude. Alex is behind on his immunization shots. When Miranda switched insurance companies she went to get him immunized but was told it couldn't be done because the paperwork hadn't been processed yet. Miranda, who most certainly qualifies as one tough cookie, seems to be insecure and unsure when dealing with health professionals.

Nisi is a yoga instructor. She's trying to make ends meet. Roger's dad is some hotshot lawyer, so the custody battle isn't exactly moving in her favor.

Ellen and her boyfriend are trying to work things out. Ellen's mom died when she was fourteen, so she doesn't have a lot of support from her family. She said her dad tries to help, but it drives her nuts to watch him screw everything up. He put Rose's diaper on backward the other day when he was babysitting. She doesn't have a car because Pete works two jobs and needs the car all the time. She says she is constantly showing Pete how to be more helpful around the house when he can. She shows him how to do everything, but then two days later he 'goes dumb.' Those are her words: 'goes dumb.' I know it's been a while since I had a husband, but that is the funniest, most honest thing I've ever heard a woman say about a man in my entire life.

'Pure genius,' my FMG says. She lies on the floor on her stomach, holding herself up by her elbows, watching Ellen's baby, Rose, try to pull herself up onto the chair. We quickly decide that Ellen is one of the smartest people we've ever met.

Ellen tells us that she and Pete really want to get Rose dedicated to a church. They've tried four different churches near their house, but none of them will do it because Ellen and Pete aren't married.

I remember when I first learned that Ellen was

a devout Christian. She made some reference about church or God and I remember thinking, *So you're a believer in everything* except *the rule on sex and marriage.* Obviously that was a snooty thing to think, which is why I didn't voice it out loud. But now, after hearing about how a baby was rejected from four churches just because of a choice her parents did or didn't make, and looking at Rose with her big, observant brown eyes, I want to personally drive to all of these churches and punch these ministers, or whoever declared such a stupid rule, in the front teeth.

'No baby-mamas, huh?' *Wham*, right to the face. And just as Pastor Ding-Dong comes to, I knee him in the groin. 'No room at the inn, huh?' *WHAM!* Then, as he pushes his chest up with his arms in an attempt to stand, I really pull out all the stops.

When a wrestling submission hold is needed, most go for the half nelson, the full nelson, or an all-out sleeper hold. When I was little, however, I was shown the greatest pressure-point move of all time. Before the guy can get back on his feet, I whip off his shoe and sock and grab ahold of his big toe and twist as hard and fast as humanly possible. This is called the Nairobi toe hold. If you aren't familiar with the Nairobi toe hold, consider yourself lucky. My uncle Kel taught us this when we were little and the painful memory of the Nairobi toe hold has never left me. The Nairobi toe hold is simple. You acquire your victim's bare foot and lock your thumb and fore-finger around his big toe. Then you pull and twist the big toe. Obviously, it is impossible to break the short bone of the big toe with such little leverage, but you basically take your victim to the point of pain where a bone is about to break but it never actually does.

So there I am with Reverend Dumb-Ass, trying to get to his feet, and just when he feels the pain subsiding out of his crotch, I pull the Nairobi toe hold on him. 'Let's get one thing straight,' I yell as he wriggles in pain, probably crying at this point. 'You either let my friend and her baby and her baby-daddy into this church—' He pleads for me to let go, but I don't. I can't keep him here too long, I can't have him pass out from the pain. After some serious Nairobi toe holding, I toss his foot aside. Then I lean toward his ear and in a very soft voice I say, 'Or I'll Carlo-Rizzi your ass so fast, you won't know what hit you.' Then I turn and calmly head for the door, but not before throwing a copy of *The Scarlet Letter* at him. 'A little bit of light reading material,' I say as I open the door. 'Maybe it'll teach you a thing or two, ya jackass!' I yell as I walk out the front door.

This is my superhero alter ego. I go around the world finding people who commit social injustices and I attack them with copies of literary classics to teach them a lesson. The kid who is suspended for racial slurs? I break into his bedroom in the middle of the night, knock out a few of his teeth, and leave him with a copy of *To Kill a Mockingbird*. The parents who get arrested because they let their twelve-year-old throw a party without their supervision and the kids break into the liquor cabinet? I visit the parents in their holding cell to drop off two copies of *Lord of the Flies*. Before the next presidential election I'll skip around the country like Santa Claus, delivering *1984* to all eligible and literate voters.

With Steinbeck sitting in on our single moms' group, I wonder what he makes of us. The beauty of Steinbeck is that it doesn't feel like he is out to teach us a lesson; he is out to show us something. I don't think he necessarily wants us to consider ourselves victims when we read his books but instead to make us aware of the challenges other people face.

'Well, why can't they just work hard and save money and buy a house like my parents did?' Eva Carmen says from the third row of Honors English. We are talking about the availability of certain opportunities in twenty-first-century America and if they really are as available as we think. Are dreams really possibilities for all Americans? All of the girls in my baby-mama group chose to have sex with a man who was not their husband. They did it without taking into account their financial situations or the status of their own romantic relationships. They made a choice. But now, because of the place where they started, everything is more challenging for them. People judge them. I judged them. Their surroundings don't support them in a way a mother should be supported. They have dozens of external factors working against them and their children. Their children, who have made no choices at all, have already inherited a tough situation.

It's so painful to read *Of Mice and Men* again because when Lennie and George talk about their dream, it's so vivid for them. You know they can see it dangling in front of them. But you also know that it will never happen. It will never happen because of the world they were born into and because of the characteristics they can never shake. I wonder if Steinbeck would look at us the same way or, more appropriately, look at our children the same way. Part of me thinks sadly, yes, he would.

In Michigan, the month of March is when the weather starts to turn. Right now winter is receding just slightly and spring is getting ready to scoot in. The gross brown snow is slowly melting. The air feels different. I love when this happens. I begin to remember that I don't live in the Arctic Circle and soon there will be a morning when I don't have to scrape my windshield before work, and maybe someday it will even be warm outside again.

There seems to be a similar thaw happening between my in-laws and me. Deedee and Ashley are great about coming over so I can have a little time to do stuff on my own. We are getting more used to being around each other and communicating. Actually, I think I am getting used to how they communicate.

Today Deedee comes over around six in the evening. When she gets here, Kai is sleeping. I hand him to her and head to the grocery store. When I get back, they are still sitting on the couch together. He is still sleeping. A few minutes after I walk in the door, he wakes up and starts to cry. Deedee immediately stands up, starts rocking him in a severe and abrupt manner, and says the following in a loud, alarmed tone. Keep in mind she is yelling this over a screaming baby.

'Oh! Oh! Well what's wrong? You were just so quiet and content the whole time your mom was gone! You were just as quiet as a mouse and now this! What's wrong? You didn't make a sound while Mom was gone, you were just perfect with Grandma and now this! What's wrong?' Kai keeps crying. She realizes that heaving him up and down is not going to do the trick. 'Okay, okay, okay, okay, not that, not that, don't want that.' She puts him over her shoulder and starts patting him on the back. 'Do you have gas? Is that what you have? A little gas? A little gas? Is that it? You were just so quiet and then all of the sudden, and then all of the sudden? You must have gas. Nat! Nat! He's got a little gas! He must have a little gas because he was just fine and then this. So it must be gas!

It's okay, it's okay, it's okay, it's okay, it's just a little gas. You must not be feeling well. Does your tummy hurt? Your tummy must hurt. Oh, does that tummy hurt!' After patting him and shushing him, he is still screaming. She then sits back down on the couch, now even more worried and anxious than before. 'Okay, okay, okay, okay, okay, okay, okay, are you wet? You must be wet, you must be a little wet. Are you wet? Is that why you're so mad?' She undoes his onesie and checks his diaper. '*Oh look!* Oh, you're wet! You're wet! Well, that must be why you are so mad, you have a wet diaper! That's it, just a wet diaper!' She picks him up and marches frantically to the nursery. She undoes his diaper; he is still screaming. His face is bright red. He is clearly very upset about something. Deedee picks up a plastic butterfly from his toy bin. The butterfly makes a clicking noise when its wings move. She puts the butterfly right over his face and starts clicking it incessantly. So now, Kai is screaming, Deedee is yelling over the scream, and the butterfly sounds like a New Year's Eve noisemaker. She shouts, 'Watch this while I change you! Watch this while I change you! Do you like the butterfly? Do you like the butterfly!' Obviously, it is not working. 'Okay, okay, okay, okay, okay, okay, okay, okay, you don't like the butterfly, okay, okay, okay, let's get this wet diaper off. Let's get this wet diaper off.' She changes him. He is still screaming.

I calmly walk into the kitchen to get a pacifier.

I walk into the room, because I feel bad for both of them, and I put my arms out. I hold Kai in my arms and I move toward the window where it's a little cooler. I hold his pacifier in his mouth and gently start rocking him a little. A few minutes later he is quiet. Eventually, he falls asleep. Deedee stares at me through this entire process. I don't say a word. Finally, she says, 'A mother's touch. He always knows his mother's touch. He knows. He just knows. You can't do anything when he knows his mother's touch. What can you do when he wants his mother's touch?'

She sits down and wipes the sweat off her forehead.

This moment makes me smile. It doesn't make me bitter or angry or frustrated or any of those negative things that I typically associate with having in-laws and no husband. She is trying so hard, she's trying hard to make Kai happy and to make me happy, and I hardly ever give her credit for that. I like this feeling of watching a situation unfold with my mother-in-law and son and not being completely saddened by it. I have no control over my in-laws, but I do have control over how I react to things or the degree to which I allow something to get to me. Lately I feel like I've been doing a better job at this. I need to keep track of these moments somehow, maybe start drawing tally marks on my wall just to remind myself that darkness doesn't get to be here all the time.

The next day, Saturday, I have to go to a bridal

shower. I need to leave by 2:30 p.m. It is now 12:27. I feed Kai lunch, clean up the kitchen, load the dishwasher, wash the bottles, pick up the living room, fold my laundry, start Kai's laundry, make my bed, have a lengthy conversation with Deedee about Michelle Arman's shower. (The one she attended yesterday afternoon. I say I don't know who Michelle Arman is. She says, 'Yes you do, from Elk Lake, J.R. and Tina's daughter, Amanda's little sister.' I have never met any of these people, but I say, 'Oh right, *Michelle*, I remember!') In addition she gives me a long dissertation about why Ashley will be in a bad mood today. I make and eat a plate of frozen lasagna. At 1:57 I say to Kai, 'We have thirty-three minutes to make and clean up broccoli white bean soup [made with fresh broccoli] so we have dinner ready by the time I get back.' I am chopping the broccoli when Kai decides that he will not partake in cooking and would rather take a nap. I immediately turn the burner off and take a fifteen-minute pause to gracefully and calmly rock Kai to sleep. I then return to the kitchen (now with seventeen minutes left) to finish cooking the broccoli white bean soup and clean up the kitchen again. Keep in mind, all of these tasks (except for the last seventeen minutes, of course) are performed with a five-and-a-half-month-old baby, a *rowdy* five-and-a-half-month-old baby, in need of constant entertainment. Right now the blender is soaking in the sink, but other than that, the kitchen, along with the rest of the house, is spotless. Snap. (Oh, did I mention the broccoli white bean soup has 11 grams of protein, 6 grams of fiber, and 94 percent of your daily vitamin C?)

Before I go to my room to get dressed, I call John Steinbeck. A stuffy secretary answers the phone.

'Mr Steinbeck's office.'

'Is Mr Steinbeck available?'

'One moment, please. I will transfer your call.' I know it will take her a while to transfer the call. It's 1939 on her end. In the meantime, I cue up my iPod. He picks up the line.

'This is Mr Steinbeck.' I put the phone down next to the iPod. I push play. M. C. Hammer's 'Can't Touch This' comes out of the speakers. I saunter back to my room to get dressed before Kai wakes up.

These small successes are somehow adding up somewhere. I'm making a small pile of positive moments. I'm slowly filling an empty bucket.

Kai and I clean up breakfast while we listen to the Valentine's Day episode of *This American Life*. As usual I'm a little behind. The opening prologue is about falling in love. Ira (we're on a first-name basis) and some psychologist talk about 'the bolt of lightning,' which all of us know about. When you see someone or meet someone and you are instantly in love. The psychologist says that this feeling of infatuation can last as long as eighteen months and then the love changes into something different. Ira explains that this week's *This American Life* will be bringing us stories about love *after* the bolt of lightning. I am so relieved. I knew I could count on *This American Life* to bring me a more realistic view of love.

The first act of the show is a short story called 'Letter to the Lady of the House,' by Richard Bausch. The story opens with a man writing a letter to his wife, Marie, after they've had an argument. They are both older, well into their seventies, and he explains that the relationship has been deteriorating for some time; after thirty years they have 'grown tired' of each other. He says he almost left her that night, but instead he decided to drink whiskey and write her a letter.

He tells Marie a story about his cousin Louise and her husband Charlie, about how when the narrator was younger, he had the opportunity to visit Louise and Charlie shortly after the two were married. It was in 1933, and even in the midst of a trying time the narrator reflects that despite their financial uncertainty and the growing doom that was sweeping over the nation, Louise and Charlie were happy simply to have each other.

The narrator then goes on to say that over time things changed. Charlie ended up suffering from a nearly fatal accident at work, and Louise became his permanent caretaker. Louise later confessed to the narrator that she had grown to hate her husband. She said that every time he was near her, she was 'overwhelmed with irritation, suffocation, and anxiety.' She tried to understand how marriage could do such a thing. How undying, powerful love can turn into such contempt.

The narrator then writes to Marie that he brings up the story because upon Louise's confession he thought it was still worth it because she and Charlie had a moment where they did adore each other. He had witnessed it. There was a time when they felt true love. He remembers hearing Louise's confession and thinking, *It must have been worth it for such loveliness.* He goes on to tell his wife that even though they do not get along anymore, even though their marriage is 'slowly eroding,' they have had wonderful times together, and if he had to go back knowing how he feels about his marriage now, he would still do it all over again, without a second thought. 'All of it. Even the sorrow.' 'Letter to the Lady of the House' is one of the most beautiful, well-written stories I have ever heard in my entire life.

At the conclusion of the story, I cry. So many of his words are in my brain. Even though I have had the hardest eight months of my life, even though I am living a life that is tragic and difficult, I would have done it all again to be with Josh for as long as I was. I've never written that or announced that or even thought about it until I heard this man's story, but I am relieved that his story prompts this conclusion. Even knowing how much pain I am in at this moment, I would not trade my days with Josh for anything in the entire world.

Part of my reaction is also because I will never get the chance to bicker with my seventy-year-old husband. I will never get to see Josh grow old and embrace old age. I will never get to know if my marriage would have lasted. But at the same time, my marriage is permanently frozen in time. I have the most wonderful memories with my husband and we were not together long enough to run into the mundaneness that most married couples encounter. We were still in the bolt of lightning phase when Josh died, which is the most tragic fact at times but also one that makes me feel better.

In so many ways, Josh reminds me of Finny from John Knowles's book *A Separate Peace*. I teach *A Separate Peace* in ninth-grade English. Finny, the idealistic teenager, dies at the end of the book. The first time I read *A Separate Peace*, before I even knew how it ended, I said to Mathews, 'Doesn't Finny remind you of Josh?' Finny is good at every sport. There is nothing he can't play. When he walks, he walks with this athletic, confident swagger. He loves life, he jokes with his teachers, and he wears pink shirts. Josh wore pink shirts. Maggie's dad even commented that Josh looked just like a Finny in one of the pictures of him at the funeral home, standing there with his handsome smile in his pink shirt. Leper Lepellier, another character, remarks, 'Everything must evolve or else it will perish.' That's why Finny dies. That is why Piggy from *Lord of the Flies* dies. These characters did not evolve. I'm not saying Josh died because he couldn't evolve. I don't think there was any sense in Josh's death. But sometimes I think that he could never live to see our marriage deteriorate into bickering. He could never live to see his friends' marriages deteriorate into bickering. He got to experience love in its purest, most wonderful form. Not everyone gets to do that.

I wish I could say something more profound. I wish I could articulate this paradox of feeling tremendous sadness about my husband's death at twenty-seven and at the exact same moment being thankful for the years we were together. But I can't. I can't think of the words, so I'm going to steal them from 'Letter to the Lady of the House.' All I can say is that I too am grateful for such loveliness.

APRIL

When the weather's nice, my parents go out quite frequently and stick a bunch of flowers on old Allie's grave. I went with them a couple of times, but I cut it out. In the first place, I don't enjoy seeing him in that crazy cemetery. Surrounded by dead guys and tombstones and all. It wasn't too bad when the sun was out, but twice – *twice* – we were there when it started to rain. It was awful. It rained on his lousy tombstone, and it rained on the grass on his stomach. It rained all over the place. All the visitors that were visiting the cemetery started running like hell over to their cars. That's what nearly drove me crazy. All the visitors could get in their cars and turn on their radios and all and then go someplace nice for dinner – everybody except Allie. I couldn't stand it. I know it's only his body and all that's in the cemetery, and his soul's in Heaven and all that crap, but I couldn't stand it anyway. I just wished he wasn't there.

—HOLDEN CAULFIELD IN J. D. SALINGER,
THE CATCHER IN THE RYE

E very day when I drive to work, I pass the cemetery where Josh's ashes were placed. I haven't been back to the cemetery since we placed the ashes there last June. I have no intention of visiting. I hardly ever get sad as I drive by. I am immune to cemeteries, or so I thought.

But this morning I am driving to work and it's pouring rain (it's April in Michigan, which means it rains a lot) and Holden Caulfield just sort of walks into my brain, completely uninvited. Holden Caulfield is the narrator in J. D. Salinger's *The Catcher in the Rye*. We teach it in tenth-grade English. I taught it my first year at Berkley. Holden, a teenager, lost his little brother, Allie, to leukemia. I haven't read *The Catcher in the Rye* in two years, but this one part comes right back to me when I see that cemetery in the midst of the gray April rain. There is a part where he talks about when it rains on Allie's stomach.

Now that it's raining so often I think about Holden all the time. Annoyingly enough, I start to look at the cemetery more and more on my way to work. I have this weird feeling when I think about the rain scene in that book. I feel relieved that Josh's remains were cremated so I never have to worry about the rain on his stomach.

I've never liked associating Josh with a cemetery. I'm not exactly sure what I think about the afterlife, but I'm certain he's not sitting in some plot at the corner of Twelve Mile Road and Woodward Avenue across the street from Uncle Andy's Pizza. Instead I tell myself his spirit is off racing around doing a million different things. I picture him snow-boarding down the Andes Mountains or juggling a soccer ball barefoot on the beaches of Fiji. Every now and then he goes back to the cemetery to check in on people – other souls who feel like they don't know where to go so they stay in the cemetery. He meets some older man named Al who passed away from old age and really misses his grandchildren. First, Josh sits and listens and goes through Al's pictures with him. Then Josh says, 'Hey Al, have you ever been fly-fishing in Mongolia?' Josh lends Al one of his Arc'teryx raincoats and his best Orvis rod and they're off.

This is how I think most of the time, but now that Holden Caulfield is in my head, I think differently. Usually I feel like my husband is too good to be cooped up in a lousy cemetery. *Lousy* – that's a total Holden Caulfield word. Maybe Josh is there. Maybe the bodies do turn gray and the ashes turn to dust and it is as sad and useless as I fear it to be.

I sign up for a grief group through my church.

I shouldn't say I signed up. Technically, I was invited to join. For some reason saying I signed up makes me sound like I'm desperate. I may be desperate, but for some reason I need you to know I was invited. I got a letter in the mail explaining that the group was for people who had lost a spouse. We would meet every Wednesday in the month of April for an hour and a half. I only work Monday, Tuesday, and Thursday, so I can make it, but I have a baby, so I can't make it.

I don't know what motivates me to call the church, but I do. For some reason, I want to go to this group. I don't see Dr G. very often anymore and this seems like a place I can go to sort of check on myself. My single moms' group is great for the camaraderie of raising a child alone, but I need a place to share my grief again. I think it will be good for me to talk about things out loud instead of just mulling stuff over in my head. I want to talk to other amputees and hear about how their lives are with one arm. Fortunately, a volunteer from the church agrees to come in and entertain Kai in the toddler room while I attend the group.

The group meets in a large room. There are four couches in a square shape and one armchair. I am the last one to arrive. I am shocked that everyone is so prompt. As I sit down and look around, I see why. It's a bit of an older crowd. *This is a huge mistake*, I think to myself.

There are six people besides me. Two female ministers lead the group, Lynne and Mary. Lynne and Mary both have short hair and soft voices. Lynne holds a clipboard on her lap. Mary opens the meeting by welcoming everyone. She explains the schedule, the parameters of the group, its intentions, and so on. She says that we'll start this week by introducing ourselves and telling our story.

Jack goes first. He sits in the armchair. He has white hair and large square glasses. He is easily in his seventies, maybe his eighties. He recently lost his wife, Carol; she was eighty years old. She had quite the life, he tells us. She served as a nurse in World War II. She had a bout of hepatitis when she got out, almost died, but made it. She went on to be a mom, then a grandmother. After retiring, she wrote two children's books. Jack says he has been fine since her death. It was expected. He basically joined the group to give him something to do.

Debbie looks like she is in her late forties. She is an attractive woman with brown hair and a nicely put together outfit. She holds a tissue tightly in her hand. Her husband worked as a minister and actually consoled a lot of people through grief. He was always concerned about the war in Iraq because he was such a peaceful man. He worried a lot about how many lives were being lost and how many families were feeling the effects of it. She says he would have done anything for anyone. 'A true Good Samaritan.'

The night he died he went off to play basketball,

just like he did every Sunday night, and collapsed in the middle of the game. No one did anything. There was a defibrillator machine on site and no one went to get it. No one tried CPR. It took EMS fifteen minutes to get there and by that time his heart had stopped beating completely. Some random guy called her and said her husband had been rushed to the ER. She went, thinking he had broken a bone, and when she got there, they put her in a room by herself. She sat there until the doctor came in, looking very scared, and said, 'Tell me about your husband's health.' She explained he was in excellent shape and exercised on a regular basis. The doctor stuttered something about his heart and then said to her, 'And we just couldn't revive him.' That's how she found out her husband was dead. She was by herself until one of her friends called her cell phone. Debbie dabs her eyes with her tissue, but she doesn't cry. Both of Debbie's kids are in college. Debbie and her husband were looking forward to traveling or just taking it easy. Two days prior to his accident, he had filed for his retirement.

Maureen sits next to Debbie. Maureen holds a tissue in her hand also. She has a little bit of an accent. She lost her husband, who had been physically disabled for about five years, in November right before Thanksgiving. They had gone out to Denver to see their son and his family. She says she remembers thinking how much energy he had on the trip. She couldn't believe it, they hadn't traveled in years. Then, one morning when he was getting dressed and she was getting ready to take a shower, he just fell backward on the bed and no one could resuscitate him. She takes the longest to tell her story. It's like she still can't believe it. Sometimes, she says, she finds herself talking to him. She admits her weekends are very lonely. She makes dinner and doesn't know what to do with all of her leftovers.

Pat has long white hair and pale skin. She wears all black to the group meeting. Her eyes are a deep brown, but they seem to droop as if her face is permanently fixed to express a sense of mournfulness. Up until Pat, everyone else had lost his or her spouse less than a year ago. Pat shrugs before starting her story. Two years ago Pat lost her 'dear friend,' Ed. Ever since Ed died, all of the deaths she has had in her life have come back to her. She says this like she's surprised and a bit annoyed. I picture her cooking dinner, and in walks the ghost of her mother and she has to yell, 'Mom! Get out of here and quit scaring me!' But as she continues to talk, I realize that she's not talking about ghosts.

For the past two years she feels like she has slipped into a hole and she 'just can't seem to get out.' She is excited for the warm weather because gardening is one of the few things that still brings her joy. Pat lost her husband early on in her life and then her daughter lost her husband at the exact same age that Pat lost hers. Pat also lost her father in 1971. She says she's really been missing him lately.

Fran is a tall, slender woman, probably in her sixties. She is beautiful. Fran's husband, Davis, was diagnosed with pancreatic cancer and died within seven months. He did not suffer and hardly complained throughout his final days at home. At one point, the hospice nurse encouraged him to start morphine, but he said he didn't want any because he didn't want to risk getting addicted. Davis played professional baseball. He played for three different teams, including the Detroit Tigers. Fran still gets mail from people requesting his autograph. She says that drives her crazy.

Bernard sits on the same couch as me. He sounds like he has a German accent. He's a handsome older guy, probably mid-fifties. His wife died in a bike accident on June 18, 2007, the day after Josh's accident. She was wearing a helmet but lost control of her bike and fell into a ravine. She died instantly. Bernard is one of two men in the group. Up until Bernard, all of the women had noted that one of the hardest parts in their initial journey was suddenly having to deal with all of the finances and the maintenance of the house. None of them knew how to file their taxes or fix the furnace or fix anything. Bernard said he obviously didn't have a problem with any of that when his wife died because he was the one who originally took care of everything. Bernard's main problem is that he just retired and he has no idea what to do or who to spend time with. He said his wife would make up their social calendar. She planned their dinner parties and arranged all of their outings with friends. 'I was just a tagalong.' Now he's not quite sure who his friends even are. Bernard has not cooked *anything* in ten months. Every night he goes out and buys something to eat.

Finally, it's my turn. This is the first time, probably in about five months, when I have to tell the whole story to people who don't know me at all. I say, 'My husband Josh' – and then I lose it. That's all I get, those three words. I am the first person in the group to cry. Up until this moment, everyone has spoken in soft voices and no one has gotten out of control with their emotions. But now I cry so hard I can hardly talk. Everyone waits and after a few minutes I try again, 'My husband Josh,' but the same thing happens. I am shocked by this. I haven't cried this hard in a long time in front of other people, let alone strangers. Everyone stares at me. They feel bad for me. I feel bad for me too. I think to myself, *Whose life is this? This is such a sad story*, which only makes me cry harder.

Finally I get it out. But when I start crying really hard and then I try to talk, everything is in this really high voice. Every now and then, in the middle of a sentence, my voice breaks and I start to cry again. Picture a little girl whose older brother has just ripped the legs off of her Barbie doll and she's trying to relay the story to her parents. Every time she gets to the hard part, all of her words run together. ('I was just putting her in the house and then he grabbed her-an'-ripped-her-legs-zoff!) That's me. At one point I say the date, 'June 17.' Bernard looks at me, almost alarmed, and says, 'That was Father's Day.' I nod.

Lynne and Mary direct a few questions at each of us. I am relieved when the spotlight moves somewhere else. Mary asks Debbie a question, which I don't hear because I'm blowing my nose still. Debbie says something to the effect of the unfairness of her husband's death, but then she pauses and looks at me.

'But then I look at this child . . .' She holds her hand out in my direction. She says that my story makes her think about what is 'unfair.'

Usually I get mad when someone references how young I am. 'Babies raising babies!' women say when they see me with Kai. But when Debbie says this, I know she's not patronizing me or trying to make me feel less mature than I am. Just in the way she says it and the look on her face, I know she sees me as too young to experience such a tragedy. She's right. I am too young. But then I look at her and think, *She's too young too.* We're all too young, too busy for our lives to be interrupted by death. All of us, despite our age difference, had a distinct plan that instantly turned to rubble. And we're not here to figure out how to clean up that rubble, or at least I'm not. I guess I'm here just to practice saying my story out loud.

At one point in *The Catcher in the Rye* the reader learns that shortly after Allie died, Holden went into his parents' garage and broke all of the windows with his bare hands. He had severe cuts all up and down his arms and he was covered in blood. The day I left the hospital with Kai, Patty, my amazing nurse, sat down on my bed and told me that I needed to ask people to help me when I needed it. With a very serious expression she said, 'If you think you're going to hurt the baby or yourself, call someone immediately.' I sat there silently. I remember thinking, *Why on earth are you saying a thing like this?* Although I would obviously never hurt Kai, there are these dark times, usually in the middle of the night when I can't get Kai to sleep and I feel the harrowing effect of Josh's absence. At those moments I fully understand why Holden shatters all of that glass. He watched his baby brother die and now his whole life is screwed up forever.

Holden seems to have Picnic, Lightning days all the time. On top of it, he's a teenage boy. I've never had the experience being a teenage boy, but a couple of Christmases ago my brother bought me this book called *Youth in Revolt*. The narrator is a fifteen-year-old boy, so you're basically inside the mind of an adolescent male. It is as if a brain with two hands has been driving the vehicle of a boy's body – at the right speed limit, obeying all traffic orders – and then one day a giant penis comes crashing through the passenger's side window, whips open the driver's side door, and kicks the brain out onto the pavement. After that the body is being driven at 120 miles per hour by a penis. The brain is long gone, never to be seen again. That's my impression of the male mind, body, and soul after reading *Youth in Revolt*. So here's Holden Caulfield in the midst of puberty and grief. No wonder he gets himself into an awkward situation with a prostitute in a sleezy hotel room. The collision of hormones and grief are catastrophic.

That's everybody's problem. All of us are trying to figure out how to operate normally at whatever phase of life we are in, and then grief turns everything inside out. Bernard and his retirement. Debbie and her empty nest. Me and motherhood.

Between my grief group, the April rain, and Holden Caulfield suddenly making a claim on my living room couch, the passing winter doesn't seem to have taken the darkness with it. These wild mood swings are forming a pattern. I walk out of the shadows for a moment, look at the sunshine, and declare that life is grand, then I go back in, shut the door, and cry for a while longer. I think about calling Dr G. again. Then I think, what kind of crazy woman am I if I call my therapist to debrief about my spousal grief group?

In the midst of my blues, I receive an e-mail from Maggie regarding Mathews. Mathews is in

Denver for a two-week hiatus before he starts his new job. Maggie is here in Michigan, but she talked to Mathews on the phone last night and had to report on what transpired.

Last night was Mathews's first night in Colorado. He went out with our friend Becky. In typical Mathews-partying fashion, he strayed away from his group and ended up roaming the streets of Denver at three o'clock in the morning by himself. Around five o'clock eastern standard time, Maggie got a phone call from Mathews. He was trying to call someone to figure out how to get back to Becky's apartment and he ended up calling Maggie, who was in Michigan. He talked to Maggie for about a half hour, relaying every moment of his late-night Denver adventure. At this point in the evening he was very drunk. As all of our friends know, when Mathews hits a certain blood alcohol level his behavior becomes very predictable. Once intoxicated he will start high-fiving random people, he becomes *obsessed* with finding something to eat, and he begins to completely disobey all pedestrian traffic laws.

In her e-mail, Maggie recounts all of the ridiculous things he said to her over and over throughout their conversation:

1. 'Sista!'
2. 'Becks – and by Becks, I mean Mags.'
3. 'I just turned the door handle to Neverland. That's right, sista!'

4. 'I am great with children; but if that baby cries, I will kick the shit out of you!' [referring to the people sitting next to/near him on the plane with a little baby]
5. 'We're in the DANGA ZONE!'
6. 'I'm ponying to the side and urinating on the grass!'
7. 'We don't know if these bushes are going to leap out at me, now, do we?'
8. 'Magrid, I love that you're on this adventure with me!'

I read this e-mail and by the end there are tears in my eyes. I can't remember the last time I laughed this hard. This is why I love Mathews. He seems to appear at just the right moments. Less than one year ago, Mathews lost his best friend in the entire world. Ever since they met in college, Mathews and Josh couldn't move through any phase of life without the other. Josh was the first person Mathews told he was gay. Josh took Mathews ring shopping when he was planning our engagement. Mathews was the first person we told when we found out I was pregnant. I have vivid memories of going to bed early and listening to the murmurs and laughter of those two in the living room. When Josh died, Mathews and I both lost our own version of a soul mate. But over the past ten months, he seems to be the one person who has tried his hardest to live despite his loss.

He is always calling me with entertaining work stories, he listens to my rants about my in-laws, and he stops by not because he pities me but because he really cares about Kai and me. He is a complete gentleman, and at the same time, as Maggie's e-mail confirms, he acts like a complete moron. A totally hilarious moron, who wastes no time in the pity pool.

I am so deeply thankful for Mathews's rich spirit and love of life. He is the only person in this world who can make me laugh when I'm stuck in a Holden Caulfield moment. He lures me out of the shadows, not because he feels sorry for me but because he knows how much more fun it is out there in the sunlight (or moonlight, depending on the occasion), which is exactly what Josh used to do when he was here. I feel like I've lost a lot of my own enthusiasm and vibrance since Josh died, but it is a tremendous relief to know that Mathews hasn't. Someday I'll catch up to him. In the meantime, I say a little prayer to the Gods of Drunk and Disorderly for once again watching over my friend Chris Mathews. They must love that guy.

This Wednesday at the grief group we were all supposed to bring in a picture of our spouse or an item that reminded us of them. Bernard has a photo of his wife and his daughter. Fran brought in an old picture of Davis in his Tigers uniform. Debbie shows us a picture from her family's last vacation to Hawaii. She starts crying a little and says that this was the last vacation she had with her husband. I forgot to bring a picture or an item. I had a picture all picked out and left it at the last minute. I found one we used for Josh's funeral. He's in his wet suit holding his surfboard and the sun is setting behind him. He has long hair. He had the most beautiful long blond hair.

Pat is wearing a bright pink hat and a camouflage army coat. Both belonged to Ed. She says it brings her joy to wear his stuff. She actually gets up and spins around to show us the whole 360 degrees. Pat passes around a picture of Ed. It was taken a while ago, or at least I think so from the brown plaid suit coat he is wearing. Ed is incredibly good looking. He reminds me of Jay Gatsby with dark hair. In the picture, he is looking dapper holding a martini glass, and he's not gazing at the camera but a little off to the side. He's got this smirk on his face. I can tell Ed and Chris Mathews would have a great time together.

As the picture is being passed around, Mary asks Pat some questions about what she and Ed did together, what some of her best memories of him were. It's still not entirely clear what the nature of their friendship was. Pat says, 'Well, he had this plane and we used to fly all over the place together.' Right as she says this, this smile creeps across her face. It's not just any smile. It's not like an 'Oh yeah, that was fun' smile. It is a distinct smile – every woman knows what it means – and suddenly li'l old Pat has transformed into Kim

Cattrall from *Sex and the City* and I know *exactly* what kind of relationship she and Ed had. I love it. I want to take Pat out for a drink and introduce her to my college friends and get her to spill her guts.

After the pictures, Mary and Lynne guide the conversation. They ask us about memories and what it's like going through pictures and clothes, how we treat these relics of our lost loved ones. They ask us about life now. Somehow we get on the topic of food and meals, and Debbie tells us that she doesn't cook anymore. She's found a few frozen meals that are okay. She says this with such a practical tone, like this is a part of the problem that she has actually solved. I feel so sad at the idea of her frozen dinners.

I imagine how Debbie probably used to walk through the grocery store when her husband was alive. She is on her cell phone with her husband talking about what to get. 'How about tilapia? Oh, that's right, you want to do Italian . . . okay, how about I make lasagna . . . Oh, Kroger has a sale on fresh peaches. Honey, can you check to see if we're out of fruit?' Or maybe they went grocery shopping together. But now she stands with her cart in the frozen food aisle debating whether to try Stouffers or Lean Cuisine. The people in the aisle get mad at her because she's in their way or she's taking too long in front of one of the glass doors. No one in the aisle knows what has happened or how this moment of picking between cold boxes for dinner is really her whole life. I don't know why this makes me sad. I want to invite her over for dinner, but I only have smashed carrots and turkey that you could drink through a straw.

In our third grief meeting we get on the topic of daily routines. We talk about what our daily routines used to be like and what they are like now. Bernard says that for the thirty-two years he and his wife were together, she always made the bed in the morning. He never made the bed once throughout their entire marriage. The morning after Marie died, the first morning he woke up without her, he made the bed. He has made the bed every day since she died.

When Bernard says this, I can tell he thinks it's a minor detail. It's not a big deal. To him it's a logical solution – she's not there, so he has to make it. But for some reason this small detail of Bernard's life sticks to me like glue. We talk about a million other things, but all I can think about is Bernard in his bathrobe or flannel pajamas pulling up the comforter. I want to put this in my pocket so that any time I hit a bad patch, I can think of Bernard stacking those pillows trying to make his bed look nice.

Moo called me a few weeks ago and said she signed up to do her first triathlon. She wants me to do it with her. Moo has always been into endurance sports. She has completed two marathons since college. I played soccer in high school and college and I only ran because I had to. When I think about running competitively it makes me want to vomit.

'Absolutely not,' I tell her.

'Nat, it's for a really good cause.' She tells me about this organization called Team in Training. Sure, I've heard of it. I get their promotional flyers in the mail sometimes with those people jogging with big smiles on their faces like that marathon they're running is no big deal. I don't buy it.

'Moo, you know what those people have that I don't? Free time. When would I train for this?'

She tells me that the grandmas would love it if they had one or two nights a week when I left to go train and they stayed with Kai. Not to mention Auntie Ashley is always around. I am still cynical.

'I don't own a bike.'

'You can borrow someone's.'

'I have never swum more than ten feet in my life.' This is actually a lie. I swam one year in the seventh grade for my middle school swim team. I had to swim the 200-meter because I wasn't fast enough to be in any of the sprints and I wasn't strong enough to do any distance farther than 200 meters. The night before the first meet I sat in my room and contemplated ways to break my foot. I ended up swimming the next day. (I didn't have the guts to actually break my foot). It was a horrible experience. I remember overhearing one of the seventh-grade boys making fun of how slowly I went. I never swam competitively again.

'You would practice.' She tells me to go to a Team in Training meeting and to think about it. I roll my eyes. We hang up.

After Moo calls me, I don't talk to anyone else about the triathlon. I think about it. I think of a list of reasons why I shouldn't do it: (1) Child care. (2) I do not enjoy running, swimming, or biking. (That seems like a really good reason.) (3) I look absolutely ridiculous in a swim cap. Yes, it is for a wonderful cause, but is clearly not the best time in my life to take on an Olympic distance triathlon. I'll let my childless, significantly more athletic sister do it instead.

It's the last Wednesday in April and the last meeting of my grief group. I think about how this group has helped. Maybe *help* isn't the right word. But I have to admit, there is something so oddly comforting in knowing that I am not the only human who wants desperately to talk to thin air, wear clothes that don't fit, and feels like the world is moving on without me. I am happy I decided to join the group. Maybe *happy* isn't the right word either. Maybe it is.

At the conclusion of the meeting Lynne says, 'I have one final question for all of you.' I sit there, expecting some female-ministerish question like 'How did this group make you feel?' or 'What did you learn about yourself?' I start to concoct my answer before she asks the question.

271

She looks over her clipboard and says, 'What are you going to do next?' I can tell from the rest of the group that we all think this is a wildly unfair question. I exhale through my mouth and contemplate. Next? What does she mean, next? I'm going to continue to do what I've been doing: go from feeling horribly sad and frustrated to joyous about my son and keep my fingers crossed that one day the former will no longer outweigh the latter. But what am I going to *do next?* I haven't got a clue.

Fran starts by saying that she is going to continue to go to other grief support groups. Beaumont Hospital offers several support groups. There is usually a speaker and then you move into break-out groups to discuss the topic. Fran pulls out a few pink sheets of paper and says she brought the information with her for anyone else who may be interested. She hands one to me. This is really nice of her, but it sort of feels like when someone gets you a gift certificate to get your eyebrows waxed. It is a kind gesture, but really they are saying, 'You really need some help.'

Bernard says he's been really good about going to church and he feels like his next step is to reconnect with people around him, his neighbors and old friends. Pat says she is going to start taking walks with a friend of hers. She needs to get out and enjoy the spring and she knows she wants to do something with someone else.

'What about you, Natalie? Where are you going to go from here?' I look up for a second. I think about what I am about to say and how much I don't want to say it, but I have to. Maybe not even for me, but for everyone else in the room.

'I'm going to train for an Olympic distance triathlon.' The whole room suddenly perks up. Bernard looks over at me. Even though we sit next to each other, we don't make a lot of eye contact during the meetings, but now he looks right at me. 'Good for you,' he says. Everyone else is nodding, smiling. I think about how I have never seen Maureen's teeth until right now. The room is buzzing with excitement. Jack wants to tell me all about his granddaughter who runs marathons and how much she loves them. They ask how I decided to do this, who I will train with, when I will start. I explain that it will raise money for cancer patients and their families. Debbie clutches her tissue to her heart and says, 'That is so wonderful.' They all want to donate money. They all want to write a check right now.

After the meeting Kai and I go home. While Kai is asleep, I go into my bedroom to put away the box I opened to find a picture of Josh to take to the meeting two weeks ago. I put back the picture of Josh in his wet suit. In the same box are two books Josh gave me years ago. When Josh and I first started dating, I was a senior in college and he had just graduated. At the start of my second semester, I had to go back to school and Josh moved out west for a few months. We knew we'd stay together; he just wanted to get some surfing in before getting a real job. When he left he gave me these two books to read. I look at their worn-out title pages. One is called *Zen and the Art of Motorcycle Maintenance* and the other is *The Gospel of the Redman. The Gospel of the Redman* is a book of Native American prayers and sayings. I have no idea where he got it. Even before we started dating I knew Josh was not a religious person. He was a chemistry major, and he answered questions with science. *The Gospel of the Redman* is the only thing I've ever seen him read that had any connection to a God, higher power, or spiritual world. But even the word *spiritual* would freak him out.

I go through *The Gospel of the Redman*, just to see what it says. I've never read it. You'd think I would considering he gave it to me, but I never have. I go through it sort of looking for a secret message from Josh. I did this with his philosophy books from college a few months ago. His favorite philosophy book was called *21 Questions*. It's all marked up in his writing and notable passages are highlighted. I went through it page by page, reading his notes, hoping he left me some sort of message about how to deal with death. I didn't find anything. It seems a little silly now, like I should've called Nancy the nurse to see if she wanted to get out the Ouija board and Josh's books and give it the old college try.

I find the section on death in *The Gospel of the Redman*. This is from a part called 'The Soul of the Redman: Death Songs.'

> *I care not where my body lies,*
> *My soul goes marching on.*
> *I care not where my body lies,*
> *My soul goes marching on.*

This is Josh. This was written for him. He isn't in a cemetery.

MAY

Stopping by Woods on a Snowy Evening, Robert Frost

Whose woods these are I think I know.
His house is in the village though;
He will not see me stopping here
To watch his woods fill up with snow.

My little horse must think it queer
To stop without a farmhouse near
Between the woods and frozen lake
The darkest evening of the year.

He gives his harness bells a shake
To ask if there is some mistake.
The only other sound's the sweep
Of easy wind and downy flake.

The woods are lovely, dark and deep.
But I have promises to keep,
And miles to go before I sleep,
And miles to go before I sleep.

Wedding season is quickly approaching. Toby and Nikki are getting married this May. Angela, my friend from college, is getting married over the July Fourth weekend – I am a bridesmaid. Terrah and her fiancé, Andy, get married in August – I am a bridesmaid. Three weddings may not seem like a lot, but for women it's not just the wedding. Nikki's shower is next week. Angela has already sent us a slew of e-mails regarding dresses, shoes, jewelry, makeup, hair, and fitting deadlines. Not to mention two bachelorette parties and two showers this spring. I am so sick of all of this that when Terrah calls me to see when I can go in for a fitting for her bridesmaid's dress I say, 'Can you just order me an eight? I'll write you a check.'

I know this is a hugely insensitive gesture considering she is the bride and I am a bridesmaid and I'm supposed to be doing everything for her, but I can't do it. I can't arrange for a babysitter to go get fitted for a dress that I'm going to wear for five minutes. I know weddings are supposed to be joyous celebrations and I really try to be happy. But part of me can't help but feel like that demographic broke up with me eight months ago.

Toby and Nikki want Kai to be a part of their wedding ceremony. Toby requests that I bring Kai to the ceremony so Claire, the maid of honor, can walk down the aisle with him and so we can get a picture of him with all the groomsmen. I am annoyed by this. I feel like Toby and Nikki are using Kai as some sort of ornament or decoration. In addition to this, I have to go to Carter's to get Kai a new outfit for the wedding.

'Well, the wedding colors are purple and black,' Nikki tells me over the phone. 'So if you could get something that matched, that would be great.'

First of all, *wedding colors* is pretty much the dumbest phrase I've ever heard. You might as well make up a wedding fight song while you're at it. Why don't you just hire some wedding cheerleaders who can get uniforms in your wedding colors? Second of all, chances are there aren't going to be any baby clothes for boys in purple and there aren't going to be any baby clothes at all in black. I vent all of this to Mathews. He says maybe I should see it as a nice gesture that they want Kai in the wedding. He asks me if they didn't invite Kai to be in the wedding, would I be annoyed at that too? I tell him his positive attitude is what is annoying.

I realize I am being incredibly grumpy about this wedding, and I know why. Most obviously, Toby is one of Josh's best friends. Josh would have been one of the groomsmen. He may have been the best man. I know that's the only thing I'll be able to think about during the ceremony.

But the other part is the dancing. Right after Josh died, I had a hard time even listening to music. I couldn't turn on the radio in the car for a while. At my brother's wedding, I realized how much music and dancing bothered me. I couldn't even watch other people dance. At Christmas when my brother and his wife, Ellie, came home we looked at pictures of them dancing together. I felt so guilty that I had missed it, but at the time I couldn't even be in the same building as people who were dancing. Every wedding after that I would sit at a table and pretend not to notice that everyone was dancing except me. I haven't been to a wedding since August, so I don't know if I can dance or not.

After Battersby lost her mom, I was always so stunned by her dad's gracefulness in accepting his widowerhood. Now that I am a widow, I think about Mr Battersby a lot. I know he thinks about me. This past December, three and a half years after her mom died, Battersby's cousin Colin got married. The day after Colin's wedding she came over to tell me all about the wedding. She said it was beautiful and a lot of fun. But the best story was about her dad.

Battersby reported that Mr B. danced like he was paid entertainment. At one point in the night the deejay played the song 'It's Getting Hot in Here.' As most teenagers know, in this song the singer informs the listeners that 'it's getting hot in here,' and you should 'take off all your clothes.' It needs to be noted that as long as I have been a friend of Katie's (since the sixth grade), we have all seen Mr Battersby as iconic. He is a lot like my dad in the sense that he is a solid, real man who keeps promises to his children and shows more than he tells. But in addition to that, he has always been a gentleman who demonstrates respectful, dignified behavior. If I was over at Katie's house in high school and the song 'It's Getting Hot in Here' came through her stereo, he would have walked in and said with his glasses pulled down slightly on his nose, 'You know, ladies, I really don't think these lyrics are appropriate. Kathleen, why don't you go ahead and turn that down.'

As Katie explained to me, however, Mr Battersby was a different man at Colin's wedding. She said that even before the song came on, he was whipping out dance moves that had some strong similarities to aerobic video workouts circa 1985. Katie started demonstrating by pulling her right knee to her opposite elbow, then the left knee to the right elbow. 'But then,' she went on to say, 'it got even worse.' 'It's Getting Hot in Here' came blaring through the speakers, and to the shock and awe of his three daughters and the rest of his extended family, he started to take off his tie. Not just take it off, like stand there and fumble with it a little, like take it *off*. After getting his tie off, he whipped it around his head and threw it out onto the dance floor. 'And then,' she paused for dramatic effect, 'he started to unbutton his shirt.' At this point, we were both laughing hysterically at the thought of Katie's dad doing an unrhythmic strip tease to a rap song. It would be like if you saw Santa Claus giving someone a lap dance. Totally unexpected and totally hilarious. For the rest of the night, Claire, Katie's little sister, strutted around the reception with her dad's tie loosely knotted around her neck.

I know Katie thought her dad's behavior was hilarious, but I could tell by the way she told the story that there was an overwhelming current of pride surging through her words. And the fact that Claire wore his tie around like a trophy only confirmed that his daughters were most certainly not embarrassed by their father, but ecstatic at his display of utter happiness.

Katie's mom died the summer after we graduated from college. Katie's older sister, Margaret, lived and worked in Chicago at the time and Claire was still in school at Michigan State. Katie decided to move back home and live with her dad for a while. I know it wasn't part of her plan – she had always thought she would end up in Chicago with Margaret. Obviously, she never made a big deal out of it. She just knew she didn't want him in a big house all alone quite yet. Although she has never told me about it, I'm sure she saw her dad up close and personal with the demon of grief. Now that I'm a widow, I understand that this is a long, hard road, and sometimes – most times – it really feels like I'm going nowhere. But when I heard about Mr Battersby dancing at Colin's wedding, I laughed and smiled because it was funny, but I also laughed and smiled because he is able to dance again. And not just dance. He is able to steal the show.

One of the hardest things about grief is that there is no accurate measure of how you are actually doing other than how much time has passed. I count months obviously. I've met people that count days, but that doesn't really tell us anything other than how much time has elapsed. So we look for little signals. We wait for times when we laugh from the gut, or for some people maybe it's falling asleep easily or getting an appetite back. But sometimes it can be hard to find those signs of life. For me, dancing is one of the few accurate barometers. It doesn't mean Mr Battersby is healed, but it does mean that he's not where he used to be. I am nervous that I will go to Toby's wedding and it will be my brother's wedding all over again. I'll have to run out and get in my car and drive home crying at eight o'clock.

There is one glimmer of hope. I've had a lot of practice dancing with Kai. At first I would just do squats while holding him. I think that's how I lost a lot of my baby weight. I would sweat in my bathrobe from repeatedly squatting with a fifteen-pound baby. Then the squatting got a little boring so it turned into dancing. Instead of just the down and up motion, we'd do down, up, right kick, down, up, left kick. Then all of the sudden we were adding side steps, hip swings, pliés, samba steps, and it grew from there. I think it's a little ironic that dancing was the one thing I couldn't do after Josh died and then after Kai was born it was the one thing he wanted. I pictured Josh whispering into

Kai's little ear while he slept in the hospital bassinet, 'Make sure she dances again.'

We dance all the time now in our pajamas or when I'm in my bathrobe. If I need to cook or clean while he is in his jumper I'll turn on the music and dance around the room to keep him entertained while I chop vegetables or clean up the house. He sees me jumping around and then he starts kicking his legs like crazy. At my parents' house, one of my favorite things to do after work is put him in the jumper next to their computer and turn on 'Shoot to Thrill' by AC/DC. He hears the opening chords and starts to laugh hysterically and jump and waits for me. I dance the whole time, or I try to. 'Shoot to Thrill' is a long song, so by the guitar solo sometimes I have to lie down and catch my breath.

My parents, like many people in this country, have been totally caught up in the recent *Dancing with the Stars* season-six fever. My mom calls me on random Monday nights and says, 'Did you see Marlee Matlin? She really is amazing.' So now when Kai and I dance, we obviously hear the announcer, 'Ladies and gentlemen, dancing their final routine, Natalie and Kai Taylor.'

Of course Kai and I have made it to the finals of *Dancing with the Baby Stars*. It is 11:26 a.m. Bottle, check. Nap, check. We are on. He starts off in the jumper in the doorway, looking nonchalant. I freeze in the middle of the living room. I unfreeze to press play on the iPod. I freeze quickly

283

again and unfreeze when the opening vocals start for 'Footloose.' An obvious choice for a final routine. I kick my legs and start whirling my hair. I am channeling Sarah Jessica Parker's performance from *Girls Just Want to Have Fun*. Kai laughs and starts jumping. I hit a combination of moves inspired by my aerobic videos (circa 2006) and a line dance my friend Trisha taught me in high school (circa 1998). The chorus kicks in. I start shaking my hips. Kai throws a smile to the audience. I grab him out of the jumper, a flawless lift. Eat that, Carrie Ann Inaba.

We are on fire. I put him on my hip, we do a little samba. Then we move into a modified tango. I go for a big dip, Kai squeals. Our technical points are spot on. I can see Len beaming out of the corner of my eye. I spin Kai and then I throw him in the air. Another spin, another throw. Then we're on the ground. I lift Kai. Superman meets a rhythmic shoulder press. Our energy is amazing. We're back on our feet, ready for our grand finale. I swing him in between my legs, bring him back up, give him a throw in the air, and grab him, and we land on the couch right as the music ends. The audience is immediately on their feet. Bruno Toniolo is out of his chair. He's throwing his arms everywhere. After Tom Bergeron gets everyone settled down, which takes a while, we stand ready for our remarks. Bruno goes first.

'Kai,' he says with this serious face. He has to pause because the audience again erupts from the mention of his name. 'Kai, you are magical. Magical! You are what makes this show.' He slams his hand down on the judges' table as he says this. 'Stupendous! Magical and stupendous!'

Carrie Ann is next. 'You know, I never know what to expect from you two.' The audience is on bated breath. Sometimes Carrie Ann does the overcritical thing just to prove she's tough, so you never know with her. She starts in again, 'But *that* was amazing.' They go nuts. 'Kai, your charisma can't be matched.' He smiles and kicks his legs. 'And Natalie, you are really improving. Your lifts were great. Your energy is up. And I'm so happy to see you took our advice and wore a bra for this week's performance.'

Len's turn. Always the toughest judge. He sits stoically for a moment. The audience quiets down. Finally he says in his British accent, 'Oi'm spea-chlus.' The audience goes crazy. He shakes his head. 'Oi'm spea-chlus.' There are tears in his eyes. He stands up and applauds us again.

We bow. Kai blows kisses. I carry him off the stage. We get back to the dressing room to catch our breaths before we do our interview with Samantha Harris. And then we'll leave for the wedding.

My mom comes with me to the ceremony. We drive separately so she can take Kai home after the wedding and I can go to the reception. Kai looks adorable.

At the ceremony, Father Jerry takes a moment

to talk about Kai and Josh, about how amazing Josh was and how even though Josh isn't there he is still a part of this special day. I start to cry when he says this. But I don't cry like I did at Ads's wedding. At Ads's wedding, I was hysterical. But at Toby and Nikki's wedding, I just sit there and let my eyes fill up with tears. I don't have a tissue, but I don't want one. I can feel everyone staring at me and I don't care. I want everyone to see those tears sitting on my face. I want everyone to see me not being hysterical but being appreciative of the words spoken about Josh. I don't bow my head and pray with everyone else throughout the ceremony. I just sit and look out at the windows at the light shining in on the altar. We take a lot of time to thank God for things and we take a lot of time to ask God for things, and I don't know how much of it I invest myself in. Sitting in my pew, I am in no mood to bow my head to anyone. But I do cry for Josh.

After the ceremony I see Deedee, Chris (he flew in for the wedding), and Ashley. They sat a few rows back. I can tell the ceremony was hard for them. All of them have red faces and their eyes are swollen from tears. I hug them, but I feel myself pulling away quickly. I can hear people around me talking excitedly about how beautiful the ceremony was, how great Nikki looked in her dress. I don't want to stand here and talk about how sad we are and how nice those words were about Josh. I heard the speech. I cried by myself

286

and took my moment. Now I want to be happy for my friends. I am not in the mood to be sad. I am so fucking tired of going to happy events and being sad. *I'm over this*, I think to myself. I'm not over Josh and I'm not over remembering and loving Josh, but I am over sitting at a table, watching all of the people dance around, and thinking about how much my life sucks. I'm over that. I'm over crying hysterically (at least for the moment). I'm over giving people long, emotional hugs and listening to people say, 'It's going to be all right.' I'm over it. Tonight is the first time I find myself thinking this.

After handing Kai off to my mom and hugging Deedee, Chris, and Ashley, I immediately find Mathews. We have about an hour and a half before the reception starts.

'Bar?' he asks.

'You know it.'

I order a vodka tonic.

My FMG orders a dirty martini.

At the reception during the toasts, Toby takes a moment to talk about Josh and I start to tear up again. I used to really hate weddings or dinners or just people in general who thought they knew what to say on joyous occasions about Josh. I was anxious about what Toby was going to say, and before he started speaking, I wished I were in the bathroom. But what he says is the best thing anyone has ever said about Josh. Toby says that Josh isn't here, but he should be. And if he were here, he would be the 'biggest clown' on the dance floor, which is completely accurate. He goes on to say that Josh would want all of us to dance and have a great time. He actually says it a lot better than that but that's the point he gets across. Then he asks us to bow our heads for a moment of silence for Josh. I don't bow my head. I don't feel like it. I sit there with my nose high in the air, taking my own haughty moment of silence. I am so proud and so relieved that Toby said what he had said. Finally someone had given me permission to dance. Someone has told me that I didn't need to sit slouched over at my empty table while all my friends get drunk and party.

I dance to almost every song they play. I dance, I point, and I throw my hair around and hustle and twist and shout and everything else. It is one of the most liberating acts I have taken in a very long time. Everyone has a great time. Maggie has her Wedding Date Cleavage out. Terrah, who has probably clocked sixty hours this week alone at the bank, dances to rap music. All of Josh's friends are here. Alex flew in from California. Marcus and Megan have been here for almost a week. The last time I saw most of these people was at Josh's funeral. It feels so nice to see them at Toby's wedding.

Back at school, the poetry unit continues in my ninth-grade class. We have the Robert Frost poem 'Stopping by Woods on a Snowy Evening' on the overhead projector. We are using the poem to talk about rhyme scheme. In the midst of labeling the AABA pattern, we start talking about the poem itself.

'It's about suicide!' Krystal with a *K* yells from the back of the room. This sometimes happens with students when one teacher, one parent, or one peer tells them one random detail about a piece of literature (or poetry in this case) and that's all they ever remember. Usually the detail doesn't do much when it's remembered in total isolation from the rest of the text. 'I heard Simon is Jesus!' they say about the small quiet boy in *Lord of the Flies*. 'Gene [from *A Separate Peace*] is gay!' 'Holden steps on the peanuts because he's given up on man!' (What? This one never makes any sense to me.)

The speaker in 'Stopping by Woods on a Snowy Evening' finds himself at a deserted barn on a dark, snowy night. It's actually the 'darkest evening of the year.' He contemplates staying, and he almost does, but then decides to move on. So I can see where some people think it's about a guy thinking about suicide. He thinks about staying in the darkness. He even admits there would be something comforting about it, but then he decides he needs to keep going. For me, when I read this poem this year (which is probably the twentieth time I've read the poem), I conclude that I connect with this poem more than any other poem in the world. For the last year, I feel like I've been in dark, cold, desolate, snowy woods. And now, as the one-year mark of Josh's death looms, I'm starting to realize that I don't have to stay here all of my life. At Toby's wedding, when I was dancing to 'Thunderstruck' and 'The Love You Save,' that was the sign of the coming light and warmth. The last four lines of Frost's poem read, 'The woods are snowy, dark and deep. / But I have promises to keep, / And miles to go before I sleep, / and miles to go before I sleep.' Sometimes I find myself thinking about these lines, or I find myself humming them under my breath. I could stay here. I could walk with grief by my side for the rest of my life. And like the snowy woods, having grief as a companion isn't necessarily a sad or tragic thing. There is something comforting about having grief loom around day after day. It can be lovely because the grief is also a testament to how much I love Josh. I never want to get rid of that pain.

But I can't stay here forever. I can't raise a son while looming in darkness and I can't pretend to be truly happy for the rest of my life. I have miles to go before I sleep. And in one month, after I have a very sad day, a day that includes a lot of long hugs, tears, and sad faces and swollen eyes, after that day, maybe not right after, but sometime after that day, I am going to get on my horse and walk out of these snowy, dark woods. I have miles to go before I sleep.

Mother's Day comes around and everyone is scheduled to go to breakfast at this nice place about a mile from my parents' house. At the last minute my mom and I decide to walk to breakfast with Kai in the stroller. We take an umbrella in case it rains; the clouds are being a little ominous. A few minutes into the walk a light drizzle starts. We consider turning back and getting the car but decide against it. Halfway there it really starts to pour. There we are clomping along in our open-toed shoes, both crouched under one umbrella that is being held over the stroller and trying to entertain Kai all at the same time.

My FMG walks behind us. She is wearing a knee-length cotton skirt that has clearly not been ironed, running shoes, and the one T-shirt she owns without any juice stains on it. It's a faded navy blue V-neck she bought from The Gap six years ago. 'I keep it for special occasions,' she says.

We are almost there. Our rear ends and the backs of our calves are soaked. The umbrella couldn't quite cover them. Deedee drives by us. 'Wanna ride?' she yells from the car. We refuse. We've made it this far. Ashley drives by. 'What are you doing? Why didn't you drive?' she shouts from the window. We wave her by.

Finally we make it. We think we are hilarious. How emblematic that our Mother's Day celebration consists of us hovering over the baby in the pouring rain, walking a mile in the cold while everyone else drives by.

I surprise myself. I have a lovely day. I don't spend

a lot of time thinking about Josh's absence. I spend time with my mom. Our walk in the rain with Kai was the most imperfectly perfect celebration I could have asked for. I spend time by myself. Kai takes a long afternoon nap. It rains the whole time he sleeps. I don't sit and cry. I think this is the first holiday since Josh died where I haven't cried.

The reality TV show *The Bachelorette* has started its fifth season. As much as I like books and literature, sometimes I can't resist a good train wreck of a reality TV show. I hate the fact that I am intrigued by this show, but I am.

The Bachelor/Bachelorette series is a show where they take one single guy *(The Bachelor)* or one single girl (*The Bachelorette*) and put them with twenty-five singles of the opposite sex. We (the audience) watch as the women (or men in this season's case) battle it out for attention and approval of the one network-deemed stud or studette. The show is ridiculously unrealistic.

Clearly these people are living in an isolated environment and are unable to receive calls from their mothers or friends who would surely say, 'What in God's name do you think you're doing making out, getting drunk, and crying in front of television cameras?' *The Bachelor*, with one guy and twenty-five single women, is obviously way more dramatic. Girls yell at each other, cry all the time, and after they get kicked off the show, most of them say something to the confessional camera like 'I just don't understand why I wasn't good enough for him.' And I always want to yell, 'Good enough for whom? The random guy that ABC picked up in the middle of a mall, threw a suit on, and gave his job some flashy name like 'entrepreneur'? I got news for you, sister, that joker doesn't even own those nice clothes, he can't afford that trip to Fiji, and 'entrepreneur' is just some fancy name they give to people who are unemployed because they got fired from being a sales clerk at Men's Wearhouse.' I don't know what prompts these people to be on this show. Whenever I see previews for a new season of *The Bachelor*, I always see all those pretty girls and think, 'You don't have to do this to yourself.' But it doesn't get me thinking about dating.

I know I was only married for a year and a half, but I think it gave me a tremendous amount of insight on what marriage and a relationship is really all about. Now that weddings and marriages are more a spectator sport for me, I watch as other people go in with a very idealistic mind-set and then I listen to the women call in to Dr Joy and talk about how things just aren't what they used to be. In addition to all of this, being a single mom has enlightened me to what really matters in life and what I would want out of a partner if I ever decided to do it again.

I think about all of this when I watch *The Bachelorette*. This show is hilarious to me because none of the women and men actually ever talk about anything. They just look at each other a lot, make out, and every now and then they say something that would make for a good commercial. So it's basically about good looks and 'having fun.' I was married for a year, and although I loved every moment of it, I know enough to know that these superficial conversations aren't enough to determine anything. With my knowledge of the reality of marriage and the demands of life, I think I would make an amazing bachelorette. Maybe they would call my show *The Widowette*.

Instead of asking, 'Okay, what's your idea of a perfect date?' I would ask, 'Is your definition of washing the dishes (A) washing and putting the dishes away or (B) taking the pots and pans and dumping soap all over them and then 'letting them soak' so that I have to clean the pots and pans at six o'clock the next morning when I get up for work?'

In addition to condescending questions, I'd also insist that the entire show be filmed here, in Michigan, in the middle of February when the days are gray and bleak and snowy and no one has a tan. The first guy to wake up early and scrape the ice off of my car and shovel the driveway gets a rose. And he doesn't get a rose for shoveling the driveway like a ten-year-old. He needs to make clean, clear lines, and no, we don't use the front walkway, but he still has to shovel it for the mailman. These are the challenges in my life, in any real life, that a man would have to meet. It would be brutal.

'Dates' would first consist of a strict interview process. I would sit and ask suitor number one a series of questions, and if any one, any *one*, of his answers does not fit what I want, there will be no second date, no suspenseful rose ceremony. I may even leave before the food arrives, and by food I mean the Primo's pizza that I ordered because we'd be sitting in my messy living room. The point is that it is simply not worth my time to pursue anything less than perfection. (The second part of the date would consist of a game of Scrabble.) I would have twenty important questions.

1. Do you have any experience in household chores such as emptying the dishwasher, folding laundry, and running a vacuum cleaner?
2. Are you willing to spend every Fourth of July in northern Michigan? Never, for the next eighteen years, will my son or I be anywhere except northern Michigan on the Fourth of July. If you have another Fourth of July location, tell me now. Personally, I don't care if it's the goddamn Hamptons, we're not going.
3. Do you read? If so, name the last five books you have read.
4. Do you listen to talk radio? If so, name your three favorite talk radio programs.
5. Are you a competent driver? (Actually,

this does not even have to be a question, but I absolutely will not be with someone who does not demonstrate impeccable driving skills. Anything subpar and they will be eliminated immediately.)

6. Are you okay with the fact that every Christmas will be spent with my family? If this is unacceptable to you or your family, speak now. Your family needs to be aware that I want nothing to do with them on major holidays. I have enough families and enough major holidays.

7. Do you play Scrabble? What is the highest score you have ever earned in Scrabble?

8. Do you play any stupid fucking video games? If so, how many hours a week, on average, do you dedicate to stupid fucking video games? (The follow-up to this question addresses YouTube videos.)

9. Identify three goals you have for yourself, both personal and professional, that you would like to accomplish in the next five years. If you do not have any personal or professional goals, please tell me now.

10. What time do you wake up on Saturday morning?

11. Do you like to try new foods?

12. Do you have any stupid friends? Identify one activity that you and your friends do for fun. Would you call that activity stupid or would you call it fun?
13. In five years, would you be willing to move to a community in Berkley, Michigan, and raise my child in the Berkley School District?
14. Do you have any financial debt? If so, how much?
15. How long has it been since you lived with your mother?
16. Speaking of mothers, tell me about yours. On a scale of one to ten in the category of 'overbearing,' where does she rank?
17. Can you throw a good punch?
18. Do you have a problem saying 'I'm sorry'?
19. Do you have a problem saying 'You were right all along'?
20. How would you describe your level of physical fitness?

If *any* derogatory language is used during the interview (fag, homo, etc.), the date will be terminated immediately. Also, there should be no swearing on the part of the suitor. I can swear, but he can't. The suitor must also demonstrate an above-average command of the English language. Any discrepancies in the area of subject-verb agreement, proper verb tense, using adjectives in place of adverbs, and so on will be noted. A double negative will also result in immediate termination of the date.

Also, during the interview, the candidate will be evaluated on character. Internally I will ask myself the following questions about the candidate. He will have no knowledge of the fact that he is being evaluated on the following criteria.

1. Are you a funny person? Have you made me laugh at all?
2. Would I describe you as stupid-funny or witty-funny?
3. Are you polite to the pizza delivery guy?
4. If it takes a while for the food to come, do you get antsy?
5. Do you make good eye contact?
6. At some point in the date, have you made some sort of effort to tell me that I look absolutely fantastic?
7. When given the opportunity, do you talk about yourself, or do you ask me questions about me?
8. When I tell you things about me, do you somehow reaffirm that I am the coolest fucking person on the face of the planet?
9. Do you talk with food in your mouth?
10. Do you seem intrigued about who I am and what I offer?

11. Do you seem like you would impress
    my grandparents?

Of course, Chris Harrison would be there to
help me along with this process. He'd be the calm,
guiding force, just as he is on the actual show.
More important, he could be our scorekeeper for
Scrabble.

I wish I could call this girl on *The Bachelorette*
and give her some advice. My FMG could give
her advice too. My Fairy Mom Godmother and
I are sitting on the couch in the basement. We
both are wearing our bathrobes, drinking a beer,
watching the show. 'Pick the guy who talks the
least but offers to clean up after other people,' she
says. 'He's a keeper.' She is *such* a genius.

Moo calls again and tells me she officially has
a Team in Training website for fund-raising. She
asks me when I am going to start mine. I neglect
to tell her that I promised a group of old people
that I would take on this triathlon as my banner
cause. I have rethought this decision since my last
grief group. I was embraced by the moment, I
made an irrational decision, and they'll never
know if I don't end up doing it. Moo puts the
heat on me. I get her off the phone by promising
I'll at least donate twenty dollars to her triathlon.

Here's the thing about my older sister: All my
life I've wanted to do everything she did. I tried
to pal around with her friends when we were little.
I was thrilled when my dad said I was old enough

to join the father-daughter group called Indian Princesses with her and my dad. In middle school I loved it when a teacher would see my name on her sheet at the beginning of the school year and say, 'Oh, you must be Sarah's sister.' When I had to make the crucial decision on whether to wear my backpack to middle school with both straps affixed to my shoulders or go for the one-strap look, I obviously consulted my older sister. I constantly stole her clothes in high school even though we went to the same high school. Sometimes she would have to leave early for school and I'd go running into her closet or her laundry basket looking for a cool shirt. She would find me in the hallways (I was a bad thief, as most ninth-graders are) and say something like, 'What the *hell* do you think you're wearing?' I would mutter something about finding it in the basement by the washing machine and I didn't know it was hers, but all the while my main concern was making sure my friends and classmates could see me getting yelled at by my cooler older sister. Even in college my mom would call me and say, 'What do you want for Christmas?' I would tell her to take Moo shopping and let her pick out clothes she liked and then just buy them for me.

Moo has always been a person I want to be like. Even into adulthood the clothing just changes into another thing that she does or wears more grace-fully than I could ever pull off. So when she calls me and tells me to think about something, I take her very, very seriously, but that still doesn't make me want to do a freaking triathlon. I meet her halfway and sign up for a meeting.

I recruit Maggie to go to the meeting with me. Maggie thinks of Moo in much the same light I do. We may only be friends so Maggie can be closer to Moo, which is fine by me. I'm 90 percent sure that's the only reason I had any boyfriends in high school. Maggie is also a marathon runner. She's done two in the last few years, so this is right up her alley.

We find a Team in Training meeting at a local high school. On the way to the meeting I give Maggie a long lecture in the car about how we are *not* going to make a snap decision. We are not going to be the victims of efficient, manipulative (though it may be for a good cause) marketing. We are going to go to the meeting and think about it and not sign our lives away on the spot and then maybe, *maybe*, we will actually commit to doing this thing.

We walk in a little late. Maggie and I have to sit on opposite sides of the room. (In retrospect, this was clearly a well-constructed marketing tactic on their part. I swear this thing is run by the same people who operate Mary Kay cosmetics.) They hand us a pile of information. Maggie, Moo, and I would be potentially competing in the Nation's Triathlon. The Nation's Triathlon is the weekend of September 15 in Washington, D.C. It is an Olympic distance triathlon. Olympic distance means it's a 1.5-kilometer swim (just under a mile), a 40-kilometer bike ride (roughly 26 miles), and a 10-kilometer run (6.2 miles). There is no way I can do this. If I ever swam a mile, I would have to take a three-hour nap afterward. Who in their right mind could get out of the water and bike, then run? Insane. I try to get Maggie's attention to signal that this is a 'no go.' She is engrossed in her literature on the opposite side of the room.

In addition to all of this, all members of the Nation's Triathlon Team have to raise a minimum of thirty-nine hundred dollars. If you fall short of that amount, you have to pay the difference out of your own pocket. Where on earth would I find the time to train, let alone time to fund-raise? Forget it. This is way more of a commitment than I thought. I look over at Maggie again. She is circling things on her sheet. She can't be seriously considering this.

A woman in a white Team in Training shirt opens the meeting. She introduces herself, tells us about the organization, and then introduces the first speaker. Bruce did a marathon in Vancouver with TNT (that's their acronym). He is a tall, slender guy who looks like his body may be prone to marathons. Bruce tells us this was his first marathon. He's never been a runner. He just followed the workouts, ran with the group a few nights a week, and met some great people. He trained with one woman who was a single mom of three kids. He said it was amazing to watch her. She was able to do it because she made time for it in her life, because she cared about the cause and achieving her goal.

I look back down at my sheet and read over the numbers again. If this woman could do a marathon with three kids, why couldn't I do a triathlon with one kid?

After two more speakers, they start a movie. It's this nice video with inspirational music and clips of people clapping and cheering and running out of the water in wet suits, the usual. Then they start talking about honored heroes and patients affected by the money raised. They show a clip of a little girl, probably younger than five years old, who has leukemia. I put my forefinger under my nose because I can feel myself start to tense up. One time I heard that putting your forefinger under your nose will keep you from crying, but then I remember that maybe it prevents you from sneezing. So I start to get tense and I hold my body in the same position to try to keep myself from getting upset. It suddenly occurs to me that not every child is born completely healthy or stays completely healthy. I am sure I knew this before in some capacity, but Kai is so perfect in every way, I can never imagine having to go to the doctor for anything except checkups and immunization shots. I look at this little girl who may not survive because she has cancer. I lost my husband almost a year ago and I thought I had the worst situation in the world. I don't.

The lights go back on. The woman running the meeting says something about an initial payment of sixty dollars to activate your fund-raising website and to register you with a team. Before she even finishes, I am vigorously writing out a check. I don't even own a bike.

I call Moo. She is excited we are all training together, even though she's fifteen hundred miles away.

After worrying about a bike, I remember that Josh's old touring bike has been sitting in the basement, upside down, collecting dust for eleven months. I go downstairs to find the bike. I get a towel to wipe off the dust. He would be so sad to know a bike of his ever collected dust.

I've found my horse with harness bells. I guess it's time to get moving.

JUNE

Changed, I headed back through the mud.
I was drenched; anybody could see it was
time to come in out of the rain.
　　　—GENE FORRESTER IN JOHN KNOWLES,
　　　　　　　　　　　A SEPARATE PEACE

Triathlon training is a bit more challenging than I thought. First of all, I was under the impression that swimming freestyle was similar to walking in that it was a natural, automatic combination of movements for the body. I thought I would jump in the water, throw my arms one in front of the other, and I'd be off. Turns out this is hardly the case. I had a similar experience when I decided to summit a fourteen-thousand-foot mountain a few years ago with Josh. I had zero experience in mountains and was convinced that hiking was merely walking on an incline. Let's just say the day ended in tears.

Hales swam in high school and she lifeguards at a local pool, so I crash their swim lane when it's not busy. When she's not on guard duty she gets in the water with me and gives me some pointers. She tells me to roll my shoulders and extend my arms to make my stroke as long as I can. I swim fifty meters and turn and look at her through my goggles, already out of breath. 'How was that?' I yell from the deep end. She squints. 'Um . . .' Hales is the most positive person in the world. Her trademark characteristic is to overcompliment everything, even highly mediocre material (she once said *The Lizzie Maguire Movie* changed her life), so when she says 'Um,' I know I'm in trouble. She says I need to close my fingers, relax my neck, and not pull my head up so high to breathe. I swim another fifty. I pull my goggles off.

'Was that better?' I yell to her. She yells something back.

'What?' I hold my hand to my ear.

'*Kick!* You keep forgetting to kick!' Kick. Right. I've got to remember that.

On the running front, things are going fine except for the fact that I am working with about a nine-minute-mile pace. Actually, let's just say it's somewhere between nine and eleven minutes. Every now and then I get Kai to go in the jogging stroller, which is awesome training. If I can push a twenty-pound baby for three miles, then maybe I'll be able to finish six on my own.

I was looking forward to getting on Josh's bike. Ever since Josh died, seeing cyclists on the road has always bothered me. Josh was an avid cyclist even after his trip across the country. When I see cyclists from a distance, they all look the same. For almost a year my heart has jumped every time I've seen riders fly down the street. I always think it's Josh. It drives me crazy that this happens to my brain, and I really, really want it to stop. Somehow I believe that if I become a cyclist I can eradicate this problem.

So far biking has been fun. Actually, I can't say I've been out cycling yet, but I have taken Josh's bike out for a few rides. I really do enjoy doing something that I know Josh loved. I feel like we get to have a conversation that we never had while he was here. Or at least it's as close as I can get.

But something else has happened in the last few weeks. Ever since I took the bike out of the basement, I feel like I've reawakened the whole house. It's like that scene in *Hocus Pocus* when the kids light the right candles and the witches appear, or when Aladdin moves the lamp. Something has changed. Now that I've turned the air-conditioning on, the house smells different. It smells the same way it did last summer right before I left for Miami. Things hit me unexpectedly during the day and I'm finding it harder and harder to keep it together. The Red Wings are in the Stanley Cup finals again and last night during game five, I cried during the first period. Who cries during the first period of a hockey game? But I could see Josh sitting on the couch in his Pavel Datsyuk jersey. We would have been in the basement together for every game.

The other day I got a letter from Dr Harnish, the minister who officiated at Josh's funeral. It was short. I opened it and read the first few lines: 'First anniversary – Josh's death.' It said that the next year may not be easier, but if I've made it through one year, I can certainly make it through the next. I just sat there and cried with the letter in my hand. I know this day is coming soon, and for some reason it hurts just waiting for it.

Every day I think about what I was doing last year at this time. What were we doing in June of last year? June 8? June 9? And we had no idea those were his last days.

The first Tuesday in June is the last staff meeting of the year for Berkley High School. I decide to make an announcement about my triathlon and let people know how they can donate money. I am nervous about this whole thing for a number of different reasons. First of all, I am a horrible salesperson. I hate asking people for money and I hate pushing a product. If I ever did go into sales, I know I would end up telling people, 'You know, you make a good point, and now that you mention it, you really don't need our product. No really . . . I totally get it.' Even this time around, I'm pushing a cure for blood disease and I still get nervous about asking people for help.

Second, even though my job as a teacher includes the skill of standing in front of a group of people and delivering important information, I am horrendously nervous about public speaking in front of my staff meeting. I have a hard time talking in front of adults as it is, but I know that the idea of the triathlon and my brief explanation will conjure up serious emotions in my brain and I don't know if I can hold it together. It may be my grief group breakdown all over again. Over the last week, I've been practicing my speech relentlessly. I say it in the shower, I say it while I rock Kai to sleep. I say it while I fold laundry and empty the dishwasher.

Finally, co-workers are such an intimidating group for me. They know what happened and they've all been incredibly supportive, but the hard part is that nobody ever has a profound conversation or connection with a co-worker. I do not like when people at work try to hug me or touch me; it makes me really uncomfortable. Adequate proximity, both emotional and physical, is a must in the workplace. Two years ago Dennis, my fellow English teacher, gave me a hug right before winter break and it was a horrible experience. I turned bright red and left awkwardly afterward, and he spent all of his Christmas vacation thinking he had done something wrong, probably because my posthug expression was similar to that of a boy who had just been made to pull his pants down for a stranger. The worst part was, after Christmas break Dennis approached me and we had to have a conversation *about* the Christmas hug. I had to explain that he had not done anything wrong, that I was just a really awkward person. He said he felt so guilty because he could sense that I was uncomfortable. We never talked about it again.

Everyone is always a little on guard at work. I, for one, have never really opened up to my colleagues, except through thankyou cards, but at school, it's just not the time or place to make an emotional connection with people. But in my little speech, which is about three minutes, I have to say certain things. I fear one reaction: I will cry. I cannot cry.

The meeting arrives. I go last, right before we do 'good of the order.' I've been thinking about my speech the entire meeting, so by this point I am sweating. Right as I stand up I start to wonder if I smell too. Despite my perspiration and potential body odor, I start to talk. I tell them I'm doing an Olympic distance triathlon and raising money for the Leukemia Lymphoma Society. Then I have to get personal. I take a deep breath.

'Last summer I really needed help from other people.' My knees start to shake. They are visibly wobbling. Shit. 'I needed help and hundreds of people, people I didn't even know, did everything they could to get me through a very difficult time in my life. The people in this room are no exception.' My face is red hot. I can feel it. I look around the room. I am starting to make people feel awkward. Shit.

'This summer I'd like to do something to help other people.' I stop and swallow. My voice is about to break. Swallowing is the first sign that

310

my nerves are slowly creeping up my body into my throat and mouth. If I don't finish this soon, the high voice is going to break through. 'Which is why I've decided to do this triathlon for the Leukemia Lymphoma Society.'

I tell them that by tomorrow morning they will have a donation form and official letter in their mailboxes. Checks can be written to the Leukemia Lymphoma Society. I sit down as quickly as possible. I feel someone pat me on the back. I need to get out of here before the patting escalates.

I am relieved once the meeting is over. I run out the door in fear that people will want to talk to me, which I can't really handle right now. I feel embarrassed that I still have a hard time talking in front of people about things that aren't even directly about losing Josh. I go back to my room to pack up my stuff.

Paul, our athletic director, walks in the door. 'Excuse me, Mrs Taylor.' He always calls me Mrs Taylor even though I'm one of the youngest people on the staff. I look up. He is holding a pen and a checkbook. 'How do you spell leukemia?' He writes a check for one hundred dollars, hands it to me, and walks out of my room.

My juniors are currently writing their college essays. At the end of every eleventh-grade year, each student's final writing assignment is to find a prompt from a college that he or she would like to apply to and write the essay. I see it as a starting point. In the fall of their senior year, they will revisit their essays with their twelfth-grade English teacher and hopefully continue to improve the essay. Some of them won't use the essay they write, but it's still good practice. Secretly, this is my favorite assignment to read.

I tell my students that I will not be grading in the traditional sense. I will be brutally honest with my feedback, but I won't 'grade them down' for a mediocre piece. If they make the necessary changes, they get full credit. The idea is that the lack of a numerical score will help them be a little more creative and edgy. These are honors students, so most of them are used to asking the question, 'What are you looking for?' They excel at following a format and analyzing a text. But the college essay is the opposite. In answer to the question, 'What are you looking for?' the college essay would answer, 'We are looking for the essay that *doesn't* ask that question.'

In giving them some guidance, I encourage them to be honest. We read a few interesting essays and articles by college administrators about the dos and don'ts on admission essay writing. Even so, I know some of them will still go home and write something like 'Being captain of the soccer team taught me a lot about myself.'

Many of the essay topics are the same from university to university. They ask the applicant to talk about a moment of personal discovery or a 'setback.' As a teacher of literature, I see it as the university asking about one moment or event where the applicants lost their innocence, or at least part of it. For these essays, so many of my students talk about a time when, for whatever reason, they realized the world was not the easy, funloving place they thought it was.

Rebecca Adler wrote about her eating disorder, which I had always worried about with her. She said for years she thought that there were two factors in her life that meant everything: the number on the scale and how other people saw her. Now after diligently working with a therapist, a dietitian, and a physician, she is back on track. She said now she focuses her 'control' on school and other healthy forms of competition. At one point in her essay she wrote, 'If my mind has the power to make my organs fail, then all factors of my life can be manifested in a constructive way.' After I read this sentence I just had to stare at it for a while. People spend a lifetime using their brains to make decisions that hurt their bodies. As a junior in high school she's realized that her brain is a powerful force – so powerful it can seriously hurt her, but now she's turned a corner. She's not even eighteen yet. Over this sentence I write, 'You are so smart.'

Emma Dorset wrote about losing her mom to cancer, which I never knew. The question asked about a setback and how you 'resolved' it. Emma wrote, 'It seems odd to try to describe how I have resolved the death of my mother.' I write, 'Yes, amazing point.' *Resolution* is a stupid word to use when talking about death, whether it is of a mother or a spouse, or at least that's how I've always felt about it. But instead of saying, Yes, I have resolved the death of my mother by appreciating each day more and not taking things for granted, she says, No, it can't be resolved. It is irresolvable. And she's right. It can't be fixed. But she doesn't wallow in this. She goes on to describe her life now. She admires her dad and helps her sister, because her mom would be terribly disappointed if she didn't.

I half-expected Leah Simon's essay to be some sort of protest against the idea of evaluating a person based on one story. With her reputation for being blunt, cunning, and horribly inappropriate, I thought it might start with something like 'This writing prompt can lick it.' But she didn't. Instead she wrote about a tradition that was important to her. When she was little, at Christmas all of her cousins and she would try to find the 'glass pickle ornament' hidden on the Christmas tree at her grandma's house. All of the kids loved the glass-pickle hunt, and all of the aunts and uncles would take pictures and then the grandma would tell the story of the glass-pickle ornament to a floor full of squirming children. It is a beautiful opening paragraph; she uses vivid imagery and creates an overall feeling of her childlike contentment for the tradition. The second paragraph reads, 'As their adorable young toddlers turned into rebellious teenagers, the tradition began to die. Half of the family would be missing due to a divorce in the family. There would be too much arguing for there to be laughing and sharing stories. The holiday times became a hassle, and rather than looking forward to it for weeks, I hoped I got the flu so I could stay home.' I didn't write anything on her paper initially because it was fucking perfect. I wish I could have said that to Leah on Monday; no student would appreciate my use of a swear word in a compliment more than Leah. She is willing to admit that there was something in her life that brought her an innocent joy and with time, it died. I want to underline the part about the flu and write, 'I can completely relate.'

There are others that are just as good as these. Some of the best essays don't talk about death, disease, or divorce at all. Andrea Davenport wrote about her teeth. When she was little, her teeth were so bad she was ostracized from social groups and stripped of all potential friendships in grades three through five. Then she got her teeth fixed and everything changed. She talks about how she realized how superficial people really are, even though we try so hard to convince ourselves we're not.

For four years I try to get them to see this happening in literature. Everyone, no matter who we are or where we come from, goes through something where we realize . . . what? Hard truths. People die. Parents fall out of love. Parents were never in love. Holidays suck. Friends are mean people too. Didn't they get this when Gene jounces the branch and sends his best friend crashing to the ground? When Roger kills Piggy? When Romeo and Juliet commit suicide? In *The Color Purple*, Celie gets raped on page *one*, for crying out loud. Almost every protagonist or main character that we have read about since the ninth grade dies. So what am I teaching them? What are the themes in literature that carry over to actual life? Equality is only a dream. Negative behavior always repeats itself. Evil conquers good. People die. We are powerless. Even when we make choices, we are still powerless.

But there's more to it than the cold realities that we have to deal with as adults. I want my students to see the symbols in their own lives, how there are things that are more than just things, there are things that hold meaning. I want my students to learn that life can change if they want it to. I want them to know that language limits our under-standing, and words like *family* and *resolution* aren't as simple as we think. I want them to see that authors and real people make choices that can change the course of where you go and how you feel. I want my students to see that some-times fiction has answers because our own lives don't, and sometimes we like seeing things resolved in books because the reality is, it's the only time where problems end neatly or where problems end at all. I want my students to see books as a way to learn about other people and other worlds, but also as a place to learn about themselves.

How would I write a college essay today? Describe a setback you have had in your life. How did you resolve it? But it seems that the first thing you realize when you lose your innocence or come face-to-face with the reality of life is that some things don't get resolved. In *A Separate Peace*, Gene Forrester, the narrator, is best friends with Finny. Through the first few chapters, however, the reader realizes that it's not the best friendship. Gene has this strange hate for Finny. Finny is perfect at everything and Gene articulates his feelings as 'enmity.' In the midst of their summer session at Devon School, Gene, Finny, and a few other friends are climbing a tree and jumping into the Devon River. Finny is out on the end of the branch, preparing himself to jump, when Gene, who is on the same branch but holding on to the trunk, jounces the branch. Finny loses his balance because of the jounce and tumbles awkwardly. He severely breaks his leg and his perfection is lost. Eventually a complicated scene involving another slip and fall results in a tricky surgery and Finny dies. The reader knows, the boys at Devon know, and even Finny knows that it all started because of Gene's jounce of the branch.

Fifteen years after Finny's death, Gene goes back

to Devon. He walks back to the athletic fields where he and Finny used to walk together every day. On the particular day of Gene's visit, it's pouring rain. He is soaking wet. His shoes are covered in mud. Knowles writes, 'Anyone could see it was time to come in out of the rain.' For fifteen years Gene has been standing in that rain. For fifteen years he's been in the same spot. What would Gene write for his college essay fifteen years after his friend's death? 'I killed my best friend. I'm still dealing with it.' And he'd probably go home and dry himself off and he'd still feel like shit. Or maybe he wouldn't. Maybe after fifteen years of thinking about one summer, he has come to peace with it. But what does that even mean?

So is this it? After we lose our innocence we spend the rest of our lives in some sort of recovery from tragic events only waiting for the next punishing blow. It is a wonder that we don't die thinking, *Ugh, thank God that's over.*

It's amazing to read these essays because these students have so much ahead of them, but some of them have already seen huge challenges. So what is my lesson to them? Buckle up, it's only going to get worse from here. What is John Knowles's lesson? What would any of our authors say about setbacks and resolutions? I don't know. I think they'd say that these are the moments that are worth thinking about and worth writing about.

I do know that for the first time in my life, I feel like I understand these books and these authors. We see characters losing their minds because they are put in incredibly challenging situations, but this year instead of calling them crazy, I realize that this is what it means to be human – to go back to the emotions and reactions in us that transcend time and space. Grief, love, pain, the ache for power, the need for acceptance, the strength of family. What could I possibly have in common with a black woman from rural Georgia in the early nineteenth century or a wealthy bachelor from New York City during the Jazz Age? What could Celie and Gatsby possibly share when everything about their lives is different? But don't you get it? We have everything in common. All of the things that make me hurt also make them hurt and all of the things that alleviate my pain are the same things that alleviate their pain.

I don't know how to show this to my students. But maybe over time, maybe little by little, I will tell them about how these books helped me and I will try to make them see what happens when you open a book and let an author tell you a story.

At the end of the year I make each student write out his or her own six-word memoir. I read my favorites over and over.

Madison Brixton is tall with long blond hair and is dropdead gorgeous. She did her ninth-grade research project on the modeling profession. Madison is very sassy and is not afraid to question teachers or administrators. She has an equally sassy, equally gorgeous twin sister. Madison's favorite character from eleventh-grade English is Lady Macbeth. Her six-word memoir: Twin versus twin: Competition's a bitch.

Steven McCain loves being the dominant force in class discussions. Even when he hasn't done the reading homework, he loves to argue with people. A few months ago he protested the administrative decision that made all students wear I.D. tags at school. He read his protest speech to our English class. During our poetry unit, he vehemently argued the D+ he earned on his essay. His six-word memoir: Self-confidence is not a crime.

Doug Treen was one of the two students to incorporate Guitar Hero into an Honors English presentation, which was the worst presentation I'd ever seen. They were outraged at their low grade. He openly admits when he doesn't do the reading and never seems fazed by his own laziness. Although I do not know any of the details, I do know he is very mischievous; he's been called out of class a number of times to see the assistant principal. Doug's six-word memoir: Tried humble pie. Tasted like shit.

How can they be so profound and so ridiculous at the same time? The beauty of being a teenager.

June 15 is Father's Day. I make the executive decision to have Kai baptized on Father's Day. My family rallies. Dr Harnish also rises to the occasion. We have a beautiful, quiet little ceremony. Later that evening my mom comes over so

I can go for a jog and enjoy the summer air. I turn down my street and see a rainbow streaking across the sky.

Then it is June 16, the day before the one-year anniversary of Josh's death. Battersby calls to talk to me about tomorrow. She says, 'Just so you know, it ends up being pretty anticlimactic.' On the one-year anniversary of her mom's death she thought something big would happen, or the day would make her feel a certain way, or she would suddenly see something differently, but it wasn't like that at all. The day comes and goes like any other.

I go through pictures of Josh. Part of me wants tomorrow to be here and gone. Part of me wants time to stand still. I go through all of the stuff from Josh's funeral. I look at the program. The picture we chose for the front of the program was taken when he was walking into the church for our wedding rehearsal. I reread all of the cards people sent me. I've kept all of them in a box near my bed. I find my speech from Josh's funeral. I haven't looked at this since the day I read it last year. I don't know why, but this feels like an appropriate time to read it again.

> As you can imagine, it is difficult for me to find the words to accurately describe my husband at a time like this. How can I possibly find the words to paint his tremendous personality and love of life? Because

321

of this, I will draw from someone else's words. My older brother, Adam, is getting married this July. A few months ago Adam and his fiancée, Ellie, created a website featuring all of the wedding party with small, concise biographies. Josh's biography reads as follows:

'QUESTION: If Superman and the Flash raced to the end of the Universe, who would win? ANSWER: Josh Taylor. Yes, the groom's Brother from Another Mother is a superhero. If Lance Armstrong, Indiana Jones, Jack Bauer, Emeril, and the cast of Jackass had a baby – a blond barrel-chested baby who was addicted to Moomer's ice cream – it would be Josh or Diz (or 'Dizzle' if you're addressing him formally).'

I couldn't think of anything better. When Adam and Ellie posted this, Josh was so complimented, he read it three times out loud. Although the short biography makes us smile, it also reminds us of who he was. Josh was the boy who lived. He lived in every moment. He tried everything, risked anything, and never wasted any time. That is why I married him, for his spontaneity and pure love of being alive. That is why so many of us were drawn to him, because when he was around, we smiled and laughed.

In addition to his heroic qualities and

super strength, Josh was also defined by the people around him. The most daunting task of being Josh's wife was trying to understand and be a part of all of his formerly developed relationships. I can remember even last spring, I would come home from work, tired, looking forward to a quiet evening at home. Josh would then insist that he wanted to run 'a few' errands, and we would be back in no time. And no matter where we went we always ended up stopping by Margaret's house, then Deedee's house, and then we'd see one of the Quarts in their yard, so we'd chat with them. And then on the way out of the neighborhood we would see the Jabborris, the Getzes, then we'd go to the pet store to visit all of his friends there, and then to my parents, and then, maybe we'd go home.

The same thing would happen at Elk Lake. I remember the first time Josh and I went up there, just the two of us, I was looking forward to a romantic weekend with just him and me. But before we even parked the car we had to stop at Aunt Cass's and Uncle Terry's, then off to see Andy and Mary, then to the Boyntons', then Moomer's, then to the Blues', stop by soccer camp, and the list goes on and on.

And finally when Josh and I planned our wedding, we had to talk about who was invited. We agreed the first people on the list would be our families. So I wrote my family down. I interpreted the word as literally as possible. My nuclear family, my cousins, aunts, uncles, and grandparents. Everybody was somehow related, everybody fit on the same tree. And when it was Josh's turn, he created a list of people, but hardly any of the people on his 'family' list were actually related to him. Not to mention I had to stop him after a hundred or so names. 'But Josh,' I would say, 'Uncle Alex and Aunt Jane aren't really your aunt and uncle. Uncle Mel isn't actually your mother's brother. Your mom doesn't even have any brothers, but there are still twenty-seven men listed as 'uncle' on your list!' But he would look at me as if I was speaking in another language. It didn't make sense to him. These people were his aunts and uncles, they were his family. But that was who he was, he loved all of you as if you were his family. And you are his family, as I have come to realize over the years.

I know a lot of you look at me and think, what will she do? And of course I ask myself the same questions. But I look at everyone in this room and think, what will they do? What will any of us do? He was loved by so many. He was a huge part of so many lives, not just mine. All of you considered him more than just a friend, but you considered him a brother and a son.

In reflection of those afternoon drives, trips to Elk Lake, and our wedding list, I have concluded that Josh was raised by a village. He has an incredible mother, and that mother was smart enough to rally the support around her. This is a sad day. But the strength of the village does not diminish when one of their own is lost. From looking at all of the people in this room, I can tell you that it is the people in this sanctuary that have carried me through the last several days. And as I think about what an upstanding human my husband was, I am incredibly saddened to think he won't be here for our son. But it fills me – literally fills me – with joy to know that I am having his son. And while I have all of you here listening to me, I need to add, as Josh would have wanted me to inform you, the work of the village is far from over.

So what do we do now? I don't know. I've been asking myself that for four days. But I do know we must remember. We must remember everything about him. And there is nothing more painful than remembering Josh, because we have to admit he is a memory, but we have to. It is the most painful but most necessary thing we can do. When Josh was here, I always thought, like so many of you thought, he was the strongest person on the planet. He really would win a race across the universe. And although he is no longer here, I feel as if his strength has been infused in me. It has to be. And it has been infused into Deedee, Chris, Ashley, and all of the rest of us. We have to be as strong as he was, as he would have been. It is our only way. Thank you for being here.

I don't know how I was able to write this. I don't know how I was able to say this out loud in front of a sanctuary full of people. I can hardly read it now. I don't think I'll ever be able to say it out loud again without crying after the first three words. I don't know who or what occupied my body in the days following his death. One time someone told me that the only time you have all of your friends and family in the same place to celebrate someone is at his wedding and his funeral. I am relieved that I was able to properly commemorate my husband, but it still perplexes me to no end that his wedding and funeral were eighteen months and one day apart.

June 17. I spend the day at my parents' house. We sit outside on our old red bench, pushing Kai on the swing that hangs from the linden tree in my parents' front yard. We don't talk about Josh. We just sit and push the swing. It is the only thing we know how to do today.

As the sun sets Kai and I go back to our house. I make dinner. Ashley, Deedee, Mathews, and Maggie come over. Everything is solemn. Even my rickety dining room chairs seem to have quieted down for the evening.

Kai is the beam of light. Everyone wants to hold him and give him a bath and make him smile. He is the only thing worth smiling about today. I don't think he will ever know how he has saved all of us.

JULY

We were talking about kissing, and we spoke rapidly and excitedly and laughed loudly. This was a t-shirt and jeans laughter, not cocktail dress laughter – it came from the belly, not the chest. It was size fourteen and not size two. When one of us made moves toward some wilting hors d'oeuvre, the rest would stall, so that nothing good said was missed by anyone.

—ELIZABETH BERG, 'THE PARTY' IN *THE DAY I ATE WHATEVER I WANTED*

Angela Anagnost, one of my best friends from college, is getting married this weekend. I have committed a lot of time to complaining about being a bridesmaid and about leaving Kai for three whole days. My family is up north for the week, so I have to leave from there to go to the other side of the state. My parents drive me to Lauren Gentry's apartment, which is right across town from where we are staying, so she and I can carpool to Angela's for

328

the weekend. Ads and Moo are with Kai while my parents drive me. I just put him down for a nap before I left. My mom keeps telling me, 'Nat, he's fine. Everything will be fine.'

Halfway to Gentry's apartment, we start to hear jets flying over us. The annual National Cherry Festival is going on this weekend in Traverse City. One of its main attractions is the Blue Angels, exhibition fighter-jet pilots. Of course, out of all the days and all the times, they are practicing right now. My brother calls, and my dad puts him on speakerphone. I can hear Kai screaming in the background. 'There are fucking *jets* flying over the house.' Adam is frantic. 'Don't they know there are babies trying to nap in this city?' He asks what he should do to calm Kai down. Try the bottle, rock him, lie with him, I tell Ads, but it's obvious that none of it is working. Finally Adam says, 'Mom, how long till you get back here?' I feel so bad for my brother, but at the same time I want to slap him across the face. My body starts to shake at the idea that my son is crying and my car is going in the opposite direction.

My parents drop me off at Gentry's place. It's a tough goodbye. Gentry is really positive about the whole thing. She keeps telling me we're going to have a great time. I do not agree with her. I get in the car and try to channel Mathews's positive attitude.

Gentry is still one of my best friends, despite the four-hour drive between our houses. We met in college and played soccer together. During our junior year of college, a group of us girls lived in the Delta Tau Delta fraternity house. The Delts had been kicked off campus for some riotous behavior, so right there in the middle of the fraternity block was the Delt house, fully occupied by women. The Delt house was my unofficial baptism into womanhood for a lot of reasons that we won't go into now, but the point is I am still very close with my Delt house friends. They were there for my wedding, Josh's funeral, and they've been arguing about who is the best auntie ever since Kai was born.

Gentry and I have about a two-and-half-hour drive to Angela's. On the car ride over, I read Elizabeth Berg's new book of short stories, *The Day I Ate Whatever I Wanted*. Each story highlights a different truth of being a woman. One chapter is all about this woman who goes to Weight Watchers and sees a woman with an oxygen tube and a blind woman weighing in. The narrator says she turns around, walks out, and in honor of these two women, she goes and eats whatever she wants for the rest of the day. Dunkin' Donuts, Kentucky Fried Chicken, White Castle – the list goes on. It's hilarious. Another story is about women at a party talking about sex and penises and giggling like sixth-grade girls, and then one of the husbands comes over and breaks everything up, saying he's ready to go. 'Mrs Ethel Menafee and Mrs Birdie Stolz' is about two women who have been friends for over fifty years. Now Birdie is in the hospital with lymphatic leukemia. Ethel comes to visit her every day, and they talk about normal things that women talk about. Their chatty visits seem to keep Birdie going more than her medical care. I haven't read a book for fun in a million years. I love Elizabeth Berg. I feel like I know her as well as I know the girls from the Delt house.

We arrive. As other girls get there, we go screaming into hotel rooms. You'd think we hadn't seen each other in fifty years. The beauty of this wedding is that most of the girls came without their husbands and boyfriends. The conversations, therefore, are much richer in nature. First we take bets on who will be making out with which of Angela's hot Greek brothers (there are three to choose from, though I'm out of the pool, of course). Then we move on to talking about sex. No matter where we start, we eventually always end up talking about sex. This is hilarious to me that we've been friends for eight years and this topic never gets boring. Every girl in our group is so different that the conversation could go in a variety of directions. Janna, for example, likes to be very serious about sex. Janna works for a planned parenting organization in Traverse City. One of her main responsibilities is to go to schools and talk to teenagers about safe sex. Janna uses technical terms, like *clitoris*, which the rest of us find ridiculous and hilarious.

But after all of the goofing around is over, we

also talk about serious stuff. Gentry is always intrigued with how my brain is doing. Gentry is big on asking me about Josh. She is one of the few people in my life who will go for the jugular of tough questions. But she doesn't ask in a gossipy way. One of Gentry's best qualities is that she is incapable of gossip. She even hates it when we're all hanging out and Terrah starts reading *Us Weekly*. Whether it's about celebrities or her friends, Gentry sees it as totally mindless.

A few months after Kai was born, Gentry came down to stay with me for the weekend. She didn't have anyone else to visit or any other agenda other than to see me. At the time, she was waitressing full-time and taking classes for her master's in counseling, so she was busy to say the least. The first night she stayed with me was the first time we were together by ourselves since Josh died. I remember she said, 'I know this sounds insensitive, but I am so sad for me,' and she started to cry. 'I just feel like I lost one of my best friends. I'm so sad for you. But I'm sad for me too.' This was one of the kindest things anyone has ever said to me about losing Josh. People are always so concerned with how I'm feeling, sometimes they don't admit how hard their own life is without him.

At some point in the midst of spending time with my girlfriends, trying to learn how to Greek dance after being overserved and sleeping in on Friday morning, I come to the conclusion that I am having fun. Jacci, bridesmaid number three, ends up making out with Dino, Angela's twin brother, the night of the rehearsal dinner. The day of the wedding arrives. I feel like I've been at Greek camp for forty-eight hours, and tonight is the big show.

At every wedding before this one in the last twelve months (Ads's, Toby and Nikki's), there has been some acknowledgment of Josh's absence. Angela's is the first wedding where this won't happen. This is the first celebration (Father's Day, Mother's Day, weddings, my birthday, Christmas, etc.) where no one has come up to me and said, 'Hey, are you okay?' or 'Hey, this must be hard for you.' This time around, everyone just carries on like it is another normal wedding. It's so strange because I remember the tension and discomfort I felt when people took time in their own wedding to talk about Josh. It was so hard for me. But I knew, deep down, I wanted them to say something. I know Josh won't be mentioned at this wedding, and he shouldn't be. This wedding isn't about Josh or me. But I still have a knot in my stomach about celebrating without the public acknowledgment that the world is still not right. Now that a year has passed, it feels like my dark cloud has disappeared, but in some ways I want it back over my head where everyone can see it.

I stand in the lobby of the church and wait for the one person who can pull me out of this slump: Chris Mathews. Mathews was up at Elk Lake last night with Deedee and Ashley. He was planning on leaving this morning. It's about a two-hour drive to the wedding from where he is. I call his cell phone. He hasn't left yet.

Ashley gets on the phone and explains that Mathews is lying on the dock in his Hanes T-shirt and boxer shorts with his eyes closed. Last night they all went to the bar in Elk Rapids, and shockingly enough, Mathews wandered off. On their way home Ashley found Mathews passed out on the grass on a side street of Elk Rapids. Ashley laughs as she tells the story.

'I *allegedly* passed out, Natalie,' I can hear him yelling in the background.

I hang up and initially curse him for being hungover and leaving me high and dry for the ceremony. But also I know that being with Deedee and Ashley at the lake might be more important than this wedding ceremony. In his own magical way he lets them know that even though Josh is gone, he still loves being with them and spending time with them on the lake. And I'm sure before going out, he probably ate dinner with Deedee on the porch and offered to take the garbage cans to the street or take care of other tasks that previously belonged to Josh. As much as I'd like him here, I know Elk Lake needs a good Chris Mathews visit this summer. I report back to the small room at the back of the church to see if I have any final duties before the ceremony starts.

Three hours later, after a very long and very hot Greek ceremony, our party bus makes it to the reception hall. Mathews is there, looking dapper as ever. I give him a huge hug. Before I can even ask how the drive was, he says, 'I just want you to know, I threw up twice on the way here.' I open my mouth to say something. He puts up his index finger and cuts me off. 'I pulled over, stopped the car, threw up, then kept driving. Twice.' He says this like I should be proud. I should be proud of the fact that he drove all the way here, by himself, with an incredible hangover. So I say it.

'I'm proud of you.'

He shrugs. 'I'm proud of me too.' And he really means it.

The reception flies by. I try to Greek dance, but I end up leaving it to the Greeks. I have an amazing time.

I watch Angela and Brad, and sure, marriage is nice, but the real lasting relationships can be found in the seven of us in matching brown strapless dresses. My friends have been a huge force holding me up over the last thirteen months. The least I can do is be here for one of my friends, despite my current feelings about eternal love. We do this for one another because we have something different than marriage and, at certain times, more powerful. So if I have to give up three days with my son to stand in three-inch heels in the non-air-conditioned Hellenic Cultural Center for an hour-long service in another language, I'll do it.

I'll do it a hundred times over. Elizabeth Berg would be proud of me.

I stumble back to my hotel room around 1 a.m. I rummage through my bridal party goodie bag to find a snack, then open my computer. In the morning I read what I've written and laugh.

So much to wrire little time. Drunk. I heart pretzels. 1: Friends are life. 2. Greek Anagnost rbothres are Corleone Family., 3. I love goijg to bed in my own hotel room. No need to sty up and impress. Marriage is for some, not for all. Notfor me anymore. Manny. Handsome manny without in-laws. MUST go to bed. Much more drunk than once perceived. Night.

Once I get home, one of the first things on my agenda is team-triathlon training. Maggie and I go to our first Team in Training practice. Maggie is about a half hour late getting to my house, which is not incredibly surprising. I get in the car. She says that her father had a list of things he needed to discuss with her, and 'per usual' he made her late. We get all of our stuff loaded in my car and take off for Kent Lake Metro Park.

I have been out biking twice so far, and it was really more like cruising than an actual workout. I signed up for this triathlon two months ago, and this is my first practice. Luckily, Maggie has gone to several, so she's scoped things out for me. She tells me that she has a crush on Coach Rick, and everyone else is 'really nice.' I am uninterested in the niceness of our team. 'Am I going to come in last during the workout today?' This is my only concern. She laughs and says no. I tell her she is absolutely not required to stay with me on the bike.

Everyone is gathered in the parking lot. Maggie and I get our bikes out and scurry over. Apparently, before every practice the coach gives a little session on important information for first-time racers. Today he is talking about 'transitions.' Transitions are the two times an athlete has to move from one event to the next in a triathlon. Transition one is from swim to bike. Transition two is from bike to run. Coach Rick takes about twenty minutes to describe what the transition area will look like and how we should arrange every single item around our bike. He says we'll need a towel to place under the bike, a place for some water and an energy supplement, that our sunglasses should hang on the handlebars and that our helmets are to be unclipped, yaddi yaddi yadda. I keep looking at my watch. It's already twenty after eight, let's go already. 'How much instruction can there be?' I want to shout. Take off your wet suit and throw on a helmet, for crying out loud!

A tall, athletic-looking woman stands next to me. She keeps raising her hand and asking for more detail. 'Coach Rick, would you suggest wearing a waterproof watch or putting it on after the swim?' Coach Rick, who is really into being Coach Rick, replies with a 'That's a great question, Tammy!' and goes on to explain the details of taking off a wet suit with or sans watch. Tammy's hand goes up three more times.

The entire time Coach Rick talks, I check out the crowd. There are a few people my age, but most of the team is older than Maggie and me. I'd say midforties. Tammy is probably fifteen years older than me. In terms of fitness, these are some fairly average-looking athletes. There is a guy with a goatee and black riding gloves, and his belly hangs over his spandex. I put my foot on the pedal of my bike, like I know what I'm doing, and think about how I'll probably be able to keep up. In addition to sizing everyone up, I also conclude that Maggie and I have widely different taste in men. Coach Rick has perfectly aligned tube socks and a buzz cut, and initially addressed the group with a 'Hey, gang!'

Finally we start. We have a fifteen-mile ride and then a fourmile run. I take off with the front of the pack. Maggie is a little ahead of me. A ways in, I'm feeling good. I'm still near the front. Tammy leads the group. I catch up to Maggie, who has a computer on her bike. 'How long has it been?' I yell. 'Four miles,' she yells back. Great.

About ten minutes later, I start to slide. I can still see Tammy up ahead. She is chatting with the women next to her like they're out for a walk.

Jack, the guy with the belly, is right behind her. The miles start to feel longer. I feel my legs slow down. My pace tapers off, and Tammy, Jack, and the rest of the team fade out of sight.

Almost an hour later, I finish my fifteen. My legs feel rubbery. I get off my bike and start to run. But I cannot run. If someone yelled *fire* at this moment, I would have a better chance of moving if I used my hands and knees rather than my feet. I start shuffling. It's slower than a walk but I'm lifting my knees, so it looks like a forward aerobic tap dance. All of the sudden I hear Coach Rick. 'You look great, Natalie! Keep it up!' I suddenly hate Coach Rick.

Some really nice person made homemade cookies and brought bananas for after the workout. I sit in the shade staring at my feet while the rest of the team talks cheerily and debriefs about the workout. I don't think Tammy even broke a sweat. 'See you next Saturday!' Jack yells on the way to his pickup truck. 'You're dreamin',' my FMG says. She is lying on the pavement with a towel over her head and a half-eaten cookie in her left hand.

Maggie gets in the car and tells me that luckily her chain fell off a few times so Coach Rick had to rescue her. She considered the morning to be a complete success. I focus on my muscles not seizing up as I drive.

'Oh, come on,' she says, 'that wasn't so bad.' She hands me a bottle of water. I didn't even bring any water. Like everything else in my life, I have gotten myself into a situation for which I am totally and completely unprepared. I glance over at her before we pull out.

'Your words, not mine.'

I decide to go back to Elk Lake for the first time since Josh died. I have to. It has to happen eventually. I have met everything else in the past year. This is the last holdout of places that I have to see without Josh. For some reason, going to Elk Lake without Josh somehow solidifies his death even further. Okay, he's not in our house, and his car isn't here, but certainly he'll be at Elk Lake, right? But I need to go to try to wrap my head around the fact that Elk Lake exists in the absence of Josh.

The drive up I-75 is hard. Every sign reminds me of when I made this drive with Josh. I feel like I am walking into my house for the first time all over again. In the backseat I try to prepare myself for the cottage. I visualize every detail. I have a conversation with myself in my brain. 'You're going to see the quilt on the bed. You're going to see the lawn mower in the garage. You're going to see the orange colander that he used for the morel mushrooms. You're going to see the charcoal grill.' Step by step, I try to picture walking through so maybe it won't be so bad when I get there.

Once we get to the cottage, I let my parents take Kai in first so I can be by myself. I stop to look at every little detail of the cottage from the driveway. It's like slowly pulling off a Band-Aid; for some reason I need to feel the pain. I can't just storm through. I listen to the sound of the back screen door as I open it. Somehow that signals the first step. I start with the back bedroom. I look at the twin bed where Josh and I slept together when we first started dating. It's so funny how as a married couple we eventually felt like our queen-sized bed wasn't big enough for two adults, but when we were in our early lightning-bolt days, we slept together in a twin bed. I look at the chair where he'd set his gaiters after fly-fishing. I look at the place where he took off his shoes. I walk by the pictures in the back hallway. They haven't changed since I was here last time. I walk down the hallway and look into Margaret's old room. She was here last time I was here too. I'm feeling okay. I think I can hold it together.

I turn the corner into the kitchen. I see the pictures on the fridge. Damn. I forgot about the pictures on the fridge. There is one of Josh riding his bike the summer he rode it across the country. It's one of my favorite pictures in the world. I forgot all about it until this moment. On his trip, he and Toby went through the Upper Peninsula just so they could stop at Elk Lake. In the picture Josh is wearing his navy Airborne jersey and his hair is flying back in the wind. He didn't cut his hair the whole ride, so he has this long, almost yellow-blond hair. The picture is a little blurry because he's riding as it's being taken. I stare at it for a long time. I just want to reach my hand into that picture and touch him.

I walk back to the bathroom to splash some cold water on my face and blow my nose. I walk outside to say hi to everyone. Deedee squeezes me so hard I think she's going to pull me to the ground. I know it means the world to her that I came back. Chris already has Kai in the water.

For my twenty-fourth birthday, Josh gave me a digital camera. That was the last birthday of mine that we spent together. I'm not one to see certain pre-losing-Josh situations as prophetic or ominous, but I feel like that gift said something. Of course, he had no idea that he would tragically lose his life between my twenty-fourth and twenty-fifth birthdays, but I will always see that camera as an indication of what he wanted me to do more of in life: stop and appreciate the amazing people around me. Sure, take a picture of the blue water of Elk Lake or the big sand beaches of Lake Michigan. But really, my job with that camera is to somehow, if I can at all, hold on to the wonderful moments I encounter with the people I love. It has been one year and almost two months since Josh died. I still hate and love looking at pictures of him. I get so frustrated that looking at a photograph is the only way I can see him anymore. But those photos mean more to me than any other inanimate object in my life. And ironically, he bought me a new camera before he died.

Over the last several weeks, I lost the charger to that camera. This is expected of me. I lose things. I've been losing things my whole life. I lost a winter coat when I was in fifth grade. One time I lost my bike. And no matter how many *Real Simple* magazines I read or how many bins I buy from the home storage section of Target, I just can't seem to hold on to things sometimes. But I recovered the twenty-fourth-birthday camera and charger just in time to go to Elk Lake again for a whole week with my in-laws. This week, instead of having my parents just outside of town, I am at the Elk Lake cottage without refuge. Twenty-four hours a day with Ashley and Deedee for an entire week.

It is awesome. You might think living in close quarters with Deedee and Ashley for five full days might spark a complaint or two. But I have absolutely nothing negative to say about the visit. We have a great time. During the week, I develop a new-found respect for Ashley. It is amazing to see her operate when she thinks no one is watching her. She doesn't do things for praise or for credit; she does things because they need to get done. I never thought she and Josh had a lot in common, but this week is the first time I realize that when it comes to working ceaselessly for their family, they are identical twins. All weekend she is cleaning out the garage, washing windows, perfecting the landscaping, taking care of the boat she bought, and carrying Kai around on her hip while doing all of it. They let me relax all weekend. I sleep in, lie around by the water, read my book. It is amazing. I keep calling it 'Spa Elk Lake,' and I mean it too. I take pictures all week long. I don't know what comes over me, but I can't stop capturing the moment. There are so many moments to capture.

Tonight Ashley takes her boat out, and it stalls out on the water. The next-door neighbors, who are year-round residents and not from 'downstate,' go out to help her. We are on the shore when she gets back, and although she is thankful for the help, I can tell she is frustrated about the boat and about how she needed to be rescued by the neighbors. Once she anchors the boat, the same neighbors offer to help Ashley put in the shore station she bought for the boat. She agrees, but it turns out to be a huge ordeal. It takes a lot of time and people standing in the water pushing a massive metal contraption at a very slow pace. I keep taking pictures of Ashley, who is getting more frustrated by the minute. I get one picture where she is trying to finally lower the hoist to get the boat on and she is looking at the camera pointing her finger at me with this look like she's going to put my lights out if I don't get out of her face. But I love it. It's really a picture of her. No makeup, no cleavage, no blow-dried hair, no three-inch heels. She looks at the picture later and calls me a bitch, in the joking way that Ashley calls people a bitch. But I think she looks beautiful.

Time hasn't exactly worked wonders on my own grief, but I certainly think it has helped me see that Ashley is not only critical to my success as a single mother, but she is a hugely important person in Kai's life also. I don't know how close they would have been if Josh were here, which is not to say I would trade one for the other or that I am in any way grateful for his absence. I'm just making an observation. It is amazing to me how she can drive me absolutely insane, while at the exact same time, I never want her to go away.

When I'm old and sick, she'll visit me in the hospital, just like Ethel and Birdie. She'll storm into the hospital room and tell everyone how to do their job and pronounce herself the Fountain of All Knowledge with all things geriatric. 'Nat, I know you said you wanted the full-length compression hose, but I talked to my friend Alice from work and she said that these short ones are way better. See? Here, feel them, feel them, aren't they *so* much softer . . . Oh *my* God, what are they feeding you? That looks completely *disgusting*. Is there a fucking nurse around here who can get you something else? Ugh! That smells *hor*rible.' We are together for a lifetime. And I am grateful.

AUGUST

Ere long, not only on these banks, but on every hill and plain and in every hollow, the frost comes out of the ground like a dormant quadruped from its burrow, and seeks the sea with music, or migrates to other climes in clouds. Thaw with his gentle persuasion is more powerful than Thor with his hammer.

—HENRY DAVID THOREAU, *WALDEN*

Terrah's wedding is at the beginning of August. It's lovely. I get to walk down the aisle with Terrah's brother Dusty, who was once described by his own mother as 'a social beast.' Mr Battersby is at the reception. He comments on how nice it is to see me having such a good time. Gentry and I have a heart-to-heart about weddings and marriage and how we both think, for a variety of reasons, it's a generally stupid idea. We are thrilled for our friends, wish them the best – we will fully celebrate with an open bar – but we're not completely convinced it's as

346

magical as they make it out to be. Obviously, I would still like to be married, and sure it is easier to cope with being a widow if I convince myself that the institution of marriage is flawed. But now that marriage is really more of a spectator sport for me, it's not that I totally resent it or think that it can never work, it's just that I think it's a lot harder to be happy over time than people my age think. Maybe my grief goggles can help me see into the future, or maybe I can just tell that not everyone considers what a lifetime commitment actually means. My grandpa always says that marriage is like an exotic plant; you've really got to work hard and pay attention if you want to keep it alive. But how can anyone except a wise old man understand that? I think my grief goggles are making me pay more attention to wise old men than to glossy women's magazines.

The one highlight was watching Terrah's parents dance. I don't slam holy matrimony when I see people like Mr and Mrs Brewer. After Josh died, Terrah told me that her mom was engaged to be married when she was in her early twenties. Right before the wedding, Mrs Brewer's fiancé was killed in a car accident. She didn't meet Mr Brewer until ten years later, and then she decided to try it again. Lo and behold, here she is in her beige mother-of-the-bride dress.

Weddings are funny events because they last one day. I am beginning to see that people my age and younger have no sense of time. We think four years is a long time. Women think a year is a long time from engagement to wedding. We expect things to happen overnight. We want to be rich and famous and accomplished in the first few years out of college. We get frustrated when things don't move at an efficient pace. We curse the Internet when it takes more than ten seconds to load a website and we get annoyed that the voice mail lady takes so damn long to give us instructions. But now that I have Kai, I look at the parents of all of my friends in a new light. Mr and Mrs Brewer, Mr Battersby, my mom and dad, Deedee – these people understand time because they have watched their children go from toddlers in jelly shoes to women in wedding dresses. They have watched something grow. My guess is if people in their mid-twenties had any concept of time, not as many of us would be promising a lifetime to a person we met four months ago.

Right now, I'm rereading *Walden* for a new unit we're creating for our eleventh-grade English curriculum. *Walden: A Life in the Woods* is written by this guy named Henry David Thoreau who spent a year living alone on Walden Pond outside of Concord, Massachusetts. He wrote down every single observation about the pond and the natural world around him. While I wouldn't exactly consider his detailed account of the woods riveting, it is interesting to read his description of the pond transitioning from winter to spring. Ever so slowly and carefully it goes from ice to water.

He records the process of the thaw, and although Thoreau's narrative of ice melting may not wow the average twenty-first-century audience, the process itself really is amazing when you think about it. Nature understands that things take time. You can't rush certain things if you want them to work correctly. It took Mrs Brewer ten years to find love again, and here she is at her daughter's wedding, having the time of her life. I guess that kind of healing and growth needs a whole decade. Sometimes I really look forward to how I will feel in ten years.

But nothing signals the passage of time more than watching my own son. He pulls himself up on his own. He stands without holding on to things. He raises his arms for me to pick him up. He smiles when I sing, he breathes deeply when he sleeps, and he laughs when he sees pictures of his aunts and grandmas around the house. He does a million other unbelievable things. I look at him and think about how happy I am to be here for him and how happy I am that despite the absence of his amazing father, he will have a great life. He used to be the size of a peanut. Literally a peanut. A little over a year later, he is learning how to walk on his own two legs. I'm sure that pond was impressive for Thoreau, but clearly the guy never had children. The concept, however, is still the same. Nature has a way of figuring it out. I hope my brain operates under a similar premise.

I am made stronger when I think of Mrs Brewer and Mr Battersby. I think about how sometimes life gets better even when you think it can't. Sometimes the thaw can work in your favor if you just let it take its course.

On Wednesday night, Maggie and I do a mini-triathlon over at Kent Lake. Training has been going well. I should say that training has been going well when I decide to train. When Kai is in a good mood, I'll put him in the jogging stroller and go as fast as I can until he cries and then we run home. I have only biked three times and I try to swim once a week. Hales is still helping me coordinate the whole lift arms, lift head, kick legs all at once thing. It's like co-ordinating a golf swing, except for the fact that you don't get to stand there for five minutes and think about it.

I am nervous for the minitriathlon. But when I get there, I decide I just wanted to survive the swim and not have the course close before I finish.

Once I get through the swim and bike and start finally running, I feel better. Running is the only thing I know how to do in a triathlon. And by running I mean jogging, but let me tell you, I am one hell of a jogger. During my run I think about how I want to speed up. Lately, when I get into a point of physical pain in my training or in a race, I talk myself into slowing down or stopping altogether. It's like I have two opposing forces in my head. One says, 'Just stop. What's the big deal? You're not going to the Olympics. Just stop and walk.' And the other side of my brain asks one question. It asks the same question over and over: 'What are you so afraid of?'

I've spent a lot of my life being scared of things. Scared of an injury during soccer, scared of failure and criticism, scared of being rejected. Then the one thing I was so afraid of happening, so afraid I could hardly acknowledge it, actually happened. So why not go faster? Why not lose? Why not try things that I know I'm not good at? What am I so afraid of now?

On Wednesday during the run, my mind is going in all different places. I start thinking about August 14 of this year and how it compares to August 14 of last year and, reluctantly, how it compares to August 14 of the year before that, the last August I spent with Josh. As I run, I think about how I am doing better, right here at this moment, than I had been one year before. Who knows if I could say the same for two years before, but there's no point in answering that question.

Time passes and things change. I feel better today than I did one year ago. If I were sitting in Dr G.'s office, I would try to keep going with this thought. I'd say, 'Yeah, but inevitably something bad will happen again. Time passes, but some-times things change for the worse!' And she would just nod quietly and say, 'Natalie, think about what you said a few moments ago. 'I feel better today than I did one year ago.' Just stop there. That is a beautiful statement.'

My grandparents on my dad's side have lived in East Lansing, Michigan, my entire life. A few years ago, my grandfather suffered from a stroke. Even two years later, he still has minimal movement in his left hand and arm and he has to use a cane to walk. Ever since his stroke, life has been more challenging for my grandma and him. My grandma has her own physical ailments to deal with, and now she has to help my grandpa on top of it.

This past March, a house went up for sale across the street from my parents' house. It was a small, quaint house that probably hadn't been redecorated in twenty years. My dad talked to my grandparents about it for a few weeks. He urged them to buy it and sell their house in Lansing, even though the Lansing house is twice as big as this one. Finally, they gave in. Without even seeing the house, they bought it and put their own house on the market. When my grandparents came to see the house for the first time, my grandma walked in and started to cry. My dad had to remind her why she had given up her beautiful house in Lansing. 'Mom, you're going to love it. We are right across the street, remember? You're going to see your great-grandson every day.'

After a few months of remodeling, the house is finally ready. Three Corrigan moving trucks arrived this morning. My parents go over to help out in the morning. Kai and I stay away until after his afternoon nap. When we get there, everyone looks tired.

'Leen,' Grammy says in her thick Polish accent, which is hard for some people, like the guys from the moving company, to understand. When she talks to my mom, she calls her 'Leen' instead of Lynn. It's hard to know what she is saying at times. One time when we were all vacationing together, Grammy was walking around the cottage asking for 'leetle seesars.' My mom kept asking her why she wanted Little Caesars when we had just eaten dinner. But she kept insisting, 'I just need some leetle seesars!' My mom went over to the phone book, not wanting to disappoint her mother-in-law. 'Okay, Mom, but if you're hungry, why do you want pizza of all things? I can make you a sandwich right here.' My grandma looked at my mom like my mom was crazy. 'Pizza? Sandwich? What? *No!* I need LEETLE SEESARS!' Finally, we realized she was saying 'little scissors.' She needed to cut some thread. It was hilarious.

'Leen, where are da box-says wid da bedding.' My mom tells my grandma that she already put them in the bedroom next to the master bed. 'Tank God!' she says, clutching her heart. 'I tought I lost dem and I need to make da bed for Grampy.' My mom tells her to sit down and relax and she'll make the bed. Grammy walks over with her walker and sits next to Kai and me at the white dining room table. She grabs her Diet Coke and takes a long sip. Grammy only drinks Diet Coke out of one specific cup and she only drinks it through a straw with a lemon. After the Diet Coke, she puts her hand on her forehead.

'How is the move going?' I ask her.

She looks at me confused. 'Movie? What movie?' This is the other thing about my grandma. She can't hear anything. She refuses to get a hearing aid. My dad thinks she secretly likes not hearing everything.

'The *move*, how is the MOVE going?'

'Oh, da move. Well, Grampy is useless. I told heem, don't poot your clothes in a place where you will loose dem. Put dem in a box so we can get to dem today. So today I say, 'George, where are your clothes?' He says, 'I don't know, Mom, I put dem in wid every-ting else.' (My grandpa calls my grandma 'Mom.') She rolls her eyes.

My dad walks in and asks my grandma if she needs anything. My grandma looks around and says, 'Yes, Vito, please, where did dey put da grape-fruit tree?'

My dad tells her that he's sure it's still in the van, but he can go check.

'What do you need now, Mom?' my grandpa yells from the other room.

'Where is *da grapefruit tree*? If dey moved dat grapefruit tree wit out me, I will be *so* mad.'

Grammy turns to look at Kai and me. 'I grew dat grapefruit tree from a seed!'

354

This is true. Grammy has had a grapefruit tree for over twenty years. She considers her grapefruit tree to be one of her greatest accomplishments. A few years ago, Josh and I went to my grandparents' house on our way up north. My grandma took him around the entire house and told him about each plant. The grapefruit tree, of course, was the main attraction. He was so into it. He asked her all about it, how she watered it, what she did with it in the winter. To my grandmother, having that grapefruit tree is like having an Egyptian pyramid in her living room.

My grandpa walks in from the living room.

'Hi, Nads!' He has to stop walking to say hi. Once he says hello, he continues to walk toward us. He walks slowly with his cane. He sits down at the white table in the middle of the kitchen.

'George, deed you hear me? Where is da grapefruit tree? And where is dat box I told you to poot out with da stuff on top?'

Grampy looks forward for a moment to think about it. My grandma stares at him, waiting for an answer. Then he says in a voice like he is proclaiming a hard-earned truth, 'I don't know!'

She flashes me a look and takes her walker to find the moving crew.

I can tell my grandma is stressed. I know this move is really hard for her. When she was eight years old, she lived in a small town in Poland. When World War II started, the Russians came to her town and kicked her and her family out of their house. Her dad was taken to a prison, and she and her brother and mother went to live in Siberia in a work camp. They stayed there for four years until the war ended. I think after being evicted to Siberia, no matter how old you get, it leaves a bad taste in your mouth when it comes to moving.

My grandpa, on the other hand, is thrilled to be moving closer to us. He loves being around my dad, and I know that seeing Kai and me is really important to him. One of the saddest things I've ever seen was my grandfather at Josh's funeral. He came in with his cane, moving at his slow pace. I remember seeing him up by the casket. I remember not really being able to articulate what was so sad about it. Or maybe it's just that at that time I didn't want to. My grandpa had been in Europe during a world war. He saw his neighbors and friends disappear. He saw the fall of a dictator. He saw people from around the world put their lives on the line for an idea, something that doesn't really happen as often as it used to. He came to America believing in the American dream, and for him, it really came true. He has seen the planet at its absolute worst, and over time he has dealt with some serious problems in his own life. But seeing him next to that casket, it was like nothing made sense to him anymore. Seeing his shaky, unsteady body up there, his body that had endured so much and his brain that had tried to work hard for his family no matter what was going on outside;

it was as if he was silently confessing to whomever, '*This* is too much.'

'Here you go, ma'am,' I hear one of the movers say. He places the grapefruit tree in the corner of the dining room. My grandma walks in behind him.

'Tank God!'

My grandpa lifts his head up like a tortoise craning to see the sun and says, 'Tank God! What would we do wit out da grapefruit tree?!' He looks at me and smiles. He is making fun of my grandma. Clearly she knows this too.

'Shut up, George!' She slowly walks out of the room. 'Eediot.'

After an afternoon with my grandparents, Kai and I go home to our house. August evenings in Michigan are the best. Things slow down, we can feel September looming, so we savor the free time and peace that comes with no school nights. Grandma Deedee has been up north for the last several weeks, or pieces of weeks, getting her last moments in at the lake. Kai and I haven't gone up in a few weeks.

Without Deedee here, I realize that I really miss her when she is away. I miss seeing her car pull up at expected times. I miss her unannounced visits and her communication with me via Kai. I miss watching her sit him up on the counter (which I never do with him) and letting him splash his feet in the sink. She always lets him do things that I don't allow. Initially this frustrated me, but now I get it. Josh would have done the same thing. Josh and Deedee are so much alike in how they play with children.

When Kai was up north with Deedee and Ashley, they took a video of him sitting in his high chair splashing water everywhere. He just kept slamming his little hands down on the plastic tray and squealing as the water flew all over the floor. There was no mom there to say in a slightly irritated tone, 'Kai, the high chair is for eating, *not* for playing.' Sometimes I really struggle with the fact that I never get to say, 'Kai, let's pull out all of the toys and make a giant mess,' because I know I'm the one that cleans up every mess we make. Josh would have made a mess with Kai. Josh knew that when you are a kid, everything, *everything* is for playing. I know that he was this way because his mom taught him that.

Now that I am a parent, I am beginning to understand that I have no idea what Deedee is going through in dealing with the loss of her child. Not a clue. I knew Josh for four years in college, then we dated for a year, and then we were married for a year and a half. Because I'm twenty-five years old, that seems like a lot of time. But Deedee grew him from a seed.

When Josh was in the hospital after his accident, I saw his body once, and then I had to leave. I never went back. Deedee stayed at the hospital for days. Long after he was pronounced dead, he had to stay so they could remove his working organs. She stayed by him until they wheeled him away for his final surgery. I couldn't be there because to me he was gone. That body wasn't him. But as a mom, I know why she had to stay. When you watch something grow from a seed, you have a very different relationship with it than the rest of the world does.

I know Deedee spent those days staring at his body, taking in the last images of the body she had watched for twenty-seven years. Dead or alive, that body was too special to leave in an empty hospital room. She had been by his side since the day she brought him into this world, not to mention the nine months prior to that. You better believe she would be there on the day he had to leave. Right up until the last second.

When I was in high school, the minister at our church lost his son to suicide. After some time passed, Dr Logan spoke about his son's death in front of the congregation. He talked about when kids are little they love to jump from high places into the arms of their parents. Every parent has the image of their son or daughter yelling, 'Catch me, Dad!' as they jump from the tree branch or the jungle gym. And the child knows that those strong arms are always there. But there are times, he went on to say, where as a parent your arms aren't long enough to reach your falling son, and that is the pain he has to live with for the rest of his life. The death of a child is something different from any other loss in the world. It is the most unnatural circumstance. Parents are hardwired to protect their offspring. Every single species since the beginning of time has one thing in common: We all protect our young. So when a child dies, it goes against the fibers of our brains and souls. Dr Logan's metaphor has never left me. I miss Deedee. I wish she wouldn't leave so often. Someday, who knows when, I want to tell her how sorry I am for her loss. Because her loss is not my loss. And it's not about whose is worse, but I just want her to know that I love her, I love Josh, and I will always love Josh. I want her to know that she can have all the time in the world.

SEPTEMBER

> One always dies too soon – or too late. And yet one's whole life is complete at that moment, with a line drawn neatly under it, ready for the summing up. You are – your life, and nothing else.
> —INEZ REGAULT IN JEAN-PAUL SARTRE,
> *NO EXIT*

This morning on my way to work I am listening to Mojo and Spike, two radio deejays, talk about how today, September 2, is the first day of school for every public school kid in the state of Michigan and they are sad for those kids because nobody likes school. They rail about how no teenager can possibly enjoy this day.

First of all, it should be noted that Mojo and Spike are radio hosts on a popular FM station, so it seems like part of their job is to say things that are so outrageous and inaccurate that I just can't change the channel because I am so appalled. *I really should be listening to Detroit Public Radio*, I tell myself. I'd be embarrassed if anyone at school, students or co-workers, knew I checked in on Mojo and Spike every now and then. But sometimes it's impossible to turn them off.

On Thursday mornings, for example, they do this thing called War of the Roses. They have girlfriends, or even wives sometimes, call in and nominate their boyfriends or husbands who they suspect are cheating. Then Mojo and Spike have one of the women at their station call the alleged cheater and tell him he's just won a free bouquet of flowers from Flowers Forever or something, and he can send one dozen roses to whomever he chooses. So, for example, Lynette calls Mojo because she suspects Ed, her live-in boyfriend, is cheating. Lynette stays on the line, and the woman from the radio station calls Ed. She pitches him this line about some contest he entered online, and usually the guy is surprised and says what anyone would say ('I never win anything!'). Finally, once she knows he's in, she says, 'All right, Ed, so who would you like to send these flowers to?' And then, you wait. All you can think is, *Please say Lynette, please say Lynette* . . . Ed thinks for a second and the whole time his girlfriend, Lynette, is right there listening. Ed takes a deep breath and says, 'Um, I'd like to send them to Renee.' I hit my forehead on the steering wheel. My heart stops every time. I so badly want to turn it off because I feel so horrible for Lynette. It's like when I watch *American Idol,* and some of those kids cry because they actually thought they were good singers and

Simon just likened them to bad cruise-ship karaoke or said something like 'You *can't* be serious.'

So then fake Flowers Forever woman says to Ed (in this real serious voice), 'Ed, you're actually on Mojo in the Morning War of the Roses. We have Lynette on the line. Lynette, what would you like to say to Ed?' Just like that. They switch it up on the guy so fast, he can hardly keep afloat. Of course, you can imagine, tears and swear words follow. 'Who's Renee, you cheap bastard? When was the last time you slept with *her*?' It's brutal. I don't even know why I listen to it. It's so sad and depressing. You'd think once in a while the guy would just play it safe or maybe he really wasn't cheating at all, but no, he's guilty every time. I'm sure they record innocent ones, but they probably never play them on the air. Nobody wants to hear the ones that end nicely. It's like casting for a reality television show. Nobody wants the stable, even-keeled people. For whatever reason, the emotionally volatile are always more intriguing. War of the Roses is the same thing. Everybody wants to know about the bad ones.

One time Mojo and Spike were giving away passes to see Justin Timberlake rehearse before his big show in Detroit. In order to win, they held a contest called 'Tattoo Your Grandma.' You had to get your grandma to get a tattoo and you got the tickets. And, no, it didn't count if your grandma already *had* a tattoo. You had to bring your grandma into the studio and have her get a tattoo right there. How can the BBC World News compete with something like 'Tattoo Your Grandma'?

That's the kind of garbage on this radio show. And now, this morning, they are going on and on about school and how much kids hate it. I desperately want to call in and yell at Mojo and Spike and tell them that they are wrong, but then I would have to publicly acknowledge that I listen to them, which I can't do. I work in a public high school, and although I've only been there for three years, I still feel like I've got some street cred – more than Mojo and Spike at least. I know, despite what any teenager or moronic radio deejay says, kids love going back to school.

This morning I walk through Berkley High School and here is what I see: a lot of girls running up to each other and screaming, 'OH MY GOD! I missed you so much! You look so cute. *Oh* my God, who do you have for math? Do you have Wayman? *Please* tell me you have Wayman . . .'

Students wave to teachers they had last year. 'Mrs Taylor! I'm in your third-hour!' Liz Adary yells from her locker. 'Yes!' I do the arm-pump thing.

They love it here. Their friends are here. The opposite sex is here. People expect something out of them here, which for a handful of students may be different from what happens at home.

I love being here again. I love setting up my

classroom, getting my class rosters, and thinking about all the things I'll do differently this year. I think for both teachers and students, there is a certain amount of relief in that no matter how bad last year was, we get to try again this year with somewhat of a clean slate. Few jobs seem to have this type of annual renewal.

During my second-block class, all of my new eleventh-grade students are chatting as I pass out the syllabus. A skinny, short boy walks in the room and looks around awkwardly. I can tell without even asking him that he is a ninth-grader and he is completely lost. He looks very scared, like he just walked in on a meth lab. 'Um . . .' he stutters, and looks around the room for a teacher. He is visibly shaking.

'Hi there, can I help you?' He pieces together that he thinks he should be in this room – 'I thought . . . my algebra class . . .' – and hands me his schedule. I look at his crumpled half sheet of paper. He is in fact a ninth-grader and has no idea how to read his schedule, which, to his credit, is more difficult than it needs to be. I tell him where to go and not to worry, that he won't be marked late. He bumbles back toward the door.

'It's okay, man!' one of my students shouts as he walks out the door. 'Happens to the best of us!' I give her a look that asks why she is shouting across the room. She shrugs. 'Sorry.' I have no idea how they come into this school being insecure and self-conscious, and by eleventh grade they think they are smarter than everyone in the world.

I had a large number of these eleventh-grade students when they were freshmen. I think about how the last time I saw them in desks, I was married to Josh. He died on Sunday, June 17, two days after these kids ended their freshman year. I know I shouldn't be mulling over these facts on a day like the first day of school, but I can't help it anymore. I have learned to let things wander in and eventually they wander out.

I direct the students to their seats and ask them to take out a pen or pencil. There is some shuffling and chatting as I walk around the room. Then I hear a voice say, 'Um, Mrs Taylor, do you have a pencil I could borrow?' I look up. I don't know this kid. You may think that I would be shocked at the idea that some eleventh-grade student did not bring a pen or pencil on the first day of school, but I'm not. This happens every single year. Even today, after second period, it will happen again.

'What's your name?'

'Eric Heller.'

'Eric, do you show up to track practice without your running shoes?' I pause for a second. I have my hand on my hips and my eyebrows are furrowed. 'Do you show up to work without your uniform? Do you show up for a Red Wings game without your tickets?' I throw four more syllabi on the table at the back of the room. I'm still facing Eric. 'No. You don't. So why would you show up to English class on the *first day of school* with no pencil?' Eric kind of does this shrug like I'm the one asking the stupid question and could I please just give him a pencil. I ask the class if anyone has an extra pencil that Eric could borrow. Some girl at the table behind him, who probably has thirty pencils, hands him one.

Teaching is this funny thing where some days you feel really inspired and grateful that this is your job. You feel like you are lucky because you get to be a part of a very important experience. You watch kids grow and change and learn. Then there are other days when a sixteen-year-old asks you for a pencil on the first day of class, and you really believe that they are paying absolutely no attention to you at all.

I think about calling Eric's mom after class, just for the hell of it. I'd explain to her that right now, American schools are on the bottom of every single academic totem pole in the world. China, Japan, India, Russia are all crushing us in math, reading, and writing. There are a million studies that try to explain why this is and a million different philosophies as to what teachers need to do to close the gap.

'Do you know what you can do to help this cause, Mrs Heller? You can do your best to make sure that your son leaves the house in the morning *without* his head up his ass. You could start with giving him a pencil . . . That's right. Let's just start with a pencil.' I would explain that the twenty-first century is a cutthroat place to be and ever since Sputnik, American educators have been doing their best to catch up. 'But, Mrs Heller, we can't do it without your help. We're not asking for much. But I think a writing implement would at least get us started in the right direction.'

At the end of the class period, I have students fill out a short survey. It asks questions about what they read over the summer, how they learn best, and some random questions like 'Identify one major character from literature that you can relate to.' Question number fifteen asks, 'Have you changed since the ninth grade? If so, how?'

During lunch, I flip through their surveys. I am most interested in the question about their transformations that may or may not have happened during their tenth-grade year. In response to question number fifteen, Delaney Rob writes, 'OMG I hope so.' Charlie Moore writes, 'Sorry if I was a jerk in your class in ninth grade. I'm better now.' Blake Forman writes, 'Yes. I am more handsome, funnier, and I can grow a beard.' What a year for Blake Forman. He wins for best answer to question number fifteen.

This year, instead of starting with *The Great Gatsby*, we start with *Macbeth* and *No Exit*. It's just as well as far as I'm concerned. *Gatsby* would not have felt the same this year as it did last year. I think starting the year off with Jean-Paul Sartre is a great idea. Every text we read after *No Exit* will challenge Sartre's idea of free will.

At the end of the year, instead of reading *The Color Purple*, we'll read *Fences*, a play by August Wilson. In *Fences*, Troy Maxson is a middle-aged African American man living in the year 1957. The audience learns that Troy was an amazing baseball player, but when he was in his prime, black men could only play in the Negro League. Now Troy is a garbage man. His son, Cory, desperately wants to pursue football and Cory tells his dad that college scouts are interested, but Troy tells Cory he has to quit football and get a job at the A&P. Because of Troy's experiences as an African American athlete, he believes that Cory doesn't stand a chance in following his football dream, no matter how good he is. Because Cory is black in America, he does not have access to such dreams, or so his father believes. The play is amazing, and makes the reader think about where people come from and how much our ancestors have to do with our destinies.

The interesting part about starting with Sartre is that we can continue to use him throughout the entire year. What would Jean-Paul Sartre say to Troy Maxson? What would Troy Maxson say back?

Of course, all of these issues are ones that we ultimately contemplate in terms of our own lives. How free are we? What kind of power do we have in life? And if we don't have power over our own lives, then who does? What do our actions say about our identity? The hope is that all of these ideas can collide, and students can be exposed to all different ways to look at the world.

On the second day of school, my English class brainstorms our classroom rules. I have them talk about it in small groups first, and then we meet as a big group. We do this so they can think about and understand why it's necessary to have rules like 'One person talks at a time' or 'Make sure you participate.' We do a lot of small-group and large-group discussions in this class. I like to take half a period at the beginning of the year and talk about what we need from each other and what they need from me in order to make those conversations successful.

'Be respectful,' Sean Hay says. I ask what the word *respect* means. We say it all the time, but what does it look like or sound like? Melanie Ritman raises her hand.

'I don't think you need to be respectful. I just think you need to be polite. You don't have to respect everyone's ideas, but you do need to have manners.' I am a little caught off guard by her shrewdness, but I don't disagree with her comment.

We go over each group's list. Sam Stafford, the girl who shouted at the ninth-grader yesterday, holds up her sheet. Under classroom procedures and expectations she wrote, 'Play Kanye West softly in the background during group work.' *Maybe starting with existentialism is setting the bar too high*, I think to myself.

My single moms' group officially ended in May. The Beaumont volunteers, Janet and Heidi, were only to be with us for six months. They explained to us that we could carry on the group on our own if we wanted. Of course, all of us were interested. Over the summer we did a really good job of holding the group together on our own. I had everyone over to my house a few times. But once we stopped meeting one another at the church, things just felt weird. Instead of meeting in a neutral space, everyone in the group had to expose a little more about their lives in these strange, unintentional ways. They would come over and look at my house and I could tell they felt a little awkward about it.

We went to Ellen's house a few times. Her house is really nice too. Rose has her own room, and there is Princess stuff everywhere. But there isn't a park anywhere, at least not within a half mile. Ellen doesn't have a car, and the only thing within walking distance is a liquor store. There is a television right across from Rose's crib. She can see it when she stands up. I think if I would have walked in here six months ago, I would have thought, *You have a* TV *across from her crib?* And it would've been in this real judging tone. But now that I know Ellen, I don't think it's fair to judge her. If I didn't have a car and I had to be home with a baby all day and I didn't have a park to walk to or neighbors to play with or family members to come over when I was ready to crack, the television would play a much larger role in our lives.

We've also been to Laura's apartment for single moms' night. Laura lives in a very tall building off of a highway. She lives on the eighth floor. All I can think about when we get there is how much of a pain in the ass it would be to get groceries and a baby from the car to the apartment building, up eight floors and into the apartment.

Laura made us Hamburger Helper and canned peas. Again, had I been here six months ago, I would've judged her about her choices in food. But now I get it. This is the best she can do. Laura is raising a daughter by herself on a single income. She works at a day care that pays her by the hour. This is the only food she can afford to buy, and if she has any plans on moving into a house or to another apartment, she'll have to continue to buy the least expensive stuff at the grocery store.

Jean-Paul Sartre had the opportunity to attend prestigious schools when he was young, and went on to study at a top university. I'm sure he had a lot of his great ideas because he had the time and space to think. The same goes for Henry David Thoreau. He could only do what he did because he was financially secure. Had he been born into a different social class or to a different racial group, even if he still retained a keen interest for nature, his career as a writer would have been completely different. I wonder what Troy Maxson would say to Henry David Thoreau. That would be one hell of a conversation. I think Troy would be pretty annoyed with him.

The other day on *This American Life* the episode was 'Going Big.' The first act was about the Harlem Children's Zone in Harlem, New York. A guy named Geoffrey Canada had been working with teenagers from Harlem for years, and he had watched as a lot of the kids he tried to help just couldn't do it. They couldn't get out of their neighborhood and create a better life. They couldn't break the cycle. The show talked about a lot of current research that basically says that from age zero to three is a crucial time in a child's life. So Canada overhauled his ideas. Instead of working with teenagers, Canada decided to work with parents and their babies. The Harlem Children's Zone is this place where parents take classes about how to enrich the lives of their kids. They have classes that help parents learn how to discipline and the importance of reading, and they have all sorts of different classes for kids of all ages.

Where we live, there are all sorts of educational structures like this already in place. We have the park, the library, the zoo, not to mention a million different preschools to choose from. Not because I did anything to get us here, but just because of where I was born. Sure, I tried really hard in high school and college, but come on, how hard is that really, when you live in a great neighborhood where safety is never an issue, and your mom cooks you dinner every night? Even kids like Eric Heller, who don't even bring a pencil to class, will have more opportunities just because of where he lives and the public school he attends.

I never realized that certain people really are stuck. And they're not stuck because they don't work hard or because they don't want to get out of where they are. They're stuck because certain forces in the world won't let them out. If Laura wanted to buy a house in my neighborhood, or a nicer neighborhood than where her apartment is, or any house at all, could she do it? Where would she go? What bank would she call? Would they give her honest information or just help her secure a loan that she could never pay off? I can see Troy Maxson shaking his head as Sartre tries to explain the idea of ultimate responsibility.' Troy would probably walk out of the room if Thoreau started going off about 'living simply.' You'd really need somebody in there to referee that conversation. I'm sure Ira Glass could handle it.

I guess the bottom line is, I'm always trying to make sense out of things. But these things, the idea that two kids the same age, born in the same hospital, will have two incredibly different futures because of factors that neither the child nor the mother can control, despite the fact that both moms work really fucking hard and want the best for their children. That doesn't make a lot of sense. There certainly are more fences than I ever knew about.

If Josh were here, I would never know any of this. I would be living my happy life getting stressed out over things like how badly we need a new refrigerator. And I know I still sound like a spoiled white girl. It's like that scene from *Clueless* in which Cher gives the speech in her debate class about immigration and says, 'It does not say *RSVP* on the Statue of Liberty!' I don't mean to sound like I know everything just because my husband died. If anything, I've realized that I don't know anything about anything. I just found out there is so much more that I don't know about. Then again, even one of the twentieth century's greatest philosophers doesn't seem to know all of the answers either.

Tonight, right before I put Kai down for bed, I sit with him in his rocking chair. Putting Kai to bed is such a joy. It is the one time of day during which he sits with me and holds on to me as much as I hold on to him. For fourteen hours, with a brief nap in between, Kai is in motion. He pulls himself up, moves while holding on to furniture, takes one scoot with a foot, then falls and gets up and does it all over. He wants to see and touch and taste everything. This is a problem when I'm trying to sweep the kitchen. He runs after the dust pile like it's a puppy. So like all eleven-month-old boys, and maybe even girls, he does not stop, literally, until eight o'clock at night.

Tonight we snuggle for a long time. Finally, after about twenty minutes, I set him down in his crib. As I walk out his door I can feel my heart rate pick up a little. Tomorrow at 5:30 a.m., Maggie is picking me up for the airport. We land in Washington, D.C., around nine a.m. The triathlon is Sunday morning.

I won't see Kai until Sunday evening, which is technically only two full days without him, but it's still hard to think about. Everyone else on the team is flying back on Monday afternoon, but I have Meet the Teacher Night on Monday evening, and I just can't risk missing it. And once I'm done with the race, I'll really have no desire to stick around.

Up until this moment, the last several weeks have been full of stuff to think about other than the triathlon. But right now, after putting Kai to bed, there are no more distractions. I go to my room and start to pack.

I call Maggie about sixty times to make sure I have everything. She guides me through the details and reads off her lists. 'Make sure you buy a CO_2 cartridge in D.C., because you can't take them on the plane.' Cyclists usually store CO_2 cartridges on their bikes in case they get a flat. With a tire tool and CO_2 cartridge, you can fix a flat in less than five minutes.

'Maggie,' I say, 'I have no idea how to fix a flat tire. I'm not buying CO_2.' There is a pause.

'What are you going to do if you get a flat?'

'Flag down a police car and do the Miss America wave out the passenger's side window.' She tells me she can teach me once we get there. I say forget it. If I get a flat, I'll be responsible for my own stupidity and pay the consequences.

A woman from our team named Diana sits next to me on the plane. I've met her a few times at the handful of practices I attended. She's probably in her forties. She's a big, strong lady and when I did see her at practice, she was always at the front of the pack with the cyclists. Diana's boyfriend, Jim, is meeting her in D.C. He came to practices with her. He's a great cyclist too.

We get to talking and eventually I ask her how she got into cycling. She says, 'Well, I got a divorce. I was an overweight divorcée who smoked. I decided to do something else other than eat and smoke. I needed something else, so I tried biking. Now I love it.' Diana ended up losing thirty pounds and she has no interest in cigarettes anymore. This is her first triathlon. She tells her story like it's no big deal. As if making the transition from overweight smoker to triathlete was as easy as deciding to make the bed in the morning. I'm sure it wasn't that easy. But she seems so far from her past life that it's not even something she considers too often.

Our conversation naturally trails off. I sit back in my seat and think about how I get to sit still for two hours. I don't have to empty the dishwasher or chase a toddler or cook a meal or change a diaper. I can't even move if I want to. I glance over at Diana. She is staring out the window. Can you reinvent yourself? Can you change from one year to the next even after high school? Do we really have any free will? Diana says sure, why not?

The night before the race, there is this huge Team in Training pasta dinner. Every athlete who is participating in the triathlon from Team in Training is at the dinner. At our table are people from Team Michigan, none of whom I really know that well because I only went to three training sessions. But now that I'm here I'm slowly meeting people. Lindsay, for example, sits on the other side of our table. She is a little older than me. She is in medical school. Yesterday I learned that Lindsay decided to do the triathlon because when she was six she was diagnosed with leukemia. She tried some very experimental treatment and ended up beating the cancer. For years, she was in a hospital almost as often as she was at school. Her battle with leukemia sparked her interest in the medical profession, which is why she is now on her way to being a doctor.

Also sitting at the table with Lindsay are her parents and boyfriend. Her parents flew in this morning so they could watch her race tomorrow. At one point during the program, one of the representatives from the Leukemia Lymphoma Society asks if the people in the room who had cancer or who are fighting a cancer can stand up. Obviously, it is a very moving moment. The room is thunderous with applause. Some of the people standing, of course, feel a little strange to be spotlighted. They look a little bashful as if they are thinking, *You're clapping for me because I had cancer?* But then there are other cancer survivors who know exactly why the room is shaking with noise. They survived. Something really bad had happened to them, and they survived. These people are applauding themselves, standing on chairs, flexing their muscles, high-fiving the whole table.

In addition to watching the response of the room, I can't help but look at Lindsay's parents. They look like they are holding back tears. Twenty years ago a doctor told them that their six-year-old daughter had cancer. Now she is about to become a doctor, and tomorrow she'll complete an Olympic distance triathlon to raise money for other cancer patients and their families. I really want the Leukemia Lymphoma Society representative to ask the parents of a cancer survivor to stand so we can clap for Lindsay's parents too. They have certainly earned it. I can't imagine those years of hospital visits. How could they go to work every day or think about anything besides their daughter?

My FMG takes her second brownie from the middle of the table. 'Nobody claps for the parents,' she says, taking a bite. 'Just get used to it.'

The morning of the triathlon is incredible. The transition area is monstrous. It feels like an entire football field filled with bikes. The swim begins at 8:20 a.m. I really don't have any sort of strategy. I should, considering I hardly trained for this. I tell myself that I'm just going to focus on the stage I'm in. When I'm swimming, I won't think about the bike or the run. When I bike, I won't think about how slow the swim was or how tired I'll be for the run. I'll just focus on not getting a flat tire.

Maggie and I stand on the platform together waiting for our group to be signaled into the water. Moo is in the group behind us. The swim is in the Potomac River. The water is brown.

'Didn't George Washington paddle a canoe across here?' I ask Maggie, trying to give myself something inspiring to think about instead of how I probably should have taken an antibiotic before jumping in here.

'That was the Delaware,' she says, staring at the water.

I pause. 'Right.'

'What happened in this one?' I ask her. She is still staring at the water.

'I don't think I want to know.' She looks at me and tells me it's all the more reason to swim faster.

Fast is not a word I am really considering right now, let alone one of its superlatives.

The gun goes off. We start. Maggie quickly disappears, as does every other person we were just standing with on the platform. I start counting my strokes. One, two, three, four, breathe. One, two, three, four, breathe. Yes, that's right, I breathe every fourth stroke. I'm not exactly Dara Torres. More like the old ladies who do laps during adult swim.

We swim down past the bridge. I come around the turn and all I can think is, *There is only one way out of this river – you have to swim back. Just keep swimming.*

I make it back to the dock and jump out of the water. I am really fucking tired, but there is an unbelievable amount of joy surging through my body at the idea that the swim is over and I never have to swim again in my life if I don't want to. I rip off my cap on my way to the transition area. I find my bike – Josh's bike – and say a little prayer to the Gods of Flat Tires.

I secretly thought that because this was Josh's bike, I would jump on and glide through the course. I would fly through the course because Josh's spirit would somehow come alive once I started riding. I really didn't need to train all that hard because the bike would do the work for me. Something magical would happen when this bike and I met the pavement of a real race. We would somehow join forces and suddenly it would be Chitty Chitty Bang Bang on two wheels. I would fly past people. 'Whoa!' spectators would yell. 'Who *was* that girl?' And miraculously, I would have one of the fastest bike times of the entire triathlon. A picture of me passing elite male riders would appear in the *Washington Post* beneath the headline WIDOW FINDS HOPE ON HUSBAND'S BIKE. The mayor of Washington, Adrian Fenty, an elite rider himself, wants to meet me. The bike and I are national heroes.

It takes me about thirty seconds to realize that my Chitty Chitty Bang Bang daydream is not coming into fruition. After a very clumsy mount and clip in, it dawns on me that the only force getting me through the next forty kilometers are my skinny legs. And I don't mean skinny in a good way. I look down at my bike computer about every four minutes. I have roughly an hour and a half on this thing. My butt hurts already.

I pass three people who are fixing flats. Somehow I convince myself that those three people are enough of a sacrifice to the gods, and I won't have a problem. It's like when Eurylochus from Homer's *Odyssey* sacrifices the cattle to make Helios the Sun God happy.

I've never biked for an hour and a half without stopping. I've never done four consecutive hours of physical activity. But the hardest part about this triathlon is that it's just me. Nobody is there to coach me or run next to me. All my life, I have played a team sport. In soccer, no matter how tired or frustrated I got, there were always at least twenty other players around me to help me out of my mental block. If I got tired or hurt, my coach could pull me. I would sit down, drink some water, talk to my teammates, think about my mistakes, then go back out. Endurance events are very different. At the start of the race, the door shuts in your own head, and it's you versus you for four hours. So I start to retreat into my own head for a while and see what's there. Somewhere around mile eighteen on the bike ride through beautiful Maryland, I think to myself, *I am better off today, September 14 of this year, than I was on September 14 of last year*. I stop there. This time I don't think about the years before or the years to come. I just absorb the scenery and try to take in the moment. I feel like a weight has been lifted. Sometimes I feel great victory in single moments. Maybe Sartre's free will isn't a big joke after all.

One hour and thirty-three minutes later, I come into my second transition. There are a lot of things to remember to do in about two minutes. I curse myself for not listening to Coach Rick. Despite my fumbling around, one single happy thought surges through my body: The bike course is over and I can't wait to put on my running shoes. I rip off my helmet, get my bike on the rack, and give it a little 'Thanks for nothing' under my breath. I try not to mentally assess how heavy my legs feel. I get my running shoes on and take off for round three.

I feel amazing. No more fear of a flat tire, no more wincing at the thought of swallowing water from the Potomac. No more staying afloat. I've made it to the run. This is what I know how to do.

I see three girls from my Team in Training team up ahead. They are all about my age. They met one another through TNT and they all attended a significant number of training sessions. They are all really strong cyclists. I start to pick up my pace to catch up with them. I bet they waited for one another after the bike so they could run together. I have no intention of running with them. Something comes over me, and all I want to do is pass them.

I have 6.2 miles ahead of me. It is probably somewhere around 11 a.m. Today is forecasted to be one of the hottest days in September. We are definitely in the upper eighties right now, and it is supposed to get to ninety-two degrees by noon. I remember someone saying earlier that there is no shade on the run portion of the course. I acknowledge all of these factors, and then I dismiss them. I start passing people who smoked me on the bike. Until this moment, I forgot what it feels like to compete. Suddenly, all I want to do is beat people. I know this is all for a really good charity, and it's not about who beats whom. But as any true athlete will tell you, that is the biggest lie anyone has ever uttered. All my life, I have been a competitor. I wholeheartedly admit that I love the feeling of victory, and I despise the feeling of defeat. Sure, that may be immature or arrogant, but if my hockey-playing dad and trash-talking brother have taught me anything in life, it is that no matter what people tell you, no matter what charity you banner across your chest, it is *always* about who wins and who loses. I start to speed up.

I catch the group of girls. They seem to be chatting. 'Good job, Natalie!' one of them yells, with a really polite wave. 'Thanks! Keep it up, ladies!' I yell back. But deep down, I really don't mean it.

I forgot this part of me existed. I haven't played soccer in over two years. I haven't had the time or energy or do anything physical since I got pregnant with Kai, which feels like a lifetime ago. After Josh died and after Kai was born, I always looked at my athletic days as someone I was. Now I jog, go for walks, or do aerobic videos in my basement. I'm a mom, I always reasoned. I don't need to be physically fit anymore. So what if I'm a little chubbier than when I was in college. What woman isn't? I don't care what I look like anyway. I'm not trying to impress anyone.

But running through Washington, D.C., I can feel the sweat rolling down my face. I have to use my tank top to wipe off my forehead about every five minutes so it doesn't get in my eyes. I find people up ahead to pass and go after them. I thought this part of me was dead. I am so happy to know it isn't. I guess it was just dormant. And dormant and dead are two very different things.

I just keep running. I don't think about mile markers or pace or feeling tired. I am smiling as I run.

There is about a half mile left. I turn a corner and I can see the Capitol Building in the distance. For some reason, the pavement feels different. I am running on blacktop instead of normal concrete. I think my endorphins are wearing off. I start to feel like I'm going to pass out or maybe fall forward. Finally, with about four hundred meters to go, I see Moo. She has finished and she's waiting for me. She sees me and starts jumping up and down and yelling.

'Come on, Nat! You can do it, Nat!' She's been

doing a quieter version of cheerleading for the last fifteen months, but seeing her here yelling for me is enough to remind me that this isn't impossible. And by 'this' I mean a lot more than the last four hundred meters, but right now that's all I can think about. What am I so afraid of? I'm not going to pass out or fall over. I keep running.

After I cross the finish line, I go have a few minutes to myself. I hope Moo doesn't find me right now. I don't think I can even talk. I feel horrible. I desperately need water, and I also suddenly really have to go to the bathroom. I sit in the shade for about ten minutes. I can hardly think in a straight line.

Finally, after sitting in the shade by myself, I find Moo. She is screaming, jumping as she runs at me, and before we can even exchange words, she hugs me. Someone takes a picture of us right at the moment when we see each other for the first time after the race. I don't know who it was, but it is the best picture you have ever seen. Moo's head is buried in my neck, the way Kai hugs me when he's tired. You can see my face. My mouth is open and smiling. I think I'm yelling. It's one of those pictures where we really didn't know we were being photographed, so you get to see how we really felt right at that moment. We are both overjoyed.

I remember how much I hated when people would take pictures of me after Josh died. I hated trying to smile. One of the worst feelings is knowing you have to force yourself to smile. But when this picture is snapped, I am smiling. It's not a fake smile either. It's the real thing.

In act 1, scene 5, of *No Exit*, Inez Regault says, 'One always dies too soon – or too late. And yet one's whole life is complete at that moment, with a line drawn neatly under it, ready for the summing up. You are – your life, and nothing else.' Up until this very moment when I hug Moo, the last year and two months of my life have not been my proudest moments. I've spent much of my time crying in a bathrobe and wishing for a life I didn't have. I have been ungrateful for my family and too hard on my in-laws. I have been made tired by my son instead of allowing him to breathe a new life into mine. But right here, right here with my sister, I feel like I've reclaimed something. I don't know what it is, but I know I just finished something. I finished a race. There was a start and a finish and I crossed the line, and now I get to be happy. Nothing else in life works this way. Nothing else has such clear-cut indications of beginning and end, so I'm going to savor the moment. You can take this moment and hang it up. This can be my life. A big challenge, a long course, a really, really tired body, but ultimately, I finish what I set out to do. The best part is, my sister is hugging me. Her arms are fully flexed as she hugs me. We know this is not just about a triathlon. This is about moving from one place to another. Maybe not far, or fast, but we are moving.

A year ago, we were in the same pose, her holding on to me like I was leaving for the moon, but our facial expressions were completely different.

In all of the pictures that people have taken of me in the last year, I have a very mediocre smile. In my friends' wedding pictures, I am smiling, but it's nothing like the one of me after the triathlon. Sure, maybe it was the endorphins or the pride I felt from having finished. I don't care what it was. It is proof, real proof, that I am in a place that can produce that smile. When I used to go to Dr G., I remember telling her all the time about how I was scared that I would always feel sad and depressed. Even though people told me that over time things would change, I never believed them. I really thought I would wake up every morning with a knot in my stomach, and all the things I used to enjoy – food, time with my family, reading a good book – wouldn't bring me joy anymore. For a long time nothing brought me joy. Over and over, Dr G. would assure me that it would pass. 'You are only visiting this place.' *Visiting.* That was her word. When I look at this picture, I finally believe her.

EPILOGUE

Right before Kai was born, one of my mom's friends, Abbey, wrote me a letter. When Abbey's son, Zach, was eighteen months, he died tragically after falling into a river. The family was crushed. Over time, Abbey and her husband decided to have another child. Cale was born a few months after the one-year anniversary of Zach's death. Initially when I got her letter, I thought it was going to be about coping with loss, but it wasn't. She wrote to tell me about the day Cale was born. In the letter she said she remembers it as a time when 'the colors were real again.'

Today is October 18, Kai's first birthday, and all I can see are colors. Kai wears a red ribbon on his jacket that says MY SPECIAL DAY. It flitters on his chest like a hummingbird as he runs across the playground. His jacket is full of yellows and blues. All of our decorations are bold primaries. Not to mention the park itself. The leaves are turning, every tree has its own palette of autumn. Kai's bright blond hair looks beautiful in the October sunshine. It reminds me of his dad.

A few months ago, I know I looked at that blond hair and thought about how I have to live without Josh, and nothing was more depressing and painful than comprehending life without my husband. But now, standing here at Kai's first birthday, I look at that hair and think about how I get to live with our amazing son. At some point in the last few months, things that used to feel like a weight or a burden are starting to feel more like an opportunity. We get a chance to celebrate.

Abbey's letter says, 'Natalie, the pureness of every emotion with a baby is so uplifting, love-soaked, and healing. They make real laughter bubble from your soul.' When I see Kai run up to hug his great-grandpa or laugh as Deedee pushes him in the swing, I think about Abbey's words. Kai has brought all of us back to life.

Josh isn't here. I've spent the last sixteen months trying to get my head around that, but I've reached a place where I can say that grief is not about recovery or resolution or being fully healed. It's about living without someone, but still embracing life. It's about understanding that time is not as linear as we thought, but perhaps it's more like laying pictures one on top of another. It's about holding our Zachs and our Cales and our Joshes and our Kais together in one space and somehow feeling the presence of all of them.

Today I know that Josh is close enough to tell me not to be sad. I get to see all of the things that he has to miss. My dad holds Kai as they flip burgers together. My mom chats with all of the guests, both children and adults. Auntie Moo flew in from Florida for the birthday. She runs around the park with Auntie Ash and Auntie Hales taking pictures and passing out cake. Everyone is there to sing. Mr Battersby, Katie, Mathews, Maggie, Terrah – all of our friends and family. And I am here to see all of these faces and sing 'Happy Birthday' to my one-year-old son. How could anything else on the entire planet matter more than singing 'Happy Birthday'?

So, yes, the colors are real again. The colors are coming back. And somehow, ever so slowly, the same has happened to me. With the help of my friends and family, my students and my school, my books and beloved authors, with the help of other people's stories of pain and triumph, and of course, with the help of my son, I can finally say that I am coming back. They have all brought me back.